Darwin's Influence on Freud

20, MARESFIELD GARDENS,
LONDON. N.W.3.
HAMPSTEAD 2002

March 1, 1964.

Dear Mrs. Ritvo,

Of course, I shall be very interested to read your paper. Please, send it to me and it will be a pleasure to see it.

My father's outline of Lamarck has not turned up and there is no chance any more that it can do so. Personally, I remember very well how imperturbed my father was by everybody's criticism to his neo-Lamarckianism. He was quite sure that he was on safe ground.

Thank you very much for the Passover invitation also from Mrs. Burlingham's side. I remember last year with pleasure. But I shall not be in New Haven until March 29th, and she probably a week later.

With greetings for the whole family,
yours sincerely

Anna Freud

Anna Freud's letter on her father's Lamarckism (March 1, 1964, to the author).

Darwin's Influence on Freud

A Tale of Two Sciences

Lucille B. Ritvo

Yale University Press
New Haven and London

20132207

Set in Century Expanded type by G&S Typesetters, Inc. Printed in the United States of America by Vail-Ballou Press, Binghamton, N.Y.

Library of Congress Cataloging-in-Publication Data

Ritvo, Lucille B., 1920–
    Darwin's influence on Freud : a tale of two sciences / Lucille B. Ritvo.
      p. cm.
    Bibliography: p.
    Includes index.
    ISBN 0-300-04131-4
    1. Freud, Sigmund, 1856–1939. 2. Darwin, Charles, 1809–1882—
Influence. I. Title.
BF 173.R515   1990   89-16672
150.19′52—dc20

The paper in this book meets the guidelines for permanence and durability of the Committee on Production Guidelines for Book Longevity of the Council on Library Resources.

10   9   8   7   6   5   4   3   2   1

To
G. Evelyn Hutchinson
for his long surviving interest in Darwin,
Freud, and this study
and in loving memory of Pauline Bessie Copel Bernstein, R.N.,
and Asher Bernstein, M.D.

Let us take, for instance, the history of a new scientific theory, such as Darwin's theory of evolution. At first it met with embittered rejection and was violently disputed for decades; but it took no longer than a generation for it to be recognized as a great step forward towards truth. Darwin himself achieved the honour of a grave or cenotaph in Westminister Abbey. . . . The new truth awoke emotional resistances; these found expression in arguments by which the evidence in favour of the unpopular theory could be disputed; the struggle of opinions took up a certain length of time; from the first there were adherents and opponents; the number as well as the weight of the former kept on increasing till at last they gained the upper hand; during the whole time of the struggle the subject with which it was concerned was never forgotten.

Sigmund Freud
Moses and Monotheism

Contents

Contents

Acknowledgments

Most recently, crucial roles in the realization of this book have been played by Emeritus Professors G. Evelyn Hutchinson and Irving L. Janis of Yale and by Peter Gay, Dr. Eric Kandel, the Connecticut Academy of Arts and Sciences, and the consummate editor, Gladys Topkis, of the Yale University Press.

I am grateful to Dr. Edward Kronold for listening carefully and patiently and, with his psychoanalytic skills, relieving me of such handicapping neurotic debris of infancy and childhood as ambivalence, penis envy, and a too-strict superego. Hearing from my husband, Samuel Ritvo, professor of psychiatry and child study, that Ernst Kris, who had known Freud, was applying "ontogeny repeats phylogeny" in the psychoanalytically oriented Longitudinal Study at the Yale Child Study Center made me wonder about the connections between psychoanalysis and biology; I had learned the axiom in embryology from Mount Holyoke professor Ann H. Morgan.

Leonard G. Wilson, now chairman of the History of Medicine at the University of Minnesota, not only provided me with a rich background in the history of biology but was my first mentor, performing duties of guidance, encouragement, and inspiration well beyond the call of duty. His suggestion for a term paper on "Evolution as Applied to Man" revealed the need to explore Darwin's influence on Freud. Professor George Mahl's rigorous psychology course provided the foundation in psychoanalytic theory essen-

Acknowledgments

tial to pursue my Darwin–Freud hypothesis. On the recommendation of Lottie Maury Newman, the doyenne of psychoanalytic editors, an invitation from the late Dr. Max Schur, Freud's personal physician, subsequently a New York psychoanalyst and professor of psychiatry, to collaborate in articles for the American Museum of Natural History and the American Psychoanalytic Association on evolution and development in psychoanalysis offered further in-depth training in the aspect of psychoanalytic theory most relevant to the study. My husband, Samuel Ritvo, has been sharing his life in psychoanalysis with me and served as consultant on psychoanalytic issues.

A term paper for Professor Mahl on "The Impact of Darwin on Freud" was expanded under the weekly supervision of Professor Wilson into a master's thesis ("Darwin of the Mind," 1963), which Professor G. Evelyn Hutchinson was the first to recognize as worth developing into a doctoral dissertation and possible book. The dissertation adapted for this book was carried out under the conscientious and expert guidance of another historian of science, Professor Frederic L. Holmes; the late Dr. George Rosen and Dr. Stanley Jackson contributed helpful suggestions from the vantage points of the history of medicine and psychiatry, respectively.

Among the many psychoanalysts who encouraged me were Doctors Heinz Hartmann, Victor Rosen, Henry Brosin, Jacob Arlow, Kurt Eissler, Richard Sterba, Sanford Gifford, Mark Kanzer, William I. Horowitz, and Professor Abraham Zaleznik. Peter Gay, Ilse Grubrich-Simitis, Dr. Robert Evans, and Dr. Albert Solnit facilitated acquisition of the appropriate photographs of Darwin and Freud. Members of the American Psychoanalytic Association, the Western New England Psychoanalytic Society, the Washington Psychoanalytic Society, the Pan-American Psychoanalytic Congress, and many other psychoanalytic organizations were generous in allowing spouses free admission to scientific meetings and offering, along with the International Psychoanalytical Congress, opportunities to present some of this material to them for discussion and publication. Dr. Haskell Norman provided an exceptionally fine discussion at an international congress. The Joint Atlantic Seminar on the History of Biology, initiated by Leonard Wilson, also provided a forum for work-in-progress. Two papers published from early stages of this work were translated for the German *Psyche* by Ilse Grubrich-Simitis, who gave me the opportunity to correct the unedited one pirated by the *Journal of the International Psychoanalytical Association*. The essential fellowship of schol-

Acknowledgments

ars was provided when Dr. Mark Kanzer helped establish the Yale Faculty and Professional Seminar on Psychoanalysis and the Humanities, which has been very stimulating since I had the opportunity to become the only female charter member. Dr. Anna Kris Wolff obtained Miss Anna Freud's permission for me to examine Freud's library for the only book of Darwin that Jones said Freud had.

Miss Freud was extremely generous in allowing me to continue using her father's library in her home at Maresfield Gardens. Paula Fichtl, the Freud housekeeper, contributed to my joy in scholarship with her Viennese hospitality and the secret of an additional row of books at the back of one of the top shelves of *Wissenschaften* in Freud's library. With the books now catalogued but less accessible as part of the Freud Museum, Richard Wells, the director, has been very helpful, as have librarians in all the many libraries I used. Special note should be made of the Yale librarians Mrs. Dorothy Kilbourne, the late Betty Greenberg, and particularly Ferenc Gyorgyey, who were indefatigable and often ingenious in tracking down materials from behind locked doors of the Medical Historical Library. We are all indebted to the late Dr. John Fulton for the riches and beauty of that library.

Eva Kessler and Leon Talalay helped with the translation of any of Claus's *Akademischedeutsch* that had not been published in English; Dr. Rosen checked the translations and provided more felicitous English phrases where needed. My ability to cope with nineteenth-century Gothic German I owe to Mount Holyoke classmate Margo Brown Harvey.

I should also like to thank inspiring teachers whose influence here is subtle but significant: Emeritus Professor Franklin L. Baumer for intellectual history; Mount Holyoke Emeritus professors the late Abby Howe Turner for advanced physiology and Roger Holmes for more than just logic, the history of philosophy, and the philosophy of history; Kathleen Witbeck for love of biology and Isadore Dressler for fun with algebra at Grover Cleveland High School; and Mrs. Vessey at PS 87 in Middle Village, Queens, for love of the English language. The late Mrs. Betty Towner gave years of devoted service in typing; Mrs. Betty Granger typed an early version. Lorraine Ragusa made many corrected copies on the computer with accuracy. Professor Kenneth Manning of MIT made the key suggestion on the photographs.

Thanks go also to my late parents and to my children, Doctors Jonathan I., David Zvi, and Rachel Z. Ritvo, all now psychiatrists, and my son-

Acknowledgments

in-law, Steven Beckman, for their cooperation and assistance at various stages.

Alex Metro has meticulously scrutinized every speck of manuscript. But the inevitable errors are the author's.

Introduction

"I was already alive when Charles Darwin published his work on the origin of species" (1933 [1932], *SE* 22:173), Freud reminded an audience seventy-five years after the historic event. Sigmund Freud was born in Moravia on May 6, 1856, two years and two months before the theory that bears Darwin's name was announced jointly by Charles Darwin and Alfred Russel Wallace to the Linnean Society of London on July 1, 1858. The life of the creator of psychoanalysis coincides almost exactly with the onset of the "Darwinian revolution." Freud's life and work reveal the impact and also the vicissitudes of the new theory. Fossilized in the extensive corpus of Freud's writings is the evolutionary theory of Darwin's day, including aspects expunged by time. Freud's own theory became subject to surprisingly similar misinterpretations and assaults.

The lives of Darwin and Freud overlapped by more than a quarter century, until Darwin's death at Down, England, in April 1882. Although the two men never met, Freud took the opportunity at the University of Vienna Medical School to train with a biologist who had just recently been privileged to call on Darwin at Down.

Freud came under the influence of Darwin's theories during his years at the Vienna *Gymnasium*, from 1865 to 1873. In 1924, in a seventy-page "account of his personal share in the development of psycho-analysis" (1925 [1924], *SE* 20:4, ed. note), Freud noted early influences in his life that he considered relevant to his development of psychoanalysis. Among

1

the influences during his school days he included "Darwin's theories" (p. 8). At the age of seventy-one, from the perspective of a long life devoted to psychoanalysis, Freud listed "the study of evolution" as essential to "a scheme of training for analysts." The study of evolution was an important part of Freud's own medical education. His evaluation of its importance for psychoanalysis may be contrasted, as Freud actually does, with his view that "the training most suitable for an analyst . . . is not the training prescribed by the University for future doctors. What is known as medical education appears to me to be an arduous and circuitous way of approaching the profession of analysis" (1927, *SE* 20:252).

Biology in the era when it was being revolutionized by Darwin's work was originally the field of Freud's earliest scientific interest and ambition; after he left it, he continued to base his work on it, even assuming that "for the psychical field, the biological field does in fact play the part of the underlying bedrock" (1937, *SE* 23:252). Darwin symbolized the biological field and was in "large measure the agent" by which biology finally achieved the willingness and ability "to operate . . . without reservation or constraint in the dimension of time" (Kroeber 1960, 2:3). Of the five metapsychological viewpoints essential to psychoanalysis, the genetic (or Darwinian) has always been present in Freud's writings, albeit never explicitly.[1] Also indebted to Darwin is the adaptive point of view; the beautiful adaptations of Nature as the handiwork of the Creator were transformed by Darwin's theory into products of a cruel and relentless battle for existence, in which the less functional were selected out. Conflict, too, is basic in Freud's psychoanalytic thinking, as it was in all post-Darwinian biology. The conflict-free ego sphere was enunciated not by Freud but by a younger colleague, Heinz Hartmann.

Not only was natural selection involved in the Darwinian struggle but also sexual selection, a duality in Darwin's theory mirrored in psychology by Freud's dual instinct theory of the aggressive and libidinal instinctual drives.[2] According to Freud's daughter and intellectual heir, Anna, "Psychoanalysis is above all a drive psychology" (letter, October 21, 1974, to J. C. Hill in Young-Bruehl 1988, p. 457). But among the many ways in which the influence of Darwin's all-encompassing thought can be discerned in Freud's work, the "historical" approach of development and evolution is predominant.

The influence of Freud's early interest in Darwin and his training in evolutionary biology has not been examined in the same historical detail as, for instance, the scientific influences of the physicist and philosopher

Introduction

Gustav Theodor Fechner (Dorer 1932), Brücke's and Meynert's neu-rophysiology (Amacher 1965, Sulloway 1979), Charcot (Andersson 1962), the so-called Helmholtz school (Bernfeld 1944), and the post-Darwinian *Zeitgeist* (Rapaport 1960, Sulloway 1979). As the late George Rosen, Yale professor of the history of medicine, rightly pointed out, what has since Bernfeld been referred to as the "Helmholtz school" had little to do with the great scientist himself but rather concerned three of his best friends, who continued to work along primarily physiological lines: Carl Ludwig, Emil Du Bois-Reymond, and Freud's professor Ernst Brücke, for whom Freud named his fourth child, born shortly after Brücke's death in 1892.

Freud was no "crypto-biologist," as Sulloway would have us believe. Freud referred to Darwin and his biological work more than twenty times in his writings (see appendix A), and always very positively; these refer-ences range from Freud's earliest psychoanalytic work, *Studies on Hys-teria* (1895) with Joseph Breuer, to his last completed book, *Moses and Monotheism*, in the final year of his life.[3] To Freud, Darwin was "the great Darwin."

Sulloway may have been misled by Freud's lifelong insistence on the no longer acceptable biological principle of the inheritance of acquired charac-teristics, erroneously named for Darwin's precursor Lamarck. Nowhere in his psychoanalytic writing does Freud mention Lamarck. Was he there-fore also a crypto-Lamarckian? Unimportant as the inheritance of ac-quired characteristics (also called "use inheritance") has turned out to be for either Darwin's or Freud's theory, it demands attention because Freud's attitude on the subject was disturbing to many of those trained by him and seems to have influenced their response to the question of the ob-servance of the Darwin Centennial. Having by 1956 become the highly in-fluential leaders of the oldest and most prestigious psychoanalytic society in the Western Hemisphere, the émigré Viennese Americans who had known Freud discouraged their younger colleagues from initiating any official observance by the New York Psychoanalytic Society (Victor Rosen, personal communication, 1963). Individual psychoanalysts personally in-terested in evolution had to participate under other auspices. The psycho-analyst Henry Brosin, for instance, spoke at the historic University of Chicago centennial, to which over ninety famous scientists and intellec-tuals came from all over the world, but not as a psychoanalyst represent-ing psychoanalysis. He was identified as professor of psychiatry at the University of Pittsburgh, director of the Western Psychiatric Institute, fellow of the Center for Advanced Study in Behavioral Sciences, and director of the American Board of Psychiatry and Neurology, but not by any psychoanalytic affiliation or accomplishments. These may have been taken for granted in an era when training in psychoanalysis was de rigueur for leadership in American psychiatry.[4] Speaking as a psychiatrist on "Evolution and Understanding Diseases of the Mind," Brosin neither focused particularly on Darwin's influence on Freud nor omitted Freud from the many relevant contributors to psychiatry indebted to Darwin. "Freud, E[ugen] Bleuler, and Adolf Meyer have furnished most American psychiatrists with their basic theorems on thinking and the thinking disorders" (Brosin 1960, 2:376). Although Brosin did "not try to present in full the relations of psychiatry, Freud, and psychoanalysis to Darwin and evolutionary theory," he did express his "belief that Freud and many of his followers are in the Darwinian tradition both by direct descent . . . and also from indirect pressures from such collateral sources as Spencer's psychological synthesis, Galton's inheritance of abilities, Lombroso's clinical studies on criminals, William James's description of animals and men in evolutionary terms, and G. Stanley Hall's phylogenetic course on human psychology" (p. 378). Freud's "Lamarckian usage" did not escape mention by Brosin, if only in a quotation from another author.

Freud's psychoanalytic theory was expounded most fully in "Evolutionary Concepts of Brain Function following Darwin and Spencer" by a non-psychoanalyst, H. W. Magoun of the University of California, best known for his work in experimental neurobiology. Magoun expressed "curiosity concerning the derivation of the views of Hughlings Jackson in neurology, of Pavlov in physiology, of Freud in psychiatry, and of Edinger in anatomy." Each had "accounted for the phylogenetic elaboration of the central nervous system in terms of a series of superimposed levels, added successively as the evolutionary scale was ascended" (Magoun 1960, 2:188). Freud had applied this "hierarchical view" from Hughlings Jackson in a prepsychoanalytic work *On Aphasia* (1891) before adapting it to psychoanalysis. Contrastingly, at this same Darwinian celebration (1958) a former president of the American Psychological Association, Ernest R. Hilgard of Stanford University, speaking on "Psychology after Darwin," was absolutely silent about Freud. According to another highly respected psychology professor, Neal Miller of the Rockefeller Institute, academic psychologists were unaware of what they were using from Freud and attributed to him only what offended them (personal communication, December 1971). Darwin's theory experienced similar neglect or maltreatment from scientists who had neither time nor interest to study carefully the vast corpus of his published works. They mistook the part they knew for the whole and felt free to attack or to assume as their own whatever they wished.

The historian of medicine Ilsa Veith of the University of Southern California mentioned her interest in "the direct influence of Darwinism on the work of" Freud among others (1960, 3:181) but did not offer anything specific. The anthropologist A. L. Kroeber described Freud as "the last great name to cling" to the idea of the inheritance of acquired characteristics (1960, 2:6). That is all there was in the three thick centennial volumes: two references to Freud's Lamarckism and scattered clues from a variety of disciplines hinting at a Darwin–Freud connection. The absence of organized psychoanalysis from the universal celebration of the Darwin centennial creates a mystery. Were Freud and his followers indeed crypto-Darwinians?

Across the ocean another member of Freud's inner circle, the Welsh psychoanalyst Ernst Jones, dubbed Freud "the Darwin of the mind" (1953–57, 3:304). In his biography of Freud, Jones described Freud's persistent belief in the inheritance of acquired characteristics "as an extraordinary part of the story, which provides us with a baffling problem in the study of the development of Freud's ideas, and also in that of his personality" (3:310). According to his daughter Anna, Freud was "quite sure" that he was "on safe ground" and remained "unperturbed . . . by everybody's criticism to his neo-Lamarckianism" (letter of March 1, 1964, to the author [frontispiece]). Trying to solve the problem with a psychoanalytic approach rather than a historical investigation, Jones was unable to find a satisfactory explanation. We shall see what history can reveal.

Part I examines the general responses to Darwin's work in the German-speaking world which might be relevant to Freud's recollection that when he was in the *Gymnasium* "the theories of Darwin, which were then of topical interest, strongly attracted me, for they held out hopes of an extraordinary advance in our understanding of the world" (1925 [1924], p. 8). Freud's *Gymnasium* years, 1865 to 1873, coincided with the popularization of Darwin in the Germanophonic world, particularly by Haeckel, as well as with the German publication of two of the three Darwin works referred to by Freud in his psychoanalytic writings, *The Variation of Animals and Plants under Domestication* (1868) and *The Descent of Man* (1871; German translation 1872). Part I reveals the complex issues evoked

5

by the Darwinian view of evolution and the complexities within the theory itself at that early stage. Advances in biology have invalidated some of the positions taken by Darwin and validated others. Freud's views are remarkably consistent with Darwin's positions whether eventually validated or discredited.

Freud's emphasis on the value of the study of evolution in the training of psychoanalysts warrants examination of his own study of evolution as a medical student. Part II therefore explores the Darwinian elements in the teachings of Freud's great professors, Carl Claus, Ernst Wilhelm Brücke, and Theodore H. Meynert, and in Freud's scientific work with them at the University of Vienna Medical School from 1873 to 1882. Here the zoologist Claus, relatively neglected up to now in the literature about Freud, becomes the major figure as a teacher of the new Darwinian biology. Brücke, who as a physiologist had no need for Darwin's theory in his work, provided a congenial laboratory setting for Freud's own important phylogenetic and ontogenetic researches. Amacher's work entitled "Freud's Neurological Education and Its Influence on Psychoanalytic Theory" points out that Meynert took issue in his psychiatric lectures with Darwin's *Expression of the Emotions* (1871, trans. 1875), specifically with Darwin's definition of instinct as inherited learning. Inasmuch as Brücke and his assistant Exner subscribed to Meynert's neurophysiological ideas, they, too, were critical of Darwin's definition of instinct, without thereby intending to question the possibility of inheritance through use and disuse per se (Amacher in Ritvo 1970). Positive contributions of Darwin's *Expression of the Emotions*, noted in Meynert's *Psychiatrie* (1884) but unmentioned by Amacher, bear a close relationship to the references to Darwin in Breuer and Freud's *Studies on Hysteria* (1893–95).

Chronological presentation of the material has been modified to acommodate two factors. The relevance of the material presented in the first two parts would be lost on all but those already fully acquainted with the writings of Freud if Freud's work awaited examination in a final section. Second, Darwin's role in reviving, emphasizing, or supporting one side or another in the biological issues aroused by his publications has to be assessed in terms of the pre-Darwinian as well as post-Darwinian history of these issues. The genius of Darwin's convincing synthesis of vast amounts of essential observations threw new light on many *old* ideas. In addition, predecessors were sought and found for individual ideas in Darwin's theory. Darwin himself sought and acknowledged predecessors. Citing prior authorities for one's ideas was still the scientific tradition for acceptability; authority, not originality, was the coin of science until the twentieth century.[5] One cannot, therefore, discuss Darwin's influence in terms of a *new* idea or ideas but must assess the reactions and issues his work evoked in the time and place under consideration.

Part One

Freud's *Gymnasium* Days
(1865–1873): "The Theories
of Darwin, Which Were
Then of Topical Interest"

Under the powerful influence of a school friendship with
a boy rather my senior who grew up to be a well-known
politician, I developed a wish to study law like him and
to engage in social activities. At the same time, the
theories of Darwin, which were then of topical interest,
strongly attracted me, for they held out hopes of an
extraordinary advance in our understanding of the
world; and it was hearing Goethe's beautiful essay on
Nature read aloud at a popular lecture by Professor
Carl Brühl just before I left school that decided me to
become a medical student.

Sigmund Freud
An Autobiographical Study

Since the discovery and posthumous
publication in 1950 of the "Fliess Papers," written in 1892, and Freud's so-
called Project for a Scientific Psychology, an 1895 attempt to survey the
field of psychology and psychopathology never intended for publication, it
has been clear that early ideas could remain dormant in Freud's mind for
twenty, thirty, and more years, to be revived and developed later in life.

Freud's own work has established the importance of early experience for later development. In the latter part of his life Freud's "interest, after making a lifelong *détour* through the natural sciences, medicine and psychotherapy, returned to the cultural problems which had fascinated me long before, when I was a youth scarcely old enough for thinking" (1935, *SE* 20:72)—that is, in the pre-university period.

Freud attended the *Sperlgymnasium* from 1865 to 1873 and, he reports, was at the top of his class for all seven years. During this period, Haeckel achieved his great success in popularizing "the theories of Darwin." In this period also, Darwin's works, beginning with the fourth edition of *On the Origin of Species* (1866, German trans. 1867) and followed closely by *The Variation of Animals and Plants under Domestication* (1868), became available in the outstanding German translations of Victor Carus, a zoology professor at Leipzig. A friend of Darwin, Carus had been eyewitness to the famous (or infamous) controversy over Darwin's theory at the British Association Meeting in 1860, where, in a heated debate with Darwin's foremost advocate, Thomas Henry Huxley, Bishop Wilberforce (known as "Soapy Sam") asked "whether Huxley was related by his grandfather's or his grandmother's side to an ape" (Lyell 1881, 2:335). The second (1860) and third (1861) editions of the *Origin* and Darwin's first subsequent work, *On the Various Contrivances by which Orchids are Fertilized by Insects* (1862), had been published in German almost immediately. But these early translations of Darwin, undertaken by the German zoologist and paleontologist Heinrich Georg Bronn until his death in 1862, were too literal to be enjoyable reading; they suffered not only from haste in translation but also from such serious censorship by the translator as deletion of the single reference to man, Darwin's cautious statement that "light will be thrown on the origin of man and his history" (1950 [1859], p. 414). It was during Freud's *Gymnasium* days that these defects were rectified by Carus's translation of the *Origin* and the *Variation* and by Haeckel's popularizations of the *Descent of Man* (1871; German trans. Carus 1872). In this period even Darwin's and Wallace's 1858 presentation to the Linnean Society was translated into German (1870).

Discussion of "the theories of Darwin" may also have been stirred by the election of Darwin in 1871 as a foreign corresponding member of the Vienna Academy of Science, a scientific body which was to accept three of the four scientific papers published by Freud during Darwin's lifetime. Darwin was elevated to honorary foreign member in 1875, just two years before Freud's first two scientific papers were presented to the academy by his professors, Claus and Brücke. Thus if, in spite of his increasing difficulty with the traditional, convoluted academic German as he aged, Darwin read the *Proceedings of the Vienna Academy* after becoming a member, he would have had three opportunities to encounter Freud's work in science before his death in 1882. Perhaps his eyes did light on Freud's name as he scanned the *Proceedings* for evolutionary contributions. The name of a zoologist whose work Darwin esteemed so highly as to allow him to visit at his home in Down a few years before might have called his attention to the paper presented by Professor Claus for his young student, Sigmund Freud. Even as a biologist Freud deviated from the academic style of the day and reported his scientific work from the beginning in a straightforward German, simple enough even for Darwin.

1

Haeckel's Popularizations
of Darwin

One of the best examples of the "missing links" between two major types predicted by Darwin's *Origin of Species* (1859) was found in 1861 in the late Jurassic limestone of Solenhofen, Germany. The *Archaeopteryx* was a virtually perfect intermediate link between birds and reptiles. This discovery, too early to be experienced by Freud at the time, contributed to the excitement over Darwin's ideas that was to grow in the Germanophonic world during the next decade. The following year the Darwinian question was placed before the forum of German science for the first time with Ernst Heinrich Haeckel's advocacy of evolution in his *Radiolaria* (1862) and again in 1863 in his address at the Versammlung deutsche Naturforscher und Arzte (Assembly of German Naturalists and Physicians) at Stettin. Haeckel, biologist and philosopher at the University of Jena from 1862 to 1909, became a successful but overzealous popularizer of Darwin's theory. Until 1862–63 German scientists, with one important exception, had preferred to wait and see.

It seemed to Thomas Henry Huxley, Darwin's public advocate and close friend, that Germany "took time to consider." He characterized Bronn's early translation of the *Origin* as "slightly Bowdlerized." Huxley could not recall any "public" declaration of support by any German "scientific notability." In 1860 the only public notice was the satiric illustrated Berlin weekly *Kladderadatish*[1] "cut[ting] his [*sic*] jokes upon the ape origin of man," as humorists of many countries did for decades. In speculating as a foreigner on this "curious interval of silence," Huxley fancied that "one moiety of the German biologists were orthodox at any price and the other moiety as distinctly heterodox." The latter, as "evolutionists, *a priori*, already," would have "felt the disgust natural to deductive philosophers at being offered an inductive and experimental foundation for a conviction which they had reached by a shorter cut." Huxley could see that for philosophical evolutionists it was "undoubtedly trying to learn" that "though your conclusions may be all right, your reasons for them are all wrong, or, at any rate insufficient" (1887, 2:186).

In August 1860 the preeminent Baltic German pioneer of embryology, Karl Ernst von Baer, prematurely expressed his "general assent to evolutionist views" (Huxley 2:186n)—good but short-lived news for Huxley and Darwin. In the light of von Baer's subsequent writings, Huxley had later to dismiss as meaningless the claim of "the man who stands next to Darwin in his influence on modern biology" that "'J'ai énoncé les mêmes idées sur la transformation des types ou origine d'espèce que M. Darwin' ('I have expressed the same ideas on the transformation of types or origin of species as Mr. Darwin')" (in Huxley 2:329). Not exactly. As both parties soon realized, von Baer had mistakenly assumed that Darwin's theory of evolution was teleological. Six years later, in an essay *On Purpose in the Processes of Nature* (1866), von Baer elaborated his theme that purpose guides the development of the embryo and the whole creative activity of the world; by 1876 he more correctly claimed only that he "had supplied some material for the foundation of Darwin's Doctrine" but that, unfortunately, "time and Darwin himself have erected on the foundation a structure to which I feel myself alien" (1876, 2:241).

The same year as von Baer's too hasty claim to Darwin's ideas, another famous German scientist, Rudolf Wagner, discoverer in 1835 of the germinal spot in the human egg, sent Darwin an abstract of Agassiz's *Essay on Classification* (1857), in which Wagner considered Darwin's views also. Just before Darwin's and Wallace's revolutionary announcement challenged the reigning scientific theory of creationism, the internationally acclaimed Swiss-born Jean Louis Rodolphe Agassiz, professor of geology and zoology at Harvard, produced his magnum opus, the definitive *Essay on Classification*, based on the paradigm in biology of the creation of each species individually. The zoological data Agassiz collected and studied did not require any other theory, and Agassiz remained one of Darwin's most powerful adversaries until his death in 1873.[2] Wagner proposed that the truth lay halfway between Agassiz and the *Origin*, thus leading Darwin to hope that "as he goes thus far he will, nolens volens, have to go further"

(1887–88; 2:330–31). But in the end Wagner too became an opponent of materialism rather than a follower or supporter of Darwin. In November 1860 Darwin was able to write to his staunch supporter at Harvard, the professor of botany Asa Gray, that he had "just heard that Du Bois-Reymond" German physiologist, successor of Johannes Müller, and since the early 1840s a friend of Freud's physiology professor Ernst Brücke,[3] "agrees with me" (2:354).

Almost a year later, in September 1861, Darwin remarked on the silence in Germany: "Many are so fearful of speaking out. A German naturalist came here the other day; he tells me that there are many in Germany on our side, but that all seem fearful of speaking out, and waiting for some one to speak, and then many will follow. The naturalists seem as timid as young ladies should be, about their scientific reputation" (1903, 1:196). Huxley recalled that none of them "dreamed" that "in the course of a few years the strength" and, he added in parentheses, perhaps also the "weakness of 'Darwinismus' would have its most extensive and most brilliant illustrations" in the "land of learning" (1887, 2:86). In an evaluation of Darwin and his relationship to Germany (*Charles Darwin und sein Verhältniss zu Deutschland* 1885), Ernst Ludwig Krause (Carus Sterne), author also of an essay on Darwin's grandfather *Erasmus Darwin* for the 1879 *Gratulationsheft* issue of the evolutionary journal *Kosmos* in honor of Darwin, credited Haeckel with being the first to speak out, although the same year as Haeckel's *Radiolaria* (1862), the physiologist Wilhelm Preyer published in his "Dissertation on *Alca impennis* . . . one of the earliest pieces of special work on the basis of the 'Origin of Species'" (F. Darwin ed. in C. Darwin 1887–88, 3:16n). Preyer, a professor at Jena, was a psychologist as well as a physiologist and later published a pioneer work on child development strongly indebted to Darwin's *Descent of Man;* in his *Three Essays on the Theory of Sexuality* (1905) Freud refers to Preyer's *Die Seele des Kindes* (1882) as "well known" (*SE* 7:174).

In 1863, the year Haeckel fired the opening salvo in his address at Stettin, Karl Vogt published *Vorlesungen über den Menschen, seine Stellung in der Schöpfung und der Geschichte der Erde* (*Lectures on Man, his Place in Creation and in the History of the Earth*), and the psychologist Wilhelm Wundt, founder both of the science of psychology and in 1878 of the first laboratory for experimental psychology, expressed his agreement with Darwin in *Vorlesungen die Menschen- und Thierseele* (*Lectures on the Human and Animal Soul*). Vogt, a German naturalist at the University of Geneva, was both a collaborator of Darwin's arch opponent Louis

Agassiz and an ardent supporter of Darwin. The early 1863 works by Vogt and Wundt are referred to and recommended by Haeckel in *The History of Creation*. Later works of Wundt are prominent in Freud's writings; Freud refers frequently in *The Interpretation of Dreams* (1900) and again in the *Introductory Lectures* (1916–17) to Wundt's *Grundzüge der physiologischen Psychologie* (*Principles of Physiological Psychology* 1874); he refers to Wundt's later *Völkerpsychologie* (*Elements of Folk Psychology* 1900, 1906, and 1916) in *The Psychopathology of Everyday Life* (1901) and *Totem and Taboo* (1913).

In December 1864, Darwin was able to write to a Cambridge friend who had in America become a successful farmer, businessman, and Illinois state entomologist, Benjamin Dann Walsh: "As you allude in your paper to the believers in change of species, you will be glad to hear that very many of the very best men are coming around in Germany. I have lately heard of Häckel, Gegenbauer, F. Müller, Leuckart, Claperède, Alex Schleiden, etc." (1903, 1:259). Freud was to encounter the work of Gegenbauer, Müller, and Leuckart in studying with Claus. A copy of Gegenbauer's *Gründriss der vergleichenden Anatomie* (*Outline of Comparative Anatomy*, 1874) is among the books Freud rescued from the Nazis in fleeing to London. Haeckel's popularizations could have introduced Freud to Fritz Müller's little book *Für Darwin* (1864), which, according to Krause, exerted the biggest influence on the general acceptance of Darwin's theory. Darwin considered it important enough to arrange for its translation and publication at his own expense. Freud certainly would have become fully acquainted with this work when he studied with Claus, as we shall see later. Leuckart was Claus's much admired teacher.

By 1865 Haeckel could write to Huxley, who forwarded the good news to Darwin, that the "Darwinian Theory, the establishment and development of which is the object [of] all my scientific labours has gained ground immensely in Germany (where it was at first so misunderstood) during the last two years, and I entertain no doubt that it will before long be everywhere victorious" (in Huxley 1901, 1:287). Writing to Darwin in 1869, Huxley identified Haeckel as "one of the ablest of the younger zoologists of Germany" and dubbed him "the Coryphaeous of the Darwinian movement in Germany" (1901, 1:287). According to Krause, Haeckel fought the battle of "Darwinismus" so fiercely that he "concentrated on himself . . . all the hatred and bitterness which Evolution excited in certain quarters" (1885 trans. in Darwin 1887–88, 3:67) so that "in a surprisingly short time it had become the fashion in Germany that Haeckel alone should be abused, while Darwin was held up as the ideal of forethought and moderation" (3:68). Freud's references to Darwin are of this idealized and unambivalent nature. We shall see the development of hostility toward Haeckel by a supporter of Darwin in the writings of Freud's zoology professor Carl Claus.

In 1866 Haeckel produced a massive, unreadable work, *Generelle Morphologie der Organismen: Allgemeine Grundzüge der organischen Formen-Wissenschaft, mechanisch begründet durch die von Charles Darwin Descendenz-Theorie (General Morphology of Organisms: General Outlines of the Science of Organic Forms based on Mechanical Principles through the Theory of Descent as reformed by Charles Darwin)*, in which he attempted to trace the series of man's ancestors. His success as a popularizer of Darwin for the educated layman began when he adapted the most important parts of the *Generelle Morphologie* and presented them in a series of popular lectures at Jena in 1867–68; two of the lectures were published in Virchow and Holtzendorff's *Collection of Popular Scientific Lectures* (1868). The popular interest in science in Germany was so strong that this volume went to a fourth edition by 1881; the public lecture that served as a source of Darwinian inspiration for Freud as a schoolboy was on comparative anatomy, a subject of public interest in the wake of Darwin's theory. Haeckel's presentation of Darwin's theories received even wider distribution with the publication of Haeckel's revised and expanded lecture notes (*Natürliche Schöpfungsgeschichte* [1868], which appeared in English as *The History of Creation: or the Development of the Earth and its Inhabitants by Natural Causes*). By 1873, when Freud enrolled in the medical faculty at the University of Vienna, the *Natürliche Schöpfungsgeschichte* was in its fourth *"verbesserte"* (improved) edition. In less than a decade there were eight foreign translations. By 1889 the *"Achte umgearbeitete und Vermehrte Auflage"* (8th revised and enlarged edition) had become a mammoth 832-page volume.

SOLVING THE RIDDLES OF THE UNIVERSE

In 1927 Freud recalled that "in my youth I felt an overpowering need to understand something of the riddles of the world in which we live and perhaps even contribute something to their solution" (1927, *SE* 20:253). Solution of the riddles of the universe by means of the clue supplied by evolution became a nineteenth-century expectation promoted by Haeckel, who wrote: "Development is now the magic word by means of which we shall

17

solve the riddles by which we are surrounded, or at least move along the road toward their solution" (trans. Hatfield 1930 in Rádl 1909, pp. 126–27). Attempting to apply the doctrine of evolution to the problems of philosophy and religion, Haeckel called his work *Die Welträtsel*, published in English as *The Riddle of the Universe at the Close of the Nineteenth Century* (1900).

Throughout the nineteenth century "development" and "evolution" were expressed in German by the same "magic word," *Entwicklungsgeschichte*. In English the word "evolution" had originated in preformationist embryology, which taught that organisms existed fully formed from the beginning.[4] Evolution came eventually to be used exclusively for phylogenetic development, the ancestral history of organisms. Darwin did not use the word in the *Origin*, but he set the stage for the future by ending his work with the word "evolve": "There is grandeur in this view of life, with its several powers, having been originally breathed into a few forms or into one; and that, while this planet has gone cycling on according to the fixed laws of gravity, from so simple a beginning endless forms most beautiful and most wonderful have been, and are being, evolved" (1950 [1859], p. 415). The history of the words *Entwicklungsgeschichte* in German and "evolution" in English reflects the fact that for almost a century after Darwin the study of embryology was dominated by phylogenetic considerations. Haeckel provided a distinction with his creation of the words "ontogeny" and "phylogeny." At the same time, he was very emphatic about maintaining a close relationship between the two. "These two branches of the organic history of development—ontogeny, or the history of the individual, and phylogeny, or the history of the tribe—stand in the closest causal connection, and the one cannot be understood without the other" (1876 [1868], 2:348). Freud's belief in this intimate relationship will be discussed in chapter 5. An example here is Freud's reference in *Beyond the Pleasure Principle* (1920) to "embryology in its capacity as a recapitulation of developmental history" (*SE* 18:26).

Haeckel proclaimed that the historical approach, which Darwin had used with such world-shaking success to find a scientific solution to the problem of species, was the key to every problem. "Every being can only be truly known when we know his becoming" (in Rádl 1930, pp. 126–27), Haeckel proclaimed. Morphology became "morphogeny," the study of the evolution of one form from another; physiology became "physiogeny," the study of the development of function; and anthropology had to become "anthropogeny," the study of man's origin from animal ancestors. Freud's application of this clue to the problem of the neuroses is basic to psychoanalysis and provides one of its four cardinal metapsychological points of view, the genetic or Darwinian.[5] Because of its importance this will be presented more fully in a later chapter. Here it may suffice to point out that Freud had been imbued since his youthful interest in Darwin with the idea of the importance of the past as a clue to the understanding of the present; this awareness no doubt added to his excitement over, and receptivity to, Breuer's communication in 1882 of his cathartic treatment of Anna O.,[6] which revealed the "fundamental fact that the symptoms of hysterical patients are founded upon scenes in their past lives" (Freud 1914a, *SE* 14:8). Others of different ages and backgrounds did not react in the same way, as Freud was to learn when he sought to share Breuer's discovery with Charcot in Paris.

Thanks to Brücke's recommendation, Freud had obtained a travel fellowship to work under Charcot at the Salpêtrière in Paris from October 1885 to February 1886. Jean Martin Charcot was a great nosographer who brought order into the apparent chaos of psychopathology by distinguishing "types," much as the pre-Darwinians had been doing with species in biology. Following up Charcot's remark that he had not heard from his German translator since the war (the Franco-Prussian War of 1870–71), Freud offered his services as translator of Charcot's lectures and thus came to be on intimate terms with the famous director of the Clinic for Nervous Diseases at the Salpêtrière. Freud described Charcot in a letter to his fiancée Martha Bernays as "one of the greatest of physicians and a man whose common sense is touched by genius" (1960 [November 24, 1885], p. 185). He was therefore disappointed by Charcot's lack of interest in Breuer's discovery. Freud came to see that "in reality Charcot took no special interest in penetrating more deeply into the psychology of the neuroses. When all is said and done," it was from "pathological anatomy that his work had started" (1925 [1924], *SE* 20:14). (Even in trying to understand the scientific interests of the great Charcot, Freud took the historical approach and looked to origins!) Freud's own interest in science, by contrast, began with the promises held out by "Darwin's theories" and with the study of zoology under a Darwinian biologist, Carl Claus. Charcot (1825–93) was of an older generation than either Freud (1856–1939) or Breuer (1842–1925); in addition, France did not embrace Darwin's work as Germany eventually did.

Although there were probably other factors determining Charcot's lack of receptivity to Breuer's finding, the negative attitude toward Darwinian thinking in France is worthy of consideration. French scientists were cold toward Darwin's theories and assumed that Darwin had added nothing to the evolutionary speculations of France's own scientists, Buffon, Lamarck, and Geoffrey St. Hilaire, which the great Cuvier, founder of the science of comparative anatomy and paleontology, had effectively discredited earlier in the century. The two contemporary leaders of French science, the physiologist Claude Bernard and the chemist Louis Pasteur, whatever else they might disagree on, shared a disregard for Darwin's theories. Among Cuvier's followers the physiologist Marie Jean Pierre Flourens, the anthropologist Jean Louis Armand de Quatrefages de Bréau, the botanist Adolphe Théodore Brongniart, the geologists Jean Baptiste Armand Louis Léonce Élie de Beaumont, Joachim Barrande, and Étienne Jules Adolphe Desmier de Saint Simon, Vicomte de'Archiac, and the all-around naturalist Henri Milne-Edwards, who became director of the Museum of Natural History in Paris after 1864, were all opposed. In France, according to Huxley, the "influence of Élie de Beaumont and of Flourens—the former of whom is said to have 'damned himself to everlasting fame' by inventing the nickname of '*la science moussante*'[7] for Evolutionism—to say nothing of the ill-will of other powerful members of the Institut, produced for a long time the effect of a conspiracy of silence."

It was many years before the "Academy redeemed itself" from the "reproach that the name of Darwin was not to be found in the list of its members." De Quatrefages, who always combated evolutionary ideas, had a strong personal respect for Darwin and later was active in promoting his election to the French Academy. An accomplished science writer, Antoine-August Laugel, "out of the range of academical influences," gave an "excellent and appreciative notice" (Huxley 1887, 2:185–86) of the *Origin* in the *Revue des Deux Mondes*, but for the most part those French scientists and popular writers who did accept Darwinism never expressed more than a mild scientific interest. The developmental approach was therefore not as highly regarded by scientists in France as in Germany, where the influences of both von Baer and Darwin were strong.

The inspiring effect of Haeckel's *Naturliche Schöpfungsgeschichte* on young men even a decade or two after Freud is vividly described by one of the many gifted young men attracted to the study of embryology or development (*Entwicklungsgeschichte*) by Haeckel's popularizations of Darwin.

Haeckel's Popularizations of Darwin

In *Portraits from Memory: Recollections of a Zoologist* (1956), the German-born American geneticist R. B. Goldschmidt, twenty years Freud's junior, vividly recalls reading Haeckel's *History of Creation* with "burning eyes and soul." It seemed to him that "all problems of heaven and earth were solved simply and convincingly; there was an answer to every question which troubled the young mind. Evolution was the key to everything and could replace all the beliefs and creeds which one was discarding" (p. 35). Even today Haeckel's *History of Creation* effectively conveys his excitement over Darwin and his conviction of "the enormous influence which the theoretical progress of modern science will have on the entire universe and on the perfecting of man's culture . . . among all these wonderful theoretical advances, the theory wrought out by Darwin occupies by far the highest rank" (1:2–3).

The modest Darwin would not make such grandiose claims for his work, although as early as the *Origin* he did write inspiringly that in "the distant future I see open fields for far more important researches. Psychology will be based on a new foundation, that of the necessary acquirement of each mental power and capacity by gradation" (p. 413). At the time of this statement in 1859 Darwin had already observed the behavior of savages; in *Totem and Taboo* Freud cites one of these observations from *The Variation of Animals and Plants under Domestication* (1868). Even more significantly, Darwin had already made detailed observations on the gradual development of expressions, such as weeping, in his own infants. He wrote on the birth of Haeckel's son in 1868, "You will be astonished to find how the mental disposition of your child changes with advancing years. A young child, and the same when nearly grown, sometimes differ almost as much as do a caterpillar and a butterfly" (1887–88, 3:104). A few years later Darwin published his careful observations of individual development in his psychological work *The Expression of the Emotions in Man and Animals* (1872), whose influence on Freud is discussed in chapter 12 below. Psychology was Freud's "tyrant . . .; it has always been my distant, beckoning goal"—a goal to which, after a long detour through biological science and psychiatry, Freud eventually returned via the neuroses; when he did, his new psychology was based on the foundation forseen by Darwin in the *Origin*, "the necessary acquirement of each mental power and capacity by gradation" (p. 413). Freud's recollection of this period, as contained in the statement from his *Autobiographical Study* given at the beginning of part I, reveals that he shared Haeckel's response to Darwin's theories as promising "an extraordinary advance in our understanding of the world," a promise which Freud himself helped to realize.

COPERNICUS AND DARWIN

Another similarity between Haeckel and Freud in their view of Darwin is in their coupling of Darwin's name with that of Copernicus. Haeckel claimed in 1894 that he had been the first to call attention to the "service rendered by these two heroes in putting an end to the anthropocentric and geocentric views of the world" (1903 [1894], p. 97 n. 6). He referred to their accomplishments as "death blows." "As Copernicus (1543) gave the death blow to the geocentric dogma, so did Darwin (1859) to the anthropocentric one closely associated with it" (p. 15). As a result of Haeckel's *Popular Lectures* at Jena in 1867–68, references to Darwin as the "Kopernikus der organischen Welt" ("Copernicus of the organic world") had become commonplace by the time of Darwin's death in 1882, when Emil Du Bois-Reymond lectured on "Darwin and Copernicus" to the Berlin Academy of Sciences (January 25, 1883). In the first of his *Popular Lectures*, "Über die Entstehung und den Stammbaum des Menschengeschlechts" (The Origin and Genealogy of the Human Race), Haeckel had "carried out in detail the comparison between Darwin and Copernicus" (1903 [1894], p. 97 n. 6). In "A Difficulty in the Path of Psycho-Analysis" (1917) Freud presented a similar discussion to which he added a third "death blow," the psychological blow dealt by psychoanalysis to man's narcissism. Although Haeckel lacked the term "narcissism" as established by Freud, he, too, had been calling attention to the self-centered or narcissistic nature of the views overthrown by Copernicus and Darwin. Freud called them the *cosmological* blow and the *biological* blow.

In discussing the biological blow Freud saw "Darwin and his collaborators and forerunners" as putting an end to man's presumption of superiority: "Man is not a being different from animals or superior to them; he himself is of animal descent, being more closely related to some species and more distantly to others. The acquisitions he has subsequently made have not succeeded in effacing the evidence, both in his physical structure and in his mental dispositions" (1917, *SE* 17:141). For Haeckel, "the necessary and unavoidable inference" from Darwin's writings "*of the animal descent of the human race*" is of such "immense importance" that it "almost eclipsed . . . the great value of the Theory of Descent . . . in its explaining to us the origin of organic forms in a mechanical way, and pointing out their active causes." According to Haeckel, Darwin had provided a mechanical basis for the origin of organic forms and at the same time determined "the position of man in nature, and . . . his relations to the totality of things" (1876 [1868], p. 6).

Freud's reference to Darwin's "collaborators and forerunners" does not specify who they are, whereas in the same discussion Freud found the forerunners for Copernicus in the Pythagoreans and Aristarchus of Samos. Comparing Darwin to Copernicus, Haeckel had included Galileo and Kepler in the Copernican story and even made Newton the real hero; Freud occasionally substituted Newton or Kepler for Copernicus. On one occasion, in place of psychoanalysis Freud coupled the name of the sixteenth-century physician Johannes Weier with Copernicus and Darwin; in response to a request for "ten good books" Freud indicated that, if he had instead to "say 'the ten most significant books,'" he "should have to mention such scientific achievements as those of Copernicus, the old physician Johann Weier on witchcraft, Darwin's *Descent of Man*, and so on" (1960 [undated (1907)], "Letter 135 to the Antiquary Hinterberger," p. 269). In an *Introductory Lecture on Psycho-Analysis* Freud added to Darwin's name "Wallace and their predecessors" (1917, *SE* 16:285). But Freud never substituted another name for Darwin's or mentioned Lamarck. For Freud it was "Darwinian lines of thought" (1895, 1:303; 1920, 8:56), "Darwin's theory of descent" (1925, 19:221), and "Darwin's theory of evolution" (1939, 23:66).

Haeckel, on the other hand, emphatically honored Lamarck as "founder of the theory of descent." Haeckel also gave credit to Goethe for *guessing* at the unity of life, which for Haeckel with his belief in Monism was a very important contribution; in his *Generelle Morphologie der Organismen* (*General Morphology of Organisms*), as Haeckel takes the trouble to remind readers of his later *History of Creation*, he had "placed as the headings to the different books and chapters a selection of the numerous interesting and important sentences in which Goethe clearly expresses his view of organic nature and its constant development" (1:88). The subtitle of his *Naturliche Schöpfungsgeschichte* is *Gemeinverständliche wissenschaftlichen Vorträge über die Entwicklungslehre im Allgemeinen und deijenige von Darwin Goethe und Lamarck im Besonderen (Public Scientific Lectures on Evolution Theory in General and Darwin's, Goethe's and Lamarck's in Particular)*.

23

DARWIN, GOETHE, AND THE UNITY OF LIFE

The names of Darwin and Goethe are linked not only in Haeckel but in Freud's previously quoted recollection that "the theories of Darwin, strongly attracted me . . .; and it was hearing Goethe's beautiful essay on Nature . . . that decided me to become a medical student" (1925, *SE* 20:8). Although "Fragment über die Natur" (1780) was actually written by Goethe's Swiss friend G. C. Tobler, the essay reflected Goethe's youthful views so accurately that fifty years later he mistook it for his own and included it in his work. The psychologist Robert Holt attributed the Darwinian biology in Freud's methodological ideas primarily to *Naturphilosophie* (1963, p. 382), of which Goethe is considered one of the pioneers. David Rapaport, a psychologist and highly respected psychoanalytic theorist, more accurately included among "the formative influences on Freud's background . . . an early developed interest in literature (particularly a devotion to Goethe . . .)" (1960, 2:11). Freud admired the psychological insights of poets—he had an extensive knowledge of the English as well as the German writers—and compared the apparent ease with which they attained their insights to the great effort he required to gain the same ends by scientific means. Freud often illustrated his scientific points with apt quotations from Goethe's work, primarily from *Faust*. One favorite quotation, which he utilized particularly in connection with the phylogentic formulations we will discuss later, is a couplet from *Faust* that appears in *Totem and Taboo* (1913 [1912–13] *SE* 13:158) and at the end of his unfinished *Outline of Psycho-Analysis* (1940 [1938], *SE* 23:207): "*Was du ererbt von deinen Vätern hast, Erwirb es, um es zu besitzen*" ("What thou hast inherited from thy fathers, acquire it to make it thine"—*Faust*, part I, scene I [Strachey translation]).

In his own time Goethe was known and honored as a scientist as much as he was as a writer. During Freud's formative years Goethe was still taken seriously as a scientist not only in Haeckel's writings but also in Darwin's *On the Origin of Species*, Claus's *Grundzüge der Zoologie*, and even Brücke's discussion of pigments, which refers to Goethe's color theory. Freud took Brücke's *Die Physiologie der Farben* (1866) to London in fleeing Nazi-occupied Austria. In 1882, the year of Darwin's death and Freud's renunciation of his academic ambitions, Brücke's friend Emil du Bois-Reymond, upon becoming rector of the King Friedrich Wilhelms University at Berlin, delivered an inaugural address in which he attempted to denigrate Goethe as a scientist. "Beside the poet," he said, "the scientist in Goethe fades into the background. Let us at long last put him to rest" (1883 [October 15, 1882], p. 35).

Although this view prevails today, it did not go unchallenged in the period immediately following Freud's graduation from medical school. A countercritique was instantly forthcoming from Solomon Kalischer, whose 1878 "Goethe's Verhaltnis zur Naturwissenschaft und seine Bedeuting in derselben" (Goethe's Relationship to and Significance in Natural Science) served Du Bois-Reymond as an example of the "unjustified and exaggerated way of praising" Goethe that was "bringing out more controversy and detailed criticism" (p. 35n). In "Goethe und Kein Ende" (Goethe and No End) Du Bois-Reymond expressed his irritation with the controversy and wondered "whether Goethe would not have done better for himself and for the world if, following Clairaut's advice to Voltaire, he had left natural science studies to those who were not at the same time great poets" (p. 31). Du Bois-Reymond claimed that it was "irrelevant whether a greater or lesser value is placed on the natural science studies," which he saw as just "filling the intervals between Goethe's poetic activities" (p. 35). Nevertheless, he chose a state occasion on which to join in the controversy.[8] The aforementioned S. Kalischer summarized some of these statements by Du Bois-Reymond for his counterattack in "Goethe als Naturforscher und Herr Du Bois-Reymond als sein Kritiker: Eine Antikritik" (Goethe as Natural Scientist and Herr Du Bois-Reymond as his Critic: An Anti-Critique [1883]). Goethe appears in Freud's work, if not as a scientist, at least as a poet who had many insights consonant with scientific findings, both Darwin's and Freud's own.

Goethe's "guess" at the unity of life included the unity of science, a belief maintained even more rigorously by his critic Du Bois-Reymond. Physiologists like Ludwig and Brücke and supporters of Darwin like Haeckel and Claus all promoted a belief in the unity of science. Biology, as Freud learned from both Claus and Brücke, must follow the laws of physics and chemistry. In the "Project" (1950 [1895]) Freud attempted to explain psychic phenomena in terms of contemporary neurophysiology. Although he was unsuccessful and had to restrict himself to the explanation of psychic phenomena in psychological terms, he maintained the belief that, when science had advanced enough, psychic phenomena would become explicable in physico-chemical terms. For instance, in *Beyond the Pleasure Principle* (1920), where Freud once again attempted to establish a biological basis for his psychological principles, he commented that "the deficiencies in our description would probably vanish if we were already [*schon*

25

jetzt] in a position to replace the psychological terms by physiological or chemical ones" (*SE* 18:60). He iterated this view in 1933 in his *New Introductory Lectures*.

Physico-chemical explanations for biological processes were very highly regarded, if not actually required, by Freud's professors Claus and Brücke and by Haeckel, who like Freud had worked in Brücke's Institute of Physiology. In 1842 Brücke had pledged with Du Bois-Reymond "a solemn oath to put in power this truth: No other forces than the common physical chemical ones are active within the organism. In those cases which cannot at the time be explained by these forces one has either to find the specific way or form of their action by means of the physical and mathematical method, or to assume new forces inherent in matter, reducible to the forces of attraction and repulsion" (Bernfeld 1944, p. 348). Freud did eventually "assume new forces equal in matter" but not without a valiant but unsuccessful attempt to "find the specific way or form of their action by means of the physical mathematical method."

Freud had to content himself with developing the structural model of the psychic apparatus by defining its organizations—the Id, the Ego, and the Superego—as physiologists define organs, that is, by their functions. But he no longer tried to establish a close link between psychological and physiological assumptions as he had in the "Project" (1895). He turned his back on this late nineteenth-century tradition of German psychology and psychopathology and instead adopted the approach of French psychiatry, which "relegates physiological viewpoints into a second plane . . . not by omission but by an intentional exclusion, that it considered to serve a purpose." With this tactic the "clinical observation of the French" psychiatrists "gains undoubtedly in independence," Freud wrote in 1892 in introducing his German translation of Charcot's *Leçons du mardi* (*Tuesday Lectures* [1892–94, *SE* 1:135]). Freud found he needed this independence.

He would be pleased that today at least one neuropsychologist, Eric Kandel of Columbia University, is finding psychoanalytic insights rewarding for some of his neurological research. "Freud's findings about the functioning of the mind provide helpful insights for exploring the functioning of the brain," Kandel concluded an article subtitled "The Impact of Psychiatric Thought on Neurobiological Research" (1979). "What my residency cohorts and I had lost sight of and what we can now again assert, perhaps with slightly more sophistication: What we conceive of as our mind is an expression of the functioning of our brain . . . [as] certainly, in their day,

Meynert, Wagner-Jauregg and Freud had little difficulty in appreciating philosophically" (p. 1037). Kandel could have included Claus.

Haeckel had made for Darwin what may seem an extravagant claim: "The great English scientist presented a theory which for the first time announced a mechanical process for the origin of species, that is on a chemical and physical basis, traceable to so-called blind, unconscious and unplanned forces" (1868, p. 23). From the modern point of view Darwin could not possibly have provided a chemical and physical basis for evolution. He did discuss in natural terms the properties and changes of living bodies which led to speciation; and according to Claus, "the properties and changes of living bodies are strictly dependent on the physico-chemical laws of matter, and this is recognized more clearly as sciences advance" (1884, 1:9).

That Darwin's theory was regarded at the time as providing a physico-chemical basis for evolution is revealed by his critics as well as by advocates like Haeckel. Von Baer had accepted evolution but rejected Darwin's natural selection because he feared that Darwin's chance variations substituted materialism for purposefulness in biology. Well into the twentieth century, the German biologist and vitalist philosopher Hans Adolf Eduard Driesch in particular criticized Darwin because Darwin and his followers refused to see that the laws of life are absolutely different from those of physics and that in the organism purpose is all.

Included among Darwin's credits at the centennial in 1957 was his abolition of "the distinction which divided biology from physics at least since Newton" (Gillespie 1959, p. 284). According to the historian Owsei Temkin, "Darwinism became the symbol of materialistic thought" in German biology. Its answers to the two problems of the origin of species and the correlation between structure and function "bolstered greatly the mechanistic and materialistic tendencies in German biology." It was "no longer necessary to believe in the creation of species"; it had become "possible to explain the apparent finality of the organisms and its parts by adaptation without recourse to plan or purpose" (1959, p. 324).

That the properties and changes of living bodies were "strictly dependent on the physico-chemical laws of matter" was still an expression of faith in an era when, according to Claus, "it must be admitted that we are entirely ignorant of the molecular arrangement of the material basis of a living organism, and it exists under conditions the nature of which is as yet unexplained" (1884, 1:9). The belief in the unity of life had similarly been an expression of faith until Darwin demonstrated its scientific basis. Darwin was more cautious than Goethe and Haeckel about claiming the unity of life in the absence of ample evidence. He waited until 1871 to make explicit in *The Descent of Man* the unity that both his supporters and his opponents considered obvious from the *Origin*. It was the unavoidable conclusion of the unity of life and the genealogical nature of that unity that aroused such opposition when the *Origin* was published and for many years afterward, and even today in fundamentalist America. On the other hand, the notion of the unity of life via descent from an organism originating in the inoganic world was in great part responsible for the excitement and promise that men like Haeckel and Freud found in, or read into, Darwin's work. This tracing of the origin of life to the inorganic world may have been the physico-chemical basis of evolution which Haeckel claimed Darwin had provided; if life were not separately created but had at some time arisen spontaneously from the inorganic world, then it was subject to the same laws as the inorganic world. In addition, the historical and developmental approach that Darwin used, which Freud was to apply later to psychology with equally striking success, had a unifying effect on many branches of science and may have contributed, along with Goethe, Haeckel, and Brücke, to Freud's lifelong conviction of the unity of the sciences. It brought together phenomena from hitherto disparate branches of science—geology, paleontology, comparative anatomy, embryology, ecology, and geography—and demonstrated their interrelatedness.

In 1915, when World War I reduced his patient load to two or three hours a day, Freud made another heroic attempt at unification, again without success. This time it was the seductively unifying principle in biology, "ontogeny recapitulates phylogeny," that liberated the fantasies of Freud and his friends. On April 8 of that year, Freud described to a similarly idled Hungarian colleague garrisoned at Pápa, Sándor Ferenczi, the "mechanism" of scientific creativity as the "succession of daringly playful fantasy and relentlessly realistic criticism" (1987 [1915], p. 83). A draft of Freud's daringly playful fantasy of 1915 was discovered in 1983 by the Frankfurt psychoanalyst editor of *Psyche*, Ilse Grubrich-Simitis, among Ferenczi's letters and published as *A Phylogenetic Fantasy* (1987 [1915]). Obviously, it had not withstood Freud's "relentlessly realistic criticism," for he destroyed the clean copy in his possession, just as he had the earlier "Project." Nevertheless, Freud joined other colleagues in encouraging Ferenczi to publish his own speculative fantasies, which Ferenczi eventually did as *Thalassa: A Theory of Genitality* (1924).

Haeckel's Popularizations of Darwin

The unity of life "guessed at" by Goethe was not, like Darwin's, based on the historical view of a common ancestry or descent through aeons of time but rather on the unified plan of Nature. Only once, in an obscure reference near the end of his long life, did Goethe acknowledge an ancestral relationship: in the morphological compendium of the skeleton of a fossil ox Goethe wrote that "this ancient ox must be regarded as a widely distributed and extinct ancestral race, of which the common and East Indian ox may be accounted descendants" (in Magnus 1949 [1906], p. 42). Goethe's *Urpflanze* and *Urtier* were not prior in time but the ideal types of plant and animal in the Greek sense. In this respect Goethe's view was closer to the paradigm in biology exemplified by Agassiz's *Essay on Classification* (1857) of individually created species, which Darwin's theory confronted and eventually replaced. Agassiz, however, rejected the unity of life and regarded man as a distinct production of the Creator whereas Goethe believed that Nature had used the same model for man as for other animals; this assumption enabled Goethe to discover the intermaxillary bone in the jaw of man, thus destroying as early as 1784 an important distinction between man and other animals.

Another significant aspect of Darwin's theory alien to Goethe is the important role of conflict, or the struggle for existence, in the production of the beautiful and seemingly harmonious adaptations visible in nature. The concept of conflict, as will be discussed later, plays a major role throughout Freud's development of psychoanalysis. A celebrant of harmony everywhere, Goethe combined his science and poetry. His evolutionary views in particular, Goethe felt could be expressed only in poetry.

Although Goethe never developed evolutionary thought as an all-embracing principle explaining the structure of the entire animal kingdom, he may have been approaching that position in his poetry closely enough to lay the groundwork for Darwin's theories and their popularization by Haeckel and others. Occasionally in his poetry Goethe introduced elements from the contemporary evolutionary thinking of Comte George Louis Leclerc de Buffon and Geoffrey St. Hilaire, such as the ocean as the point of origin in *Faust* for homunculus seeking to be created, but he seems to have been unaware of the evolutionary work of their fellow Frenchman Lamarck. From Goethe's poetry alone, without recourse to his or any other scientific writings, members of the educated German public (like Freud) could be acquainted with the idea that man was not a distinct creation but part of a series from the lowliest organic forms through the ape. The German reader could be familiar from Goethe's poetry with slow geological changes that had shaped the world, and also the long time required for homunculus to go through many forms before he became man. From reading Goethe's poetry one learned that organic forms were related to function but purpose played no role in creating forms, that organic forms were influenced by external conditions as well as by inner laws of formations, and that fossils could be "arranged by their relationship to the various epochs in the earth's history" (p. 208) and vice versa.

Without studying science, the German reader of Goethe had many of the bits of information about nature that Darwin's theory served to unify. The unifying effect of Darwin's theory could be appreciated by, and arouse excitement in, a young reader like Freud even before he had studied science. Freud might have been particularly susceptible to the concept of unity. Even if he were a "Godless Jew," as he once described himself to his minister friend Oskar Pfister, he was reared and lived his life among a people dedicated to remembering a history too rich in ancestors who went to the scaffold or stake, but not yet the gas chambers reserved for his four sisters, proclaiming the only creed of their ancient religion, "God is One."

2

Darwin, Lamarck, and
Lamarckism

Today, Darwin's name and Lamarck's are readily identified as representing two opposing theories of evolution. Darwin's is commonly assumed to signify evolution by natural selection and Lamarck's the inheritance of acquired characteristics. But their works were not always interpreted in this fashion. The abstraction of these single items from the many faceted theories presented by Darwin and Lamarck obscures, even falsifies, their differences and similarities. This modern oversimplification led to the remark by Freud's protégé Ernst Kris, on a BBC centennial broadcast (1956), that "Freud's Lamarckian propensities were much regretted by many of us" (5:631–33). He was, of course, referring to Freud's adamant insistence on the inheritance of acquired characteristics.

The notion of the inheritance of acquired characteristics did not originate with Lamarck. It is an age-old folk belief found in the Old Testament and Greek mythology. Until the end of the nineteenth century, when it was challenged by August Weismann's germ-plasm theory, there was little cause to doubt it, and few did: only the first century B.C. Roman poet Lucretius and two men in the eighteenth century, the Swiss naturalist Charles Bonnet and the German philosophical godfather of biological empiricism, Immanuel Kant. Otherwise it went unquestioned throughout the ages. Darwin's grandfather Dr. Erasmus Darwin, whose *Zoonomia* (1794–96) contained some evolutionary predictions, believed it. So did the eighteenth-century French encyclopedist Denis Diderot, whom Freud credited with recognizing the "essential characteristics, . . . universality, . . . content and . . . fate" of the Oedipus complex with his "remarkable sentence: 'Si le petit sauvage était abandonné à lui-même, qu'il conservât toute son imbécillité, et qu'il réunît au peu de raison de l'enfant au berceau la violence des passions de l'homme de trente ans, il tordrait le col à son père et coucherait avec sa mère' ('If the little savage were left to himself, preserving all his foolishness and adding to the limited reason of a child in the cradle the violent passions of a man of thirty, he would strangle his father and lie with his mother'" (1916 [1917], *SE* 16:338; 1931 [1930], 21:251; 1940 [1938], 23:192). Around Darwin's time a few scientists began to express doubts about use inheritance but not until Weismann, toward the end of the century, did anyone point out "how thoroughly our conceptions as to the causes of transmutation of species must become changed if such an inheritance should not occur" (1894, p. 14). The twentieth century and the development of genetics took off from there.

The history of the two theories of evolution and an attempt to reconstruct what they meant to Freud strongly suggest that Freud associated Darwin rather than Lamarck with the inheritance of acquired characteristics, and that he associated Lamarck with evolution, or adaptation, by "will" and "volition,"[1] as we are about to see.

LAMARCK BEFORE DARWIN

Fifty years before Darwin, in his *Philosophie Zoologique* (1809), Lamarck had proposed a theory of ascent from the inorganic to the higher animals. Darwin's work renewed interest in Lamarck's evolutionary writings. Haeckel in particular, who made the promulgation of Darwin's theory his mission in life, searched everywhere for precursors and claimed the descent theory for Lamarck, stating in his typically exaggerated manner that "for fifty years it was not spoken of at all" (1876 [1868], 1:112). Darwin, on the other hand, did not mention Lamarck in the *Origin* until the third edition in 1861 and then wrote, "Passing over authors from the classical period to that of Buffon, with whose writings I am not familiar, Lamarck was the first man whose conclusions on this subject excited much attention" (p. xiii).

The truth probably lies somewhere between Haeckel's assertion and Darwin's generous remark. Lamarck himself once observed bitterly, "I know full well that very few will be interested in what I am going to propose, and that among those who do read this essay, the greater part will pretend to find in it only systems, only vague opinions, in no way founded in exact knowledge" (1802, p. 69; translated by Gillespie, p. 267). Many of Lamarck's scientific colleagues had been embarrassed by what they regarded as the aberrations of a gifted observer and preferred to meet Lamarck's evolutionary speculations with silence. Although there was some debate, Goethe, for example, who was informed about and interested in the evolutionary thinking of Buffon and Geoffrey St. Hilaire, remained unaware of Lamarck's evolutionary work. On the other hand, Darwin, who knew of it, probably from Lyell, reveals in his 1844 correspondence with his botanist friend Joseph Hooker that the two younger men were highly critical of Lamarck: "Heaven forfend me from Lamarck nonsense of a 'tendency to progression,' 'adaptation from the slow willing of animals,' etc!" (1881, 2:23) Darwin wrote Hooker on January 11. In other letters dated Down 1884 and September (no date) Darwin referred to "Lamarck's book on descent" as "veritable rubbish" (2:29) and to "his absurd though clever work [which] has done the subject harm" (2:39). Hooker's attitude toward Lamarck is reflected in Darwin's expectation that when he writes to Hooker "the conclusions I am led to are not widely different from his [Lamarck's]" and that "you [Hooker] will now groan and think to yourself 'on what a man have I been wasting my time and writing to'" (2:23–24).

Haeckel was not alone in his belief that "Lamarck's descent theory had been dead until suddenly renewed in 1859 by the exceptionally higher contribution of Charles Darwin's *On the Origin of Species in Plants and Animals by Natural Selection*" (1868, p. 22). Emil Du Bois-Reymond, sixteen years older than Haeckel, also testified that "the older attempts by Lamarck and others who tried with inadequate means to arrive at a new point of view in Natural Philosophy were forgotten." Scientists "had become accustomed to the idea that the problem could not be solved by natural means. Some independent spirits had some doubts [about] the valdity of the old dogma of the immutability of species—but kept quiet" (1876, pp. 9–10). The recollection of August Weismann, who was born the same year (1834) as Haeckel, makes it appear likely that Haeckel was reflecting the subjective experience of his own generation of German scientists: "We, who were then the younger men, studying in the fifties, had no idea that a theory of evolution had ever been put forward." It seemed to Weismann as if "all the teachers in our universities had drunk of the waters of Lethe" and had "utterly forgotten that such a theory had ever been discussed." In reaction to the "philosophical flights on the part of natural science" in the previous period of *Naturphilosophie*, German scientists had developed a "deep antipathy to all far-reaching deductions" and strove after "purely inductive investigation."

Half a century later Weismann could recall the motto inscribed under the picture of one of his "most stimulating" teachers, the gifted anatomist Jakob Henle: "There is a virtue of renunciation, not in the province of morality alone, but in that of intellect as well." The theory of evolution, whether Lamarck's or Darwin's, fell into the class of "more general problems of life" and of "far-reaching deductions" that the virtuous intellect was called upon to renounce. The young students "nourished only in the results of detailed research . . . uncorrelated, unintelligible in the higher sense . . . without being clear as to what was lacking . . . missed the deeper correlation of the many separate disciplines." Into this setting Darwin's synthesis fell like "a bolt from the blue. . . . The world was as though thunderstruck" (1904 [1902], 1:27–28).

"How will it be with you, dear reader, after you have read this book?" (trans. in Weismann 1:28), Bronn, the translator, queried in the preface to the earliest German edition of Darwin. Students like Haeckel and Weismann "eagerly devoured" Darwin's book with "delight and enthusiasm," aware of the "cool aversion" and even "violent opposition" of their seniors. In "their legitimate striving after purely inductive investigation" the older naturalists "forgot that the mere gathering of facts is not enough, that the drawing of conclusions is an essential part of the induction, and that a mass of bare facts, however enormous, does not constitute a science" (Weismann 1:27). For these older naturalists Darwin's theory "was a blow unlike any seen before in the history of science, so long prepared and yet so sudden. So quietly introduced and yet so powerful" (Du Bois-Reymond 1876, p. 10).

Lamarck's arguments, when rediscovered, had been made obsolete or proved erroneous by evidence brought to light since 1809 by various branches of burgeoning science. In that half century the "elucidation of the structure of the lower animals and plants had given rise to wholly new conceptions of their relations; histology and embryology, in the modern sense, had been created; physiology had been reconstituted." The facts of geographical and geological distribution had "prodigiously multiplied" and been "reduced to order" (Huxley 1887, 2:189). These facts were receiving their most up-to-date and exciting interpretation in the works of Darwin.

It is unlikely that Freud would have turned to Lamarck before reading Darwin. Nor is there any evidence of his interest in Lamarck's evolutionary work until 1916.

"LAMARCK'S DESCENT THEORY . . .
RENEWED . . . BY . . . DARWIN'S"

Unlike the students of Haeckel's and Weismann's generation twenty years earlier, Freud probably would have known during his *Gymnasium* days not only about evolution but that the name of Lamarck as well as that of Darwin was associated with it. Opponents of Darwin, such as the English moralist Samuel Butler and the French scientists, called attention to Lamarck's priority in order to demonstrate Darwin's lack of originality. Haeckel considered Lamarck's contribution important enough to maintain that "it is proper to call natural selection theory and not the whole descent theory 'Darwinism.' If one is to call the theory of descent by its earlier founder, it must be called 'Lamarckism'" (1868, p. 23).

When, at the suggestion of Bronn, Darwin added "An Historical Sketch of the Recent Progress of Opinion on the Origin of Species" to the 1861 edition of the *Origin*, he described Lamarck's evolutionary theories at length. Whether Darwin had actually developed an appreciation of Lamarck's contribution or was just being tactful in print, the tone is in sharp contrast to that of his 1844 correspondence with Hooker. "This justly celebrated naturalist," Darwin now wrote, "first published his views in 1801, . . . enlarged them in 1809 in his 'Philosophie Zoologique' and . . . in 1815, in his Introduction to his 'Hist. Nat. des Animaux sans Vertèbres.'" Darwin acknowledged that "in these works" Lamarck "upholds the doctrine that all species, including man, are descended from other species."

Darwin overgenerously credited Lamarck rather than himself with being the first to do the "eminent service of arousing attention to the probability of all change in the organic as well as in the inorganic world being the result of law, and not of miraculous interposition." Following the scientific tradition of citing the authority of predecessors, not his own originality or priority, to make his work acceptable, Darwin even conceded to Lamarck three of his own reasons for espousing the theory of evolution: (1) "Lamarck seems to have been chiefly led to his conclusion on the gradual change of species by the difficulty of distinguishing species and varieties," a task that had become impossible in the interval between Lamarck and Darwin, particularly for botanists like Hooker and Asa Gray and for beetle collectors like Darwin and Wallace; (2) "the almost perfect gradation of forms in certain organic groups," which Darwin and Wallace were able, as Lamarck had not been, to observe in their collections of English beetles; and (3) "the analogy of domestic productions" of animal breeders.

Although Darwin included "the analogy of domestic productions" as a basis for Lamarck's theory of the gradual change of species, it did not play the same role in his predecessor's theory. Lamarck recognized the gradual changes in domestic productions but did not draw the analogy between the breeder's and nature's selection of gradual changes, so obvious since Darwin called attention to it. But it is not as obvious as it at first appears. The gradual changes have to appear somehow for the breeder or nature to select them. Therefore Darwin is uncritical in listing most of the means of modification in Lamarck's theory. Lamarck "attributed something to the direct action of the physical conditions of life, something to the crossing of already existing forms, and much to use and disuse, that is, to the effects of habit. To this latter agency he seems to attribute all the beautiful adaptations in nature; such as the long neck of the giraffe for browsing on the branches of trees." Darwin was not critical of modification through use and disuse but only of Lamarck's seeming to attribute *all* nature's beautiful adaptations to it.

Darwin omitted entirely any mention of Lamarck's "adaptations from the slow willing of animals" that had so offended him in 1844. What in the privacy of his youthful correspondence he called "Lamarck nonsense of a 'tendency to progression,'" he designated in publication as "a law of progressive development," indicating his reservation very subtly with the word "but" to separate it from the other acceptable means of modification: "But he [Lamarck] likewise believed in a law of progressive development; and as all forms of life thus tended to progress, in order to account for the existence at the present day of very simple productions, he maintained that such forms were now spontaneously generated" (p. xiii). Darwin never accepted either "progressive development" or "adaptations from the slow willing of animals" or, for that matter, "spontaneous generation" as valid explanations. But the other means of modification that he attributed to Lamarck, including "use and disuse," Darwin found place for in his own work, which disseminated them more effectively than had Lamarck's. Darwin intuitively favored natural selection over modification through use and disuse, but he lacked scientific support for what seemed a personal preference. Good scientist that he was, he dutifully increased his references to use and disuse in each new edition of the *Origin*.

Except for the "Historical Sketch" the name of Lamarck is nowhere associated in Darwin's writings with the inheritance of acquired characteristics. In reading the remainder of Darwin's *Origin* Freud would have encountered Lamarck's name, not in relation to the inheritance of acquired characteristics, but for being the first to call attention to "the very important distinction between real affinities and analogical or adaptive resemblances" (1869 [1859], p. 362). In the *Variation*, where, as will be discussed in the next chapter, Darwin applies the inheritance of acquired characteristics and suggests a theory of inheritance to accommodate it, Lamarck is not mentioned. In *The Descent of Man* Darwin is happy to mention forerunners and puts Lamarck at the head of the list of those who had concluded "that man is the co-descendant with other species of some ancient, lower, and extinct form" (1888 [1871], p. 3). But unlike Lyell, Darwin does not acknowledge Lamarck as the originator of the idea of the inheritance of acquired characteristics.

DARWIN'S CRITICISM OF LAMARCK'S LAW OF PROGRESSIVE DEVELOPMENT

Darwin also added to the body of the third edition of the *Origin* his criticism of Lamarck's belief in an interior orthogenetic force, or law of progressive development toward perfection. Darwin regarded this, not use-inheritance, as a crucial difference between his theory and Lamarck's. Darwin rightly objected that "if all organic beings thus tend to rise in the scale, how is it that throughout the world a multitude of the lowest forms still exist?" And "how is it that in each great class some forms are more highly developed than others?" And why have not "the more highly developed forms everywhere supplanted and exterminated the lower?" Lamarck could solve this problem by supposing that new and simple forms were continually arising by spontaneous generation, the still scientifically respectable theory of his day that organisms could arise de novo, as anyone could see for himself in the eruption of maggots or fruitflies where dung heaps were prevalent and refrigeration was nonexistent. But by Darwin's time this belief in spontaneous generation was no longer acceptable. "I need hardly say," Darwin wrote, "that Science in her present state does not countenance the belief that living creatures are now ever produced from inorganic matter."

Darwin stressed that his theory of natural selection includes "no necessary and universal law of advancement of development." It only "takes advantage of such variations as arise and are beneficial to each creature under its complex relations of life." Therefore the "present existence of lowly organized productions offers no difficulty" and requires no resort to scientifically discredited spontaneous generation. If there were no advantage to "an infusorian animalcule—to an intestinal worm—or even to an earth-worm, to be highly organized," then "these forms would be left by natural selection unimproved or but little improved" for "indefinite ages." And that is just what geology shows us, that "some of the lowest forms, as the infusoria and rhizopods," have remained in "nearly their present state" for an "enormous period" (1861 [1859], pp. 134–35). They were neither newly formed by spontaneous generation nor predestined to advance to perfection.

Outstanding German biologists such as von Baer and the Swiss botanist Karl Wilhelm von Nägeli, professor at Munich from 1858, were among those who came to support evolution or transformationism on the basis of an innate tendency toward perfection. By analogy with the development of the embryo, where tissues are more plastic in the earlier stages than later, von Baer postulated that this interior orthogenetic force had "acted much more potently formerly in the youthful period of the earth than at present" (1876, 2:24; trans. in Holmes 1947, 37:12). Von Baer, in congratulating Darwin in 1860, had overlooked this basic discrepancy in their views. When he realized it, he regretted the use to which Darwin had put his (von Baer's) work.

Nägeli presented his first real evolutionary paper six years after the *Origin* as an address at a public meeting of the Royal Academy of Sciences at Munich, March 28, 1865. Darwin wrote to his new German translator, Carus, suggesting that if he were adding an appendix to the *Origin*, as Bronn had done, Nägeli's paper "Über Entstehung und Begriff der naturhistorischen Art" (On the Origin and Concept of Natural Species) would be "worth noticing as one of the most able pamphlets on the subject." However, Darwin was "far from agreeing" with Nägeli that the "acquisition of certain characters which appear to be of no service to plants, offers any great difficulty," or "affords a proof of some innate tendency in plants towards perfection" (1887–88, 3:49). He wrote as much to Nägeli: "On one or two points, I think, you have a little misunderstood me, though I dare say I have not been cautious in expressing myself. The remark which has struck me most, is that on the position of the leaves not having been acquired through natural selection from not being of any special importance to the plant. I well remember being formerly troubled by an analogous difficulty." He excused himself: "It was owing to forgetfulness that I did not notice this difficulty in the 'Origin.'" Although Darwin could "offer no explanation of such facts" and could "only hope to see that they may be explained," he could "hardly see how they support the doctrine of some necessary development." It was "not clear" to him "that a plant, with its leaves placed at some particular angle, or with its ovules in some particular position, thus stands higher than another plant" (3:51). Darwin himself discussed some of Nägeli's points in the fifth edition of the *Origin*, thus giving them even wider distribution.

With rare exceptions, Freud was not enough of an optimist to be attracted to a belief in an innate tendency toward perfection, whether the belief was espoused by Nägeli, von Baer, or Lamarck. Freud's famous dictum "Where id was, there let ego become" (*Wo Es war, soll Ich werden, Gesammelte Werke* 15:86; "where id was, there ego shall be," Strachey translation *SE* 22:80)[2] could not be realized without effort on man's part. Like Darwin, Freud saw struggle; and the most Freud dared hope for in "the eternal struggle between the trends of love and death" was that "the other of the two 'Heavenly Powers,' eternal Eros, will make an effort to assert himself in the struggle with his equally immortal adversary. But who can foresee with what success and with what result?" (1930 *SE* 21:145). Thus for Freud there was no Lamarckian orthogenetic force toward progress but two forces eternally struggling. A notable exception is in Freud's letter to Einstein on "Why War?" (1933 [1932], *SE* 22:214–15), where, "perhaps to reassure himself against the devastating reality, Freud says that an innate trend towards higher culturization makes men allergic to war" (Sterba in Ritvo 1970, 18:201).

THE ROLE OF ENVIRONMENT

Freud subscribed to the view of evolution or development through the pressure of environmental demands, which he called the "exigencies of life," whether operating by natural selection or by habit. Freud even went so far as to say that in the "last resort it may be assumed that every internal compulsion which makes itself felt in the development of human beings was originally—that is, in *the history of mankind*—only an external one" (1915b: *SE* 14:282). In his *Philosophie Zoologique* Lamarck had recognized the importance of environmental changes as one step in the chain leading to organic changes. His readers and interpreters for the most part seemed to have overlooked it in favor of either an internal factor such as the "innate tendency to progression" or the "will" or "volition" of the animal. According to E. S. Russell, "Almost his [Darwin's] greatest service to biology was that he made biologists realize as they never did before the vast importance of environment" (1916, pp. 231–32). Haeckel, in promoting Darwin, invented the term *ecology* and introduced it in his *Generelle Morphologie* (1866) to designate what he regarded as one of the many notable aspects of Darwin's thought.

The question of the innate versus the accidental occupied Freud for a long time, until he resolved it with the "complemental series" in 1915. Freud in his lifetime traversed the entire gamut of the nature-nurture controversy: from the emphasis on heredity (Charcot), then on experience (childhood seductions), back to the innate (the Oedipus complex), to the recognition of the interplay between them (also recognized by Goethe), and finally to the study of the intricate nature of that interplay (the complemental series). When Freud entered practice, the etiology of hysteria was explained by hereditary taint, a view supported by the great Charcot. Freud did not discard this view as rapidly as he did Erb's popular electrotherapy. In "Fragment of an Analysis of a Case of Hysteria" (1905 [1901]) Freud still mentioned the syphilitic history of the patient's father, as he had done in his earlier hysteria papers. But that same year, in his *Three Essays on Sexuality*, he pointed out that "writers who concern themselves with explaining the characteristics and reactions of the adult have devoted much more attention to the primaeval period which is comprised in the life of the individual's ancestors—have, that is, ascribed much more influence to heredity—than to the other primaeval period, which falls within the lifetime of the individual himself—that is, to childhood. One would surely have supposed that the influence of this latter period would be easier to understand and could claim to be considered before that of heredity" (1905, *SE* 7:173).

One view of the etiology of neurotic illness did emphasize the experiential: neurosis was likened to a foreign body that needs to be excised. The cathartic method that Freud learned from Josef Breuer, co-discoverer of the Hering–Breuer reflex,[3] attributed the source of the symptoms to a forgotten trauma—a repressed memory—which Freud found was always of a sexual nature and always, when traced to its source, an infantile sexual trauma. Freud's realization of the importance of experiential factors was derived from the tales of early childhood seduction of his hysteria patients. Today we are constantly bombarded by reports of the sexual victimization of children but in the 1890s such information was restricted for the most part to the consulting room and the confessional, and not, as today, widely available in autobiographical literature. "Sexual assaults on young girls by their fathers had been canvassed in public since the beginning of the nineteenth century," but the "matter was treated with considerable reserve in the medical literature" (Gay 1988, p. 95n).

Not having heard of it in his training, Freud had good reason to believe that he was about to achieve the fame and fortune he sought through his discovery that the origin of neuroses was the experiential in his patients' histories—that is, childhood seductions—and not heredity, as he had been taught. By 1897 Freud had to recognize that not all his patients were telling him the truth. Freud's greatness lay in his willingness to admit that, even though in several cases he had been able to obtain corroboration of the patients' reports from such outside sources as physicians, governesses, parents, or siblings, for the most part the seductions were fantasies and therefore innate. Turning this defeat into victory was one of Freud's triumphs. He confided to Fliess in a letter of November 21, 1897: "Were I depressed, jaded, unclear in my mind, such doubts might be taken for signs of weakness. But as I am in just the opposite state, I must acknowledge them to be the result of honest and effective intellectual labour, and I am proud that after penetrating so far I am still capable of such criticism. Can these doubts be only an episode on the way to further knowledge?" (1954 [1887–1902], pp. 216–17). It did indeed lead to knowledge of the importance of the early fantasy life in mental development—to the discovery of "psychic reality."

From there Freud was able to put hereditary disposition and experiential factors in their proper perspective, at least ontogenetically. He did not relinquish completely what he regarded as his "great discovery" of the importance of the experiential—the trauma of childhood seductions—but displaced it from the ontogenetic to the phylogenetic, from the childhood experience of the individual to the childhood experience of the race (Benjamin 1961, p. 23). The discoverer of the Oedipus complex followed Darwin in assuming that an innate or inherited characteristic had behind it the developmental or experiential history of the species.

The possibilities of an innate tendency to evolve and the development of necessary organs "at will" in Lamarck's theory made the experiential or accidental in developmental history less significant than did Darwin's theory. Nevertheless, Freud's attempt to displace the importance of the experiential from the ontogenetic to the phylogenetic is one of the most famous (or infamous) uses he made of the neo-Lamarckian idea of the inheritance of acquired characteristics. His displacement of the prime importance of

41

the experiential from the ontogenetic to the phylogentic, plus the restriction of psychoanalytic observation to a single species, may explain the very marked difference in the fate of Freud's ontogenetic and phylogenetic formulations. The phylogenetic were for the most part speculative and controversial; some—for instance, the death instinct—contributed to a great deal of confusion (Schur 1966). The ontogenetic led to important discoveries.

Freud saw the nature-nurture controversy as "a case in which scientifically thinking people distort a cooperation into an antithesis" whereas for Freud, Goethe's "Δaimon kai Tyxh [fate and chance] and not one or the other is decisive" (1960, "Letter October 1, 1911, to Else Voigtländer," p. 284). For the interplay of the accidental and constitutional factors Freud developed the etiological or complemental series, which he added to the 1915 edition of the *Three Essays:* "To cover the majority of cases we can picture what has been described as a 'complemental series,' in which the diminishing intensity of one factor is balanced by the increasing intensity of the other" (*SE* 7:239–40). Here and in "Analysis Terminable and Interminable" (1937), he explained the importance of the concept of the complemental series for the etiology of mental illness: At one end of the series the *anlage* can be so "lethal" that, even given a normal, "average-expectable" environment, mental illness develops, whereas at the other extreme of the series severe environmental noxae can be mainly responsible for pathology.

Outside psychoanalysis "the traditional heredity-environment dilemma" raged on as a "pseudo-problem" even though "further evidence" collected by students of animal behavior "indicates that in all animals intrinsic and extrinsic factors are closely related throughout ontogeny." More than forty years after Freud, the evolutionary biologist T. C. Schneirla, a curator at the American Museum of Natural History, reached the same conclusion as Freud and restated the mature-nurture problem for his colleagues: "The question is how development occurs in the particular animal under prevailing conditions, not what heredity specifically contributes or environment specifically contributes, or how much either contributes proportionally, to the process" (Schneirla 1957, pp. 78–108).

In 1915 Freud applied the series not only to differences between individuals but to ontogeny. "We shall be in even closer harmony with psychoanalytic research if we give a place of preference among the accidental factors to the experiences of early childhood" (7:240). Near the end of his life Freud found an analogy in embryology: "The damage inflicted on the ego

by its first experiences gives us the appearance of being dispropor-
tionately great; but we have only to take as an analogy the differences in
the results produced by the prick of a needle into a mass of cells in the act
of cell-division (as in Roux's experiments) and into the fully grown animal
which eventually develops out of them" (1940 [1938], *SE* 23:185).

"CONCLUSION ON THE GRADUAL CHANGE OF SPECIES"

Saltation, the theory that evolution proceeds by huge leaps or jumps,
became an issue after the publication of the *Origin*. Darwin found the inheritance of acquired characteristics compatible with natural selection but
opposed all attempts to explain evolution either by an internal orthogenetic force or by monstrosities, as huge jumps were also called; he always
maintained his belief in gradualism, or development by minute changes.
Even his close friend and staunchest advocate, Thomas Henry Huxley,
was critical of Darwin for too frequently reiterating in the *Origin* that "nature does not make jumps." In an 1894 letter to the British naturalist
William Bateson, Huxley recalled his own protracted difference of opinion
with Darwin on this point. Bateson, in a book *On Variation* published that
year, "inclined to advocate the possibility of considerable saltus"; Huxley
responded that he "always took the same view, much to Mr. Darwin's disgust." Huxley and Darwin "used often to debate it" (Huxley 1901, 2:394).

There was much consideration of saltus following Darwin's publication
of the *Origin*. Another close and long-time friend of Darwin's, the botanist Joseph Hooker, regarded it as "a middle way, loosely much written
about, often broached and attempted." He cited Owen as "hedging" for
saltus in his 1860 review of Darwin for the *Edinburgh Review* and thought
there was "a deal to be said for" it. Hooker had been carefully examining
plants at London's Kew Gardens for saltus for fifteen years, even before
publication of the *Origin*. Darwin could have drawn support for his arguments with Huxley about saltus from Hooker's failure in the fifteen years
to find "any reasonably cumulative support in facts, and none in Geog. dis-
trib. or classification." Hooker expected other views to turn up but "in the
present state of science" he looked to "an advance on Darwin's *general*
views" as the "most hopeful future" (1918, 1:518–19).

Darwin wrote of saltus to Asa Gray, whom he asked to thank his American critic, Professor Parson, "for the extremely liberal and fair spirit" of
his essay in *Silliman's Journal* of July 1860. "Please tell him that I reflected much on the chance of favourable monstrosities (*i.e.*, great and

sudden variation) arising. I have, of course, no objection to" great and sudden variation: "indeed it would be a great aid." But "after much labour," Darwin "could find nothing which satisfied" him "of the probability of such occurrences." There seemed to him "in almost every case too much, too complex, and too beautiful adaptation, in every structure to believe in its sudden production." He pointed out that he had "alluded under the head of beautifully hooked seeds to such [a] possibility. Monsters are apt to be sterile, or *not* to transmit monstrous peculiarities. Look at the fineness of gradation in the shells of successive *sub-stages* of the same great formation; I could give many other considerations which made me doubt such [a] view. It holds, to a certain extent, with domestic productions no doubt, where man preserves some abrupt change in structure." But it "amused" Darwin "to see Sir R. Murchison," director general of the Geological Survey of Great Britain, "quoted as judge of affinities of animals," and it gave him "a cold shudder to hear of any one speculating about a true crustacean giving birth to a true fish!" (1887–88, 2:333–34).

What made Darwin shudder was nevertheless soon to be seriously proposed and supported in Germany as Kölliker's theory of heterogeneous generation, according to which an organism might suddenly produce an offspring belonging to a quite different class. Von Baer favored the theory of the Swiss anatomist and physiologist Albert von Kölliker and conjectured that the sudden flowering of past types such as trilobites and cephalopods without apparent transitional stages could be accounted for by his notion of the greater plasticity and modifiability of newly arisen types. In contrast to von Baer's antagonism toward Darwin's theory of natural selection, which stemmed from his fear that it would substitute mere chance for purpose in the production of the adaptations of life, Kölliker's presentation of his theory of heterogeneous generation in "Über die Darwin'sche Schöpfungstheorie: Ein Vortrag" (On the Darwinian Creation Theory: A Lecture [1864]) misinterpreted and attacked Darwin for the opposite reason for being "in the fullest sense of the word, a Teleologist" (p. 199, translated in Huxley 1893, 2:88).

Freud must have experienced a feeling of déjà vu when his own complicated theory was similarly misinterpreted and attacked for opposite reasons: by some critics as excluding the experiential in favor of the constitutional ("biology is destiny") and by other critics as excluding the constitutional in favor of the environmental (childhood experiences cause neuroses), whereas Freud, as we have seen, promulgated a complemental series of the interaction of constitution and environment. Lesser minds assume that only one or the other, DAIMON *or* TYXH (Fate *or* Chance) can be operative and gratuitously attribute the same limitation to Freud. There seems to be a tendency in all but our greatest minds to prefer to choose sides rather than consider the possibility that seemingly contradictory ideas can coexist. Newton included both a wave theory and a corpuscular theory of the motion of light in his *Opticks* (1704). It took almost two centuries of advances in physics before physicists understood that a belief in the motion of light as both wave and corpuscular was no aberration on the part of their great predecessor. Lamarck, Goethe, Darwin, and Freud all recognized that neither heredity nor environment operates in isolation but of necessity through interaction with each other.

Kölliker gratuitously assumed that Darwin's belief in minute variations involved variations in the single direction of a necessary and continued progress of organisms, whereas Haeckel, Huxley, and others regarded as "one of the many peculiar merits of Darwin's hypothesis" (Huxley 1893, 2:88) that it involved no such belief. The variations according to Darwin, as von Baer rightly feared in opposing Darwin, were all chance in all directions; only the functional ones survived. Kölliker's other objections to Darwin's theory of variation by gradation were more telling: "No transitional forms between existing species are known," and "no transitional forms of animals are met with among the organic remains of earlier epochs" (1864, p. 190 trans. in Huxley 1893, 2:89).[4] Huxley agreed with Kölliker that "Mr. Darwin has unnecessarily hampered himself by adhering so strictly to his favourite 'Natura non facit saltum.' We greatly suspect that she does make considerable jumps in the way of variation now and then, and that these saltations give rise to some of the gaps which appear to exist in the series of known forms" (2:97). The Swiss botanist Oswald Heer was another of the Germanophonic scientists who, after the publication of Darwin's *Origin*, promoted the idea of evolution by suddenly arising monstrosities. In his correspondence with Heer, Darwin referred to "extremely gradual evolution, to which view I know you are strongly opposed" (1903, 2:239).

Darwin's staunchly maintained view that "nature does not make jumps," although subject to much controversy and attack during his lifetime and into the twentieth century, did not originate with Darwin, as such controversy might seem to indicate. Its lengthy historical development has been traced by Lovejoy in *The Great Chain of Being* (1936). For our purpose, it is sufficient to point out that Freud, who felt bound to development by gradation, could have found gradualism expressed in some form in Goethe and Lamarck as well as Darwin. On this point the views of all three men converged. When Darwin added the "Historical Sketch" to the *Origin*, he praised Lamarck not only for "the eminent service of arousing attention to the probability of all change in the organic, as well as in the inorganic world, being the result of law, and not of miraculous interposition," but also for "his conclusion on the gradual change of species" (1861 [1859], xiii). Darwin's unmistakable insistence in the *Origin* that "natura non facit saltus" and the controversy it aroused made this a lively issue in this period of Freud's life. The close identification of Darwin's name and theory with the concept of variation by minute gradations contributed to the assumption in the early years of the twentieth century, following Hugo de Vries's mistaken "discovery" of sudden large mutations, that Darwinism was moribund.

The difficulties besetting natural selection from the state of knowledge in physics and biology during the nineteenth century might have been alleviated had Nägeli appreciated the pioneer work on heredity sent to him by the Austrian priest Gregor Johann Mendel in 1865. Mendel's work remained unknown to the scientific world until its simultaneous rediscovery in 1900 by three other botanists, Carl Franz Joseph Erich Correns at the University of Tübingen, Erich von Tschermak-Seysenegg in Austria, and Hugo de Vries at the University of Amsterdam. This was not the first time in the history of science that some early scientific finding has had to await further developments to prepare other scientists to recognize its worth. De Vries's mistaken "discovery" of large mutations once again militated against the theory associated with Darwin's name of change occurring through the slow accretion of characters. Huxley's grandson Julian (1958) points out that if Darwin had been familiar with Mendel's work he too might very well have been misled into some sort of saltational mutationism, like de Vries, Bateson, and other Mendelians.[5] It was only as the twentieth century progressed and the American zoologist T. H. Morgan extended the work of Weismann that "biological thought swung around to the opinion that however wrong Darwin may have been in certain details, he had been justified in his view that small changes are less apt to be detrimental to the organism and are the more likely modes of evolutionary change" (Eiseley 1958, p. 229). Today criticism of Darwin for his gradualism has reopened under the leadership of Stephen Jay Gould, professor of geology at Harvard.[6]

THE IMPORTANCE OF "WILL" IN LAMARCK'S THEORY

In 1903, a few years before his work on *Drosophila* revealed the discrete physical basis of heredity that he called the chromosome, the American zoologist Thomas Hunt Morgan tried to correct what he considered a
long-standing misconception of the importance of the role of "will" in
Lamarck's theory and to relegate its function to exercise or "use." His success may be responsible for the identification today of the term *Lamarckism* with the belief in use-inheritance. Use-inheritance had not yet been
discredited; it had only been called into question by Weismann and his followers. In 1903 Morgan obviously thought he was elevating Lamarck by
emphasizing use-inheritance and denigrating "will" in the interpretation of
Lamarck's theory. The issue for him was not between use-inheritance and
natural selection. Shortly afterward his own research on the common
fruitfly, *Drosophila*, led to the discovery of the chromosome that would
make it no more fortunate for Lamarck's theory to be associated with the
inheritance of acquired characteristics than with "will" and "volition."

In 1909, the discoverer of the chromosome published an article, "For
Darwin," in *Popular Science Monthly*. It was the year in which France
celebrated the Lamarck centennial; "For Darwin" had been presented at
Columbia University the previous year, when England and America were
observing the Darwin semicentennial. It testifies that at that time, when
Freud was turning fifty-three, there were still "three rival claims" attempting "to explain how evolution takes place: (1) that which adopts the
theory of natural selection in one or another of its aspects; (2) that which
maintains that acquired characters are inherited; (3) that which, in trying
to penetrate deeper into the mystery of life, ascribes to living matter a
purposefulness—an almost conscious response to 'the course of nature.'
Today [that is, in 1908], the claimants to the second are designated
Lamarckian or neo-Lamarckian evolutionists." Morgan, in honoring Darwin, emphasized that "Darwin himself adopted the first and the second of
these views. His whole philosophy stands opposed in principle to the third
view" (p. 378). During the next two decades evidence accumulated from
biological research validating natural selection and invalidating use-inheritance. Although "Lamarckian assumptions," as Freud's younger psychoanalyst friends Heinz Hartmann, Ernst Kris, and Rudolph Loewenstein
pointed out, "strictly speaking . . . were not invalidated" (1964, p. 96), for
biologists' purposes they were by 1930, when Sir Ronald Aylmer Fisher
published *The Genetical Theory of Natural Selection*.

47

If, as Morgan claimed in 1903, the misconception of the role of "will" in Lamarck's theory was of long standing, Freud would have had ample opportunity to encounter it. Enough, at least, to be aware, when his scientific interest turned to problems of will and volition, that Lamarck's theory of evolution might be relevant. Morgan's effort to associate Lamarck's name with the more acceptable idea of use-inheritance also publicized the existence of a relationship between "will" and Lamarck's theory of evolution. "Since plants and the lower animals," as Lamarck supposed, "have no central nervous system, or at least no such well-defined nervous system as have the higher animals, Lamarck thought that they could not have evolved in the same way as have the higher animals." Morgan believed this distinction by Lamarck to be "responsible, no doubt, for a misconception that was long held in regard to a part of his views. It is often stated that he supposed the desire of the animal for a particular part [of the body] has led to the development of that part." Morgan explained that "in reality" Lamarck "only maintained" that "the desire to use a particular organ to fulfil some want led to its better development through exercise and the result was inherited" and that "Lamarck also supposed that the *decrease* in use of a part which leads to its decrease in size accounts for the degeneration of organs" (1903, p. 223).

Morgan may have succeeded in winning for Lamarck credit for the commonly accepted theory of use-inheritance, which his own genetic studies would soon invalidate. It is more likely that he prepared the way for scientists to transfer to Lamarck what turned out to be an unacceptable aberration in their hero Darwin. Until Freud revolutionized the intellectual world, all great men were presented as perfect. Their aberrations were hidden by their followers. For instance, during the centuries when the findings of physics supported the corpuscular theory of the motion of light, physicists acknowledged Newton's priority for it in the *Opticks* but left unmentioned what they considered an aberration, his wave theory, and vice versa. With the Freudian revolution it has become popular to magnify the warts of great men. Lamarck's presentation of his ideas seems to have confused his readers so that when these ideas were revived they were interpreted, or misinterpreted, in opposite ways by different scientists. Some saw Lamarck's views as purely vitalistic and others interpreted them to be mechanistic; some thought they were following Lamarck in believing that it is the *activity* of the living organism which is all-important while others were just as convinced that they were following in Lamarck's footsteps by emphasizing the passivity of the organism. Morgan's interpretation of

Lamarck could be arrived at only by someone strongly opposed to the idea of "will" as an explanation. Vitalists could as easily find in *Philosophie Zoologique* evidence for the importance of "will."

At times Lamarck expressed his evolutionary theory teleologically, as though nature purposefully pursues a course from the simplest to the most highly organized or complex. For example, in discussing the development of the nervous system, Lamarck wrote: "When nature had supplied the nervous system with a true brain, that is, with an anterior medullary swelling, capable of giving rise immediately to at least one special sense such as sight, and of containing in a single nucleus the centre of communication of the nerves, she had not yet completed the development of the system. Indeed she long continued to be concerned with the gradual development of the brain, and started the rudiments of the senses of hearing in the crustaceans and molluscs." Modern evolutionary biologists may talk in a teleological fashion among themselves as a shortcut, but never in writing where it might be misunderstood. When Lamarck wrote, biology was still teleological. One studied nature as God's handiwork. Modern physicists like Einstein and the late Nobel Prize winner I. I. Rabi have also expressed their feeling that they were studying God's handiwork but without implying will or intention in nature.

Lamarck outlined a series of steps, apparently all equally important, involving environmental changes, "need" or "will," and "habit" or "exercise": "Thus to obtain a knowledge of the true causes of shapes and habits found in the various known animals, we must reflect that the infinitely diversified but slowly changing environment in which the animals of each race have successively been placed, has involved each of them in new needs and corresponding alterations in their habits" (1963 [1809], p. 308). Lamarck insisted that function or need creates the necessary forms although the adaptations he cited could as easily support the view that form creates function: "If an animal, for the satisfaction of its needs, makes repeated efforts to lengthen its tongue, it will acquire a considerable length (anteater, green woodpecker); if it requires to seize anything with this same organ, its tongue will then divide and become forked" (p. 120).

It is this adaptation of the organism to its environment through its own efforts that distinguishes Lamarck's theory from Darwin's natural selection. And it is with this willed adaptation that Freud associated Lamarck's name in the earliest reference found so far. Freud had been in correspondence with his Hungarian colleague Sándor Ferenczi about their mutual interest in biology, particularly the implications of phylogeny for ontogeny, which we will come to later. Here is that earliest and singular reference to Lamarck: "Don't we now know two conditions for artistic endowment? First, the wealth of phylogenetically transferred material, as with the neurotic; second, a good remnant of the old technique of *modifying oneself instead of the outside world* (see Lamarck, etc.)" (1987 [1915], p. 93).

Lacking the Darwinian idea of chance variations that might be selected out because they functioned to give the animal an advantage in surviving "the slowly changing environment," Lamarck bridged the gap between the need created by environmental changes and the acquisition of the form required to perform the new function by inserting, as though it were self-explanatory, the "will," "wish," or "effort" of the animal. It is this unsatisfactory intermediate and seemingly vitalistic step of the "will" that struck many of Lamarck's readers, including Darwin. Lyell, for instance, writing after publication of the *Origin* in *The Geological Evidences of the Antiquity of Man with Remarks on Theories of the Origin of Species by Variation* (1863), gives Lamarck credit for the law of inheritance of acquired characteristics as "legitimate speculations" but reiterates arguments he had made as early as 1832 against Lamarck's "purely imaginary causes" of variation, that is, volition. It was these criticisms by Lyell that Darwin had in mind when writing to his friend Hooker from the *Beagle* about his evolutionary thoughts. Lyell credited Lamarck with "clearly" presenting "some of the laws which govern the appearance of new varieties." Among these "acceptable laws" Lyell included what we label Lamarckian today, "that as the muscles of the arm become strengthened by exercise or enfeebled by disuse, some organs may in this way, in the course of time, become entirely obsolete, and others previously weak become strong and play a new or more leading part in the organization of a species." And the same "with instincts, where animals experience new dangers they become more cautious and cunning, and transmit these acquired faculties to their posterity."

Lyell took issue with Lamarck for not being "satisfied with such legitimate speculations" and for having "conceived that by repeated acts of volition animals might acquire new organs and attributes" (1870 [1863], p. 391). Lyell thus affirmed the distinctive role of "will" in Lamarckian evolution. Huxley, too, referring the reader to Lamarck's "Phil. Zoologique, vol. i 222, et seq.," found it "curious that Lamarck should insist so strongly as he has done, that circumstances never in any degree directly

modify the form or the organization of animals, but only operate by changing their wants and consequently their actions for he thereby brings upon
himself the obvious question, how then do plants, which cannot be said to
have wants or actions, become modified?" (1871 [1860], p. 289). Lamarck
had answered this queston but not in a fashion that would satisfy successive generations of less philosophically oriented zoologists like Huxley.
He postulated for plants, as Lyell noted in 1863, "certain subtle fluids or
organizing forces" that might work out effects analogous to those of "will"
in animals. Even Lamarck's attempt to call attention to the importance of
environment diverted readers like Huxley into thinking that his emphasis
was on the role of "wish" or "will."

Thirty years after Morgan had claimed use-inheritance as Lamarck's
scientific contribution, Morgan received the 1933 Nobel Prize in Physiology and Medicine for his theory that hereditary unit characters are dependent on genes in the chromosomes; he studied and mapped them in detail. Use-inheritance was scientifically dead.

No longer concerned with use-inheritance, genetics advanced to discovery of the "DNA double helix with its extraordinarily stable structure infrequently subject to spontaneous degradation and errors in replication,"
Darwin's chance variatons. "Furthermore, discovery of all the elements
that lie between DNA sequence and protein structure gave rise to the central dogma of microbiology," that of the randomness of variations essential
to Darwinian evolution, denying "any possible effect of a cell's experience
upon the sequence of bases in its DNA."

This dogma has recently been challenged in experiments by three scientists at the Harvard School of Public Health. Heinz Hartmann, in defense
of Freud, had noted that it is impossible to prove a negative. In *Nature*
(September 8, 1988) John Cairns, Julie Overbaugh, and Stephen Miller of
the Department of Cancer Research, "describe some experiments suggesting that cells may have mechanisms for *choosing* which mutations will
occur" (335:42, italics added). They had altered a gene in *E. coli* so that
the bacteria could not use sugar lactose for energy essential to reproduction. The altered bacteria were placed on culture plates containing only
lactose. The experimenters found that some bacteria were able to correct
the genetic abnormality in the lactose gene and produce descendants who
could also thrive on lactose.

In considering "what mechanism might be the basis for the forms of mutations" they had found, the researchers learned that "molecular biology

51

was deserting [the] reduction[ist dogma]. Now almost anything seems possible. In certain systems, information flows back from RNA into DNA, genomic instability can be switched on under conditions of stress, and switched off when the stress is over; and instances exist where cells are able to generate extreme variability in localized regions of their genome. The only major category of informational transfer that has not been described is between proteins and the messenger RNA (mRNA) molecules that made them." The authors consider how such a connection might be made by cells to provide the "kind of versatility and adaptability" their experiments seemed to reveal. They suggest processes, each of which "could, in effect, provide a mechanism for the inheritance of acquired characteristics." The possibility of "will" is also raised. "If a cell discovered how to make that connection [informational transfer between proteins and the messenger RNA (mRNA) molecules that made them], it might be able *to exercise some choice over which mutations to accept and which to reject*" (italics added).

In describing "a few experiments and some circumstantial evidence suggesting that bacteria can choose which mutations they should produce," the authors "realize that this is too important an issue to be settled by three or four rather ambiguous experiments." But they have succeeded in showing "how insecure is our belief in the spontaneity (randomness) of most mutations," a doctrine which it seems "has never been properly put to the test" (335:149).

Freud, only ten years older than Morgan, had branched off from biology after publishing his paper "Über den Ursprung des N. Acusticus" (On the Origin of the Acoustical Nerve) in 1886, at age thirty. Forced to leave his research at the university in order to earn the comfortable bourgeois life with Martha Bernays that he longed for, Freud diverged in his subsequent research from the main trunk of biology. In Freud's writings can be found elements of the Darwinian biology of the era in which he was a student and then a researcher at the cutting edge. Similarly, a knowledgeable student of Freud's writings can usually discern in what stage of Freud's development of psychoanalysis a particular contemporary critic has immersed himself and whether the critic has kept up-to-date as a scholar of Freud and psychoanalysis or is only an intellectually interested outsider. Freud became such an outsider in relation to biology after 1886, retaining interest but no longer a student or a participant abreast of its advances as he had once been.

FREUD'S INTEREST IN LAMARCK

To the end of his life Freud maintained a staunch belief in the theory associated with Lamarck's name, the inheritance of acquired characteristics (see Anna Freud letter [frontispiece]). He believed that the Oedipus complex was the ontogenic repetition of the phylogenetic experience of Darwin's primal horde in killing the father. He hypothesized that "the experiences of the ego . . . transform themselves, so to say, into experiences of the id, the impressions of which are preserved by heredity" (1923, *SE* 19:38). In his last completed book, *Moses and Monotheism* (1939), Freud insisted on retaining neo-Lamarckian statements in the face of Jones's objections that they contradicted the biologists in their own field. According to Hartmann, Kris, and Loewenstein, "when he [Freud] became aware of the fact that biological studies had not confirmed Lamarckian assumptions (though strictly speaking they were not invalidated), he 'postulated' the phylogenetic explanation 'for psychological reasons'" (1964, p. 96). With rare exceptions, most notably Anna Freud, psychoanalysts find it possible to dispense with neo-Lamarckian explanations; several have even "suggested alternate explanations which seem fully to account for the phenomena in question" (p. 86).

Neither Haeckel nor Darwin claimed that natural selection was the only mechanical process forming new species; both men assigned an important role to the inheritance of characteristics acquired by habit, use or disuse, and as a consequence of environmental influences. According to Haeckel, "the theory of Selection or Darwinism is, up to the present time, the most important of the various theories which seek to explain the transformation of species by mechanical principles, but it is by no means the only one." Haeckel criticized Lamarck, not for believing in use and disuse, but for *overemphasizing* it and for failing to provide a mechanical principle for the theory of descent, of which he is the founder. Haeckel wrote that "mutability by nutrition is observable." In addition, "not only those qualities of organisms are transmitted by inheritance which they have inherited from their parents, but those also which they themselves have acquired"—a thought Freud repeated decades later—"acquired through their own life, through the influence of outward circumstances, such as climate, nourishment, training, etc." (1876 [1868], 1:158).

With one exception there are no references to Lamarck in any of Freud's scientific writings and none at all in his psychoanalytic publications. In an early nonevolutionary work, "Über Coca" (1884), Freud mentioned Lamarck's work on cocaine. Freud's only references to Lamarck's evolutionary work are in correspondence with three of his colleagues, Ferenczi and the German psychoanalysts Karl Abraham and George Groddeck at about the time of World War I. Freud's published correspondence with Jung contains no reference to Lamarck but only to Darwin, even in the period when Freud was reading Lamarck's *Philosophie Zoologique* at Ferenczi's urging. Nor is any reference to Lamarck revealed by Masson's 1985 restorations of the material expunged thirty-five years earlier by the original editors of the Freud–Fliess correspondence, Princess Marie Bonaparte, Anna Freud, and Ernst Kris. Even in his work on the nerve-cells of crayfish in Brücke's institute during his undergraduate summers of 1879 and 1881, Freud did not refer to Lamarck, who was famous for his classification of invertebrates. Rather, Freud paid high tribute to the latest evolutionary work by Darwin's friend and protagonist Thomas Henry Huxley, *"The Crayfish: An Introduction to the Study of Zoology"* (1880). In the Freud Library at Maresfield Gardens is a volume by Huxley, *Gründzuge der Physiologie in Allgemeinverständlichen Vorlesungen* (*Lay Lectures on Basic Physiology*), edited by Dr. J. Rosenthal (Leipzig: Leopald Voss, 1871), inscribed "from the private library of Martha Freud 16/Jan 83"—a gift perhaps, from Sigmund, or an attempt to share the interests of her fiancé.

In the "Project for a Scientific Psychology" (1895), which adumbrates much of his later thinking, Freud made use of Darwin but not Lamarck in sketching out "The Biological Standpoint" of his psychology. He hypothesized "two systems of neurones, Φ and Ψ, of which Φ consists of permeable elements and Ψ of impermeable," in order "to provide an explanation of this one of the peculiarities of the nervous system—that of retaining and yet of remaining capable of receiving." As "morphologically (that is, histologically) nothing is known in support of the distinction" that Freud finds it necessary to make, he asks: "Where else are we to look for this division into classes?" Freud, who received his biological training when Darwinism was at its zenith, looked for the answer denied by histology "if possible in the biological development of the nervous system." He pointed out in his correspondence with Fliess that this development "in the eyes of natural scientists, is, like everything else, something that has come about gradually." What for Freud "would be most satisfactory, of course, would be if the mechanism" by which his two classes of neurones "developed characteristics so different as permeability and impermeability . . . should itself arise out of the primitive biological part played" (*SE* 1:302) by these two classes of neurones. A page later Freud was explicit about the possibility of using "a Darwinian line of thought" to solve the dilemma of the "unfortunate tinge of arbitrariness" he found in assuming "an ultimate difference between the valence of the contact-barriers of Φ and Ψ." His "Darwinian line of thought" is "to appeal to the fact of impermeable neurones being indispensable and to their surviving in consequence" (1:303).

In the early years Freud's references to Darwin were to *The Expression of the Emotions* (1872) in *The Studies on Hysteria* (1893–95) and to the physiology of laughter in *Jokes and their Relation to the Unconscious* (1905). In 1907 he revealed in a letter his high regard for Darwin's *Descent of Man* as one of the great scientific achievements, and most of the later references are to this work. In all there are one or more references to Darwin or his work in seventeen works by Freud (see appendix A for a complete list).

In contrast, Lamarck does not appear in any of Freud's published writing on psychoanalysis. Except for two letters in 1916, Freud's interest in Lamarck appears exclusively in his correspondence of 1917, when his practice was reduced to two or three hours a day. His earliest mention of Lamarck was on January 6, 1916, in a letter to Ferenczi, similarly idled by World War I. Jones reports that "during Freud's visit to Pápa in Hungary, he discussed with Ferenczi the project of writing a work together on the relation of Lamarckism to psychoanalysis. Other preoccupations intervened" (1953–57, 3:312), but on December 22, 1916, Freud notified Ferenczi that he had ordered "the Lamarck" from the University Library: "I cannot stay completely idle, and our project, 'L and PsA' [Lamarck and psychoanalysis], suddenly came to mind as hopeful and rich in content." Ferenczi promptly confirmed the "joint plan of work" on December 28. Freud responded on New Year's Day 1917 with a "sketch of the Lamarck-work" and the fact that he had begun reading Lamarck's *Zoological Philosophy*. Ilse Grubrich-Simitis, who in 1983 discovered Freud's "Phylogenetic Fantasy" (1915) and is preparing the Freud–Ferenczi correspondence for publication, reports that in a "rapid succession of letters suggestions were then exchanged about the procedure for obtaining the literature as well as for dividing up the work, and notes and suggestions for precise wording were sent back and forth."

But reading Lamarck and what literature was available under war conditions quickly proved disappointing to Freud. On January 28, he conceded: "My impression is that we are coming completely into line with the psycho-Lamarckists, such as Pauly, and will have little to say that is completely new. Still, PsA will then have left its calling card with biology." By March 2 he was reassuring Ferenczi that he "need not worry about neglecting our work on Lamarck," for, he confessed, "I have not progressed either; in the weeks of cold and darkness I stopped working in the evening—and have not got back to it since then." By May 29 Freud was "not at all disposed to doing the work on Lamarck in the summer and would prefer to relinquish the whole thing" to Ferenczi, whom he had assured the year before, "This is your real field, in which you will be without peer" (1987 [1915], p. 93 and 94n). A few days later, on June 5, Freud wrote to George Groddeck, creator of the term *Das Es*, adopted by Freud and translated by Strachey as "the id," that Ferenczi was making "a biological experiment for me to show how a consistent continuation of Lamarck's theory of evolution coincided with the final outcome of psychoanalytic thinking" (1960, p. 317).

Freud's interest in Lamarck appears at a time when, according to Hugh Elliott in his 1914 translation of Lamarck's *Zoological Philosophy*, biologists could no longer accept the inheritance of acquired characteristics although most other educated people still did. Elliott himself commented in a footnote that the discoveries being made just then about hormones might reveal the way in which acquired characteristics could be inherited.

Freud's letters to Karl Abraham show that it was not the inheritance of acquired characteristics but what Darwin had called "Lamarck nonsense of . . . 'adaptations from the slow willing of animals'" that Freud meant when he referred to Lamarck's theory of evolution. On November 5, 1917, he wrote to Abraham: "As I write to you so seldom, I do not know whether I have as yet mentioned the paper on Lamarck, the point of which is to be that even the 'omnipotence of thoughts' was a reality once" (1965, p. 258). The concept of the "omnipotence of thoughts" had occurred to Freud in 1908 while analyzing the case of "The Rat Man," which he published in 1909 as "Notes upon a Case of Obsessional Neurosis." The patient, a successful lawyer, "ascribed to his thoughts and feelings, and to his wishes, whether good or evil," the power to become true in the outer world. The patient referred to "omnipotence of wishes," and Freud observed that "indeed, all obsessional neurotics behave as though they shared this conviction." Freud saw their belief as "a frank acknowledgment of a relic of the old megalomania of infancy" (*SE* 10:233–34). All of us as children once believed that our thoughts and wishes had the power to come true; consequently we felt responsible if a hostile wish, as for the death of a parent or sibling, actually occurred. Freud was soon able to correlate the "omnipotence of thoughts" also with attitudes in the unconscious mind; and in 1913, in *Totem and Taboo*, he correlated it with various beliefs in the efficacy of magic. He had earlier, in the *Studies on Hysteria* (1895), recognized the power of unconscious thoughts over the body in creating hysterical symptoms.

According to Freud, "anyone who is engaged in the construction of hypotheses will only begin to take his theories seriously if they can be fitted into our knowledge from more than one direction" (1895, *SE* 1:302). The direction of Freud's thoughts in 1917 was toward the structural theory that he realized in 1923 in *The Ego and the Id*. When in 1915 Freud turned his attention to the ego, its role in adaptation became apparent. The ego is the organ of will and volition. As an organ of adaptation capable of functioning autoplastically and alloplastically, it makes man appear singularly free of natural selection. As this view of the ego was emerging in Freud's thinking, he turned from Darwinian natural selection to explore the possibility of a biological foundation in Lamarck's evolutionary theory with its "will" and "volition." Freud hoped to find in Lamarck's theory of evolution, with its basis presumably in "volition" and "innate tendency" or "necessity," an additional correlation of the "omnipotence of thought," this time with evolutionary biology, particularly adaptation. In 1915 he had applied the "biological point of view" to the instinctual drives on which he had up to then chosen to concentrate his attention: "If now we apply ourselves to considering mental life from a *biological* point of view, an 'instinct' appears to us as a concept on the frontier between the mental and the somatic, as the psychical representative of the stimuli originating from within the organism and reachng the mind, as a measure of the demand made upon the mind for work in consequence of its connection with the body" (*SE* 14:121–22). Freud considered Lamarck for the biological point of view of the concept of the ego as he was developing it in this period.

Abraham "did not quite follow" the "hint about a paper on Lamarck" in Freud's letter of November 5 connecting Lamarck with the "omnipotence of thought," so on November 11 Freud provided a fuller account: "It [the Lamarck idea] arose between Ferenczi and me, but neither of us has the time or spirit to tackle it at present. The idea is to put Lamarck entirely on our ground and to show that the 'necessity' that according to him creates and transforms organs is nothing but the power of unconscious ideas over one's own body, of which we see remnants in hysteria, in short the 'omnipotence of thought.' This would actually supply a psycho-analytic explanation of adaptation." More than that, "it would put the coping-stone on psycho-analysis. There would be two linked principles of progressive change, adaptation of one's own body and subsequent transformation of the external world (autoplasticity), etc." (1965, pp. 261–62).

There are links in this passage, not only to the aforementioned "omnipotence of thought" and hysterical symptoms and to the structural theory established by Freud in 1923 in *The Ego and the Id*, but also to Haeckel's popularizations of Darwin. Haeckel's presentations are filled with "two linked principles of progressive change": "inheritance and adaptation" (the inner formative principle and the outer formative principle, which Haeckel also credits Goethe with having recognized), "reproduction and nutrition," and "the instincts of propagation and of self-preservation." Haeckel, with his propensity for linked principles, distinguished a conservative principle of inheritance directly connected with the functions of reproduction and a progressive principle of adaptation connected with nutrition. Haeckel is here generalizing the common term *nutrition* to a much wider field than is usually subsumed in the everyday use of this term just as Freud was to do later with *sex* and *sexuality*. According to Haeckel, "Darwin assumes no kind of unknown forces of nature nor hypothetical conditions, as the acting causes for the transformation of organic forms, but solely and simply the universally recognized vital activities of all organisms, which we term *Inheritance* and *Adaptation*" (1876 [1868], 1:169).

Haeckel was quite right that Darwin did not assume any unknown forces of nature, but Haeckel himself believed at this time that there were as yet undiscovered causes in addition to natural selection active in the formation of species: "If we assume that most species have originated through natural elimination, we also now know on the other hand that many forms distinguished as variations are hybrids between two different varieties and can be propagated as such, and it is equally well worthy of consideration that other causes are in activity in the formation of species of which, up to the present time, we have no conception." Therefore, "it is left to the judgment of individual naturalists to decide what share is to be attributed to natural selection in the origin of species, . . . authorities differ widely on the subject. Some give it a large share and some a very small one in the result" (1879, p. 5).

By the end of 1917 Freud was acknowledging to Ferenczi that "I cannot make up my mind about getting back to Lamarck." Before going on by himself, Ferenczi pressured Freud one last time on May 18, 1918: "It would be good if the *work on Lamarck* took recognizable shape this summer." But to no avail. Just before the war ended Freud explained: "Not disposed to work . . . too much interested in the end of the world drama." Ferenczi continued on without Freud toward "the final realization of the paleobiological speculations" they had engaged in during the war. Before publishing *Thalassa: A Theory of Genitality* (1924), Ferenczi asked Freud on July 25, 1923: "Will you permit me . . . [in the biological part] to come back to the assumptions about Lamarckism that were jointly constructed in Pápa and elsewhere?" (in Freud 1987 [1915], pp. 94–95). Freud regarded Ferenczi's "little book" as a "biological rather than a psychoanalytic study; . . . an application of the attitudes and insights associated with psychoanalysis to the biology of the sexual process and, beyond them, to organic life in general . . . the boldest application of psycho-analysis that was ever attempted" (1933, *SE* 22:228). Ferenczi, an analysand of Freud's before the war interfered, may have been identifying with Freud's application in *Totem and Taboo* (1912–13) "of the attitudes and insights associated with psychoanalysis" to anthropology with his primal horde theory.

Only in 1917, when Freud read Lamarck's *Philosophie Zoologique* with great expectations, did he refer to Darwin's "collaborators and forerunners." But that is as far as Freud went in acknowledging in his professional work the interest in Lamarck that he was discussing at the time with his friends and colleagues. In 1920, in *Beyond the Pleasure Principle*, Freud returned to and developed much of the thinking sketched in the "Project" under the heading "The Biological Standpoint." There is no evidence that he had derived anything applicable from his recent exploration of Lamarck. Rather, he utilized once again "a Darwinian line of thought," this time called "sober Darwinian lines": "The origin of reproduction by sexually differentiated germ-cells might be pictured along sober Darwinian lines by supposing that the advantage of amphimixis, arrived at on some occasion by the chance conjugation of two protista, was retained and further exploited in later development. On this view 'sex' would not be anything very ancient; and the extraordinarily violent instincts whose aim it is to bring about sexual union would be repeating something that had once occurred by chance and had since become established as being advantageous" (*SE* 18:56–57).

3

Adaptation
and Conflict

With the structural theory established by Freud in the *Ego and the Id* (1923) the ego became the organ of adaptation. Haeckel sometimes referred to "the theory of adaptation" as though it were one of "Darwin's theories." According to Haeckel adaptation and inheritance are "the two organic functions . . . necessary . . . to . . . arrive at a right understanding of Darwinism. . . . These two functions, by themselves, have been able to produce all the variety of animal and vegetable forms" (1876 [1868], 1:252–53). Darwin defined as "the main subject of my second work," *The Variation of Animals and Plants under Domestication* (1868), "this problem of the conversion of varieties into species,—that is, the augmentation of the slight differences characteristic of varieties into greater differences characteristic of species and genera, including the *admirable adaptations* of each being to its complex organic and inorganic conditions of life" (1:5, italics added).

Before Darwin, adaptation was celebrated as an important revelation of the handiwork of a beneficent Creator. At Cambridge Darwin had delighted in the ethical textbook of the theologian William Paley, *The Principles of Moral and Political Philosophy* (1785), and in his orthodox refutation of the deists, *View of the Evidences of Christianity* (1794), which Darwin, without any consideration of their premises, classed with Euclid for the beauty of their logic. In seeking the origin of species Darwin discovered that the marvelous adaptations in nature were not the result of design and the happy planning of the Creator but the gradual accumulation over a long period of time of beneficial variations through the ruthless elimination of maladapted variations by the inexorable blind forces of nature, what Freud later called "the exigencies of life": "We shall therein [in the main subject of *The Variation*] see that all organic beings, without exception, tend to increase at so high a ratio, that no district, no station, not even the whole surface of the land or the whole ocean, would hold the progeny of a single pair after a certain number of generations. The inevitable result is an ever-recurrent Struggle for Existence. It has truly been said that all nature is at war; the strongest ultimately prevail, the weakest fail; and we well know that myriads of forms have disappeared from the face of the earth. . . . the severe and often-recurrent struggle for existence will determine that those variations, however slight, which are favourable shall be preserved or selected, and those which are unfavourable shall be destroyed" (1:5–6).

The view of adaptation revealed by Darwin's theory called attention to and emphasized the strife and conflict underlying the seemingly harmonious workings of nature celebrated by poets like Goethe and incorporated into science by pre-Darwinian biologists. Lamarck's evolutionary theory seen as "innate tendency to evolve" and "volition" did not, like Darwin's "struggle for existence," stress conflict. The idea of conflict is omnipresent in Freud's work and remained basic to his thinking throughout his life. Freud found not only that neurotic symptoms are based on pathogenic conflicts but also that conflicts are the essential core of the normal human personality. In 1895 in *The Studies on Hysteria* Freud looked upon the symptoms of his patients as the result of conflict between an unacceptable wish or thought and the dominant ideational mass or ego. Later he conceptualized the conflict as being between the unconscious and the conscious, that is, between the instinctual drives (whose developmental characteristics Freud studied first and described in detail) and the ego (which remained ill defined for a much longer time until the structural theory in *The Ego and the Id* [1923]).

With the structural theory of an ego, id, and superego, the ego becomes defined as an organ of adaptation mediating or avoiding conflict both intrapsychically (between two or more of these three structures) and also between any or all of these structures and the outside world. In the letter on Lamarck discussed in the preceding chapter, Freud referred to these two types of adaptation, the autoplastic and the alloplastic (the internal and the external). In the Lamarck reference he was considering the autoplastic as affecting bodily changes, as in hysteria; with the structural theory the autoplastic is extended to include psychical changes as well. Heinz Hartmann, who in the next generation developed adaptation more fully as the fifth psychoanalytic viewpoint, called attention to "a most effective adaptation process (which, by the way, transcends the common antithesis of autoplastic and alloplastic adaptations)." It is the "avoidance of the environment in which difficulties are encountered—and its positive correlate, the search for one which offers easier and better possibilities for action" (1958 [1939], pp. 19–20), as Hartmann and his colleagues were doing by fleeing from Hitler to England and America.

Freud's propensity for two opposing (conflicting) forces has been understood until now, on the basis of Bernfeld's 1944 research, in terms of the so-called Helmholtzian school, Bernfeld's designation for the physiology of Carl Ludwig, Ernst Brücke, and Emil Du Bois-Reymond. Freud himself called attention to the fact that psychic phenomena are multiply determined.[1] The great role that "conflict" plays in Freud's work had also as one of its determinants the new philosophy that arose from Darwin's work and dominated biology for a time, as it was later to dominate Freud's biologically oriented psychology, psychoanalysis. According to the German popularizer of Darwin, Ernst Krause, in his 1885 evaluation of Charles Darwin and his relation to Germany (*Charles Darwin und sein Verhältnis zu Deutschland*), Darwin's "struggle for existence" had become in Germany in 1869, following a speech by Hermann Helmholtz to the *Versammlung der deutschen Naturforschern* (Meeting of the German Natural Scientists) at Innsbruck "*das oberste Erklärungsprincip, vor dem nicht einmal mehr die Molekule in der Mutterlauge und die Sterne im Himmel sicher bleiben*" ("the highest principle of explanation in the face of which not even the molecules in the mother liquor and the stars in heaven were safe" p. 166). During the period covered by Krause, "the struggle for existence" appears in quotation marks in Freud's correspondence with his fiancée, Martha Bernays.

According to Eiseley: "So complete was the triumph of the new philosophy that the struggle for existence, the 'war of nature' was projected into the growth of the organism itself. Darwin's shadow dominates, in this respect, the rest of the century. . . . The cooperative aspects of bodily chemistry remained to a considerable degree uninvestigated. Instead 'struggle' was the leading motif of the day. . . . Neither Darwin nor his immediate followers seem to have had any particular feeling for the internal stability and harmony of the organism" (1958, pp. 335–36). Physiologists like

Claude Bernard who did have a feeling for the internal stability and harmony of the organism showed little interest in Darwin.

Younger men, Freud's contemporaries in biology, particularly in Germany, like Wilhelm Roux, who had come under the influence of Darwin and/or Haeckel, applied the struggle for existence and the survival of the fittest to the inner workings of the organism. In discussing the "complemental series" in the posthumous publication of "An Outline of Psycho-Analysis" (1940 [1938]), Freud referred to Roux's embryological experiments. Roux was one of Haeckel's pupils. In *Der Kampf der Theile im Organismus* (*The Battle of the Parts in Organisms*, 1881) Roux sought to explain the adaptiveness of even the minutest structures in animal tissues on the basis of intraselection, that is, on the grounds that equivalent parts of the organism, no matter how small, are contending with one another for survival. Roux's thesis in *Der Kampf* was well-known and well accepted. Weismann, who discussed it almost fifteen years later in his Romanes Lectures of 1894, considered it of great importance and differed with Roux only "in that he [Roux] believed that these histological structures arose entirely by intra-selection, and not by individual selection at all" (p. 13).

Freud, like his contemporary Roux, was attracted by the idea of "the struggle for existence" in Darwin's theory of evolution and like Roux and Weismann considered it applicable internally as well as externally. From the very beginning of psychoanalysis Freud was highly successful in applying the concept of conflict to the understanding of the psyche. It remained for a psychoanalyst of the next generation, Heinz Hartmann (1894–1970), to enunciate in 1939 the extremely fruitful concept of the "conflict-free ego sphere," which by its very designation reveals the prevalence of conflict in Freud's view of the ego and adaptation. The year of Freud's death, 1939, Hartmann wrote: "So far, psychoanalytic ego psychology has been predominantly a conflict psychology; the conflict-free avenues of a reality-adapted development have remained peripheral to it." This was corrected in the years following Freud's death, for "a science is entitled to feel its way from one result to the next" (p. 13). Freud, like some of his contemporaries in biology who had similarly come under the influence of Darwin and Haeckel, had concentrated on conflict and obtained fruitful results. Freud's successors have demonstrated that conflict is not the whole story for psychoanalysis any more than it has turned out to be for biology.

4

Ideas from Darwin's Publications during Freud's *Gymnasium* Days: The Inheritance of Acquired Characteristics

I n his *Autobiography* Darwin recalled that he had begun to arrange his notes for the *Variation* on January 1, 1860, but it was not published until 1868, the same year as Haeckel's successful popularizations. The two men were in correspondence, and Haeckel revealed in the *History of Creation* that he had had word from Darwin that "Darwin himself characterized" the *Origin* "as only a preliminary extract from a larger more detailed work, which is to contain a mass of facts in favour of his theory, and comprehensive and experimental proofs." The first part "of the larger work promised by Darwin appeared in 1868, under the title 'The Variations of Animals and Plants in the State of Domestication,'" and "has been translated into German by Victor Carus. It contains a rich abundance of the most valuable evidence as to the extraordinary changes of organic forms which man can produce by cultivation and artificial selection" (Haeckal 1876 [1868], 1:136). Freud, with his well-known "preference for comprehensive monographs on each subject" (Jones 1953–57, 1:21) even as a schoolboy, referred to three of the "larger, more detailed" works by Darwin and never to the now more famous "preliminary extract," the *Origin*.

Freud acquired the *Origin* "2/XI/81." This is the date inscribed after "Dr Sigmfreud" in volume 2 of Carus's 1876 translation of Darwin's *Gesammelte Werke* in Freud's library at Maresfield Gardens. Volume 1, *Reise eines Naturforschers um die Welt*, (*A Naturalist's Journal of Researches into the Natural History and Geology of Countries Visited during a Voyage of the Beagle Round the World,* 1875 [1845]), is also in the library signed "Dr. Sigmfreud 2/xi/81."

By 1881 Freud already owned one or both volumes of *The Descent of Man* and also Darwin's *Insectivorous Plants*. For Freud *The Descent of Man,* rather than the *Origin,* appears to have been the great book by Darwin; it was, according to Jones, the only Darwin book Freud owned (3:310). With the help of Freud's housekeeper, Miss Paula Fichtl, I found in August 1969 seven other Darwin volumes in Freud's library in England. The library has since become part of the Freud Museum and been catalogued. *The Descent of Man* in Carus's 1875 translation was the first Darwin book Freud possessed and proudly inscribed "Sigismundfreud stud. med. 1875"; Volume 2 was missing. *Insectivorous Plants* is inscribed "SigmFreud 79" (day and month illegible) and is in the 1875 London edition. Along with "such scientific achievements as those of Copernicus, [and] Johann Weier on witchcraft," Freud in 1907 named Darwin's *Descent of Man* among his choices for "the ten most significant books" (1960, "Letter 135 to the Antiquary Hinterberger," p. 268). *The Descent of Man* and *The Variation of Animals and Plants under Domestication* were published in German while Freud was still in *Gymnasium;* both are referred to by Freud in *Totem and Taboo* (1912–13), where for the first time Freud developed his case for an actual historic killing of the father by Darwin's primal horde.

In Freud's library both volumes of the English first edition of the 1868 *Variation* are inscribed "DrSigmFreud 6/6 83." Also in his library is the English edition of *The Effects of Cross and Self-Fertilization in the Vegetable Kingdom* (1876), signed "DrSigmfreud 6/9/81." All the volumes are uniformly bound. A later 1933 edition of *The Voyage of the Beagle* is stamped from the library of Martha Freud. The second volume of *The Descent of Man* I was seeking in Freud's library is said to have remained in Jones's library upon his death shortly after completion of his pioneer three-volume biography of Freud (L. Newman, personal communication, 1988).

THE VARIATION OF ANIMALS AND PLANTS UNDER DOMESTICATION (1868)

Freud would have found Darwin's *Variation* discussed and recommended both in Haeckel's popularizations and later in his work with Claus. In the *Variation* Darwin wrestled with the problem of the share to be given natural selection and the share to be given other causes such as environment and habit. Darwin was careful to avoid the error of making his principle "all-important." Haeckel criticized Lamarck for such an error. Darwin, too, was critical on this point when in 1860 he discussed with Bronn a suitable translation for "natural selection": "It is folly in me, but I cannot help doubting whether 'Wahl der Lebensweise' expresses my notion. It leaves the impression on my mind of the Lamarckian doctrine (which I reject) of habits of life being *all-important*" (1888, 2:279, italics added). *Natürliche Zuchtung* was finally used by Bronn; Claus changed it to *Zuchtwahl*. To a modern reader Darwin's objection to "Wahl der Lebensweise" may seem to indicate that he was opposed to the idea of the inheritance of acquired characteristics. He was only opposed, as were Haeckel and other Darwin supporters of the time, to making it "all-important" as an explanation for evolution. Darwin tried to avoid committing a similar mistake of making natural selection "all-important," and so he, and Haeckel at that time, acknowledged that other mechanisms such as sexual selection, habit, and inheritance through use and disuse might also play a part.

Darwin's partiality for natural selection is revealed in some of his private letters and in the *Autobiography*, which he intended only for the eyes of his family. But in writings intended for the public Darwin, cautious scientist that he was, scrupulously assigned a share in the transformation of species to causes other than natural selection. At the beginning of the first edition of the *Origin* Darwin stated that "some slight amount of change may, I think, be attributed to the direct action of the conditions of life—as, in some cases, increased size from amount of food, colour from particular kinds of food and from light, and perhaps the thickness of fur from climate." But he assigned to the direct action of food and climate a lesser role than Haeckel did. In most instances natural selection provided a better explanation.

Darwin attributed a greater share to inheritance through habit, or use and disuse. "Habit also has a decided influence as in the period of flowering with plants when transported from one climate to another. In animals it has a more marked effect." As an example, Darwin reported his findings "in the domestic duck that the bones of the wing weigh less and the bones of the leg more, in proportion to the whole skeleton, than do the same bones in the wild duck." He presumed that "this change may be safely attributed to the domestic duck flying much less, and walking more than its wild parent." We know a century after Darwin that bones do respond to use and disuse; but we also know that only the *capacity* to retain or lose calcium through use or disuse can be inherited but not the retention or loss of weight itself. The examples of inherited characteristics that Darwin gave in the first edition of the *Origin* are all of domestic animals and might better have been attributed to man's power of selection than to use and disuse: "The great and inherited development of the udders in cows and goats in countries where they are habitually milked, in comparison with the state of these organs in other countries, is another instance of the effect of use" (p. 9). Darwin's final example can be attributed to the protection from natural selection afforded by domestication, but according to Darwin disuse is the probable cause: "Not a single domestic animal can be named which has not in some country drooping ears; and the view suggested by some authors, that the drooping is due to the disuse of the muscles of the ear, from the animals not being much alarmed by danger, seems probable" (p. 10).

The first edition of the *Origin* was a hastily prepared resumé of Darwin's life work. The more careful preparation of his later publications, including all further editions of the *Origin*, permitted Darwin to give greater consideration to the role of the inheritance of acquired characteristics. Expansion of the first chapter of the *Origin* into the two-volume *The Variation of Plants and Animals under Domestication* focused attention on the vexing question of the source of the variations acted upon by selection: "No doubt man selects varying individuals, sows their seeds and again selects their varying offspring. But the initial variation on which man works, and without which he can do nothing, is caused by slight changes in the conditions of life, which must often have occurred under nature." In the *Variation* Darwin treated "as fully as my materials permit, the whole subject of variation under domestication," in the hope of obtaining "some light, little though it be, on the causes of variability" (1:3). Darwin, here too, regarded as false "the belief that an innate tendency to vary exists, independently of external conditions" even though this "seems at first sight probable." Such a view would deny Darwin's conviction that "each separate variation has its own proper exciting cause" (2:252–53).

As examples of the laws that govern variability Darwin started with "direct action of climate and food, the effects of use and disuse, and of correlation of growth," and in the case of domesticated animals "the amount of change to which domesticated organisms are liable" (1:3). Of these, Darwin seemed to give the greatest role to the effects of use and disuse, even relating the effects of the correlation of growth to the effects due to use and disuse. In the pigeon, for instance, "we may confidently admit that the length of the sternum and frequently the prominence of its crest, the length of the scapulae and furcala, have all been reduced in size in comparison with the same parts in the rock-pigeon. And I presume that they may be safely attributed to disuse." Although "the feet as well as the tarsi conjointly with the middle toe have likewise in most cases become reduced and this it is probable has been caused by their lessened use," nevertheless, "shown more plainly than the effects of disuse" is the "existence of some sort of correlation between the feet and beak" (1:176–77).

Many of Darwin's statements supporting use-inheritance occur in connection with Freud's interests, that is, closely related to psychology. For instance, Darwin states that "the inheritance of any habit may be believed" (1:56). Even the brain, "the most important and complicated organ in the whole organization, is subject to the law of decrease in size from disuse" (1:129). And learning may be transmitted: "When man first entered any country, the animals living there would have felt no instinctive or inherited fear. . . . I have elsewhere shown (Journal of Researches 1845, p. 393) how slowly the native birds of several islands have acquired and inherited a salutary dread of man" (1:20). To this day, as in Darwin's, animals and birds in the Galapagos allow tourists to walk among them like Adam and Eve in the Garden of Eden. Even the little bird remains unperturbed on its branch while a photographer takes a close-up snapshot.

Darwin felt that recurrence over many generations is important in increasing the effect of direct action of climate and food as well as of use and disuse, so that in one example he wrote: "The nature of the food during many generations has apparently affected the length of the intestines." As Darwin advanced in his discussions in the *Variation*, the role of experience "over many generations" became increasingly prominent.[1] The three elements, (1) the inheritance of acquired characteristics, (2) the repetition over many generations, and (3) the application to the psychological that we find in Darwin's *Variation*, are present in Freud's formulation in *The Ego and the Id* of the formation of the superego: "The experiences of the ego . . . when they have been repeated often enough and with sufficient strength in many individuals in successive generations, transform themselves, so to say, into experiences of the id, the impressions of which are preserved by heredity. Thus in the id, which is capable of being inherited, are harboured residues of the existence of countless egos; and when the ego forms its super-ego out of the id, it may perhaps only be reviving shapes of former egos and bringing them to resurrection" (1923, *SE* 19:38). Freud here used Darwin's view of inheritance as the biological basis of a psychological structure. His own work has made it possible to explain psychologically the formation of the superego by identification without invoking phylogenetic speculations. But Freud believed that identifications arising in later generations could, like Darwin's "habits and experience," also be inherited.

The revival or resurrection of former shapes referred to by Freud in the above passage was also dealt with at length by Darwin in the *Variation*. It is called reversion or atavism in English. Darwin saw in reversion to old or long-lost characters one of the sources he was seeking for variations from which man or nature selects; it was important enough to Darwin to warrant a whole chapter in the *Variation*. Reversion to or reappearance of earlier characteristics was distinguished by Freud in man's psychosexual development and called regression. The complex concepts Freud developed around his observations of these phenomena were influenced by Hughlings Jackson and Josef Breuer.[2]

Darwin did not always recognize examples of reversion. The most famous was Darwin's belief that the quagga[3] that had crossed with Lord Morton's mare was responsible for the stripes on progeny of the mare resulting from later matings with stallions. He also believed that a woman's children by a second marriage could resemble her first husband. For Darwin there was no problem in inheritance of any characteristic whatever its source; he found it more difficult to understand how the failure of inheritance, or its discontinuity, could occur. Therefore, it was Darwin's view that the influence of a former mate could be transmitted to later progeny through the female; habits and experience could be inherited, if repeated frequently and strongly enough through successive generations.

In contrast to Weismann's germ-plasm theory, which, when confirmed, established the non-inheritability of acquired characteristics, Darwin proposed in the *Variation* a "provisional hypothesis" of heredity, long known as pangenesis, which was intended to include the inheritance of acquired characteristics and "so many large classes of facts" which Darwin "could not endure to keep . . . all floating loose in my mind without some thread of connection to tie them together in a tangible method" (1903, 2:371). Similarly troubled by "large classes of facts . . . floating loose in" his mind, Freud found the inheritance of acquired characteristics useful. Pangenesis, in Darwin's own words, "implies that the whole organization, in the sense of every separate atom or unit reproduces itself. Hence ovules and pollen grains—the fertilized seed or eggs, as well as buds—include and consist of a multitude of germs thrown off from each separate atom of the organism" (1868, 2:357–58). Darwn saw in pangenesis, discredited by Aristotle, "a tangible method bearing on bud-variation, the various forms of inheritance, the causes and laws of variation . . . as well as the several modes of reproduction."

Darwin's *Variation* nowhere suggests that anyone, least of all Darwin, questions the inheritance of acquired characteristics. Rather, in Darwin's opinion "everyone would wish to explain to himself how it is possible for a character possessed by some remote ancestor suddenly to reappear in the offspring; how effects of increased or decreased use of a limb can be transmitted to the child; how the male sexual element can act not solely on the ovule, but occasionally on the mother-form; how a limb can be reproduced on the exact line of amputation, with neither too much nor too little added; how the various modes of reproduction are connected, and so forth" (2:357).

The alternative hypothesis to pangenesis, that of the continuity of the germ plasm, was not unknown to Darwin but he did not make his readers aware of it. Darwin's cousin Sir Francis Galton, with whom he was on good terms, published a "Theory of Heredity" early in the 1870s in which he raised the question of the transmission of acquired characteristics and answered it in much the same manner as Weismann was to do independently in the period following Darwin's death. Darwin wrote a letter to *Nature* (April 27, 1871) crediting Galton for the ingenious experiments designed to test the truth of the hypothesis of pangenesis which Galton had presented in a paper to the Royal Society (March 30, 1871), but Darwin would not allow that pangenesis had "as yet received its death-blow, though from presenting so many vulnerable points its life is always in jeopardy" (1887–88, 3:195).

According to the experimental biologist George Romanes at University College, who worked on this problem for his friend Charles Darwin, "the idea of what is now called a 'continuity of germ-plasm' was present to Darwin's mind as a logically possible alternative to the one which he adopted in his theory of pangenesis—an alternative, therefore, which he was anxious to exclude by way of experimental disproof." In his *Examination of Weismannism* (1881) Romanes recalled: "As far back as 1874 I had long conversations with Darwin himself upon the matter, and under his guidance performed what I suppose are the only systematic experiments which have ever been undertaken with regard to it. These occupied more than five years of almost exclusive devotion; but, as they all proved failures, they were never published" (p. viii). Although Darwin's tentative hypothesis of pangenesis makes it difficult to understand the reversion, or the discontinuity in inheritance, which Darwin found a problem, it seems almost specifically to account for the inheritance of acquired characteristics, in which Darwin preferred to believe.

THE DESCENT OF MAN (1871)

Typical of the thoughtful way in which Darwin considered and evaluated each of the possible causes of variation in each individual situation is a passage from his discussion of rudimentary organs at the beginning of *The Descent of Man*. In trying to understand the origin of rudimentary organs Darwin considers "disuse" the "chief agent"; natural selection is relegated to a secondary position as operative "in some cases," with other factors lending assistance. "Disuse at that period of life, when an organ is chiefly used, and this is generally during maturity, together with inheritance at a corresponding period of life, seems to have been the chief agent in causing organs to become rudimentary." For Darwin, the term *disuse* applies to more than merely the "lessened action of muscles." It also "includes a diminished flow of blood to a part or organ, from being subjected to fewer alternations of pressure, or from becoming in any way less habitually active." It is only in "*some* cases" that "organs have been reduced by means of natural selection, from having become injurious to the species under changed habits of life."

The process of reduction is "probably *often* aided through the two principles of compensation and economy of growth" (1:12, italics added). The principle of economy of growth "as applied to natural species, was propounded by Goethe and Geoffrey St. Hilaire at nearly the same time." Botanists in particular subscribed to the idea that, "when much organized matter is used in building up some one part, other parts are starved and become reduced." As Darwin found it "scarcely possible to distinguish between the supposed effects of such compensation of growth, and the effects of long-continued selection, which may at the same time lead to the augmentation of one part and the diminution of another" (1868, 2:342), he considered that its importance had probably been exaggerated. However, he thought it occasionally held good. Recognizing that neither compensation nor the principle of the economy of growth could "come into play" where a part was "already useless and much reduced in size," Darwin turned to the hypothesis of pangenesis introduced in the *Variation* because the "final and complete suppression of a part . . . is perhaps intelligible by the aid of the hypothesis of pangenesis, and apparently in no other way" (1871, 1:12).

After the publication of the *Origin* Darwin had found that "my critics frequently assume that I attribute all changes in the corporal structure and mental power exclusively to the natural selection of such variations as are often called spontaneous." Darwin was eager to disabuse his readers of this interpretation of his work. In the *Descent* he protested that "even in the first edition of the 'Origin of Species,' I distinctly stated that great weight must be attributed to the inherited effects of use and disuse, with respect both to the body and mind" (1874 [1871], 1:v–vii). With each publication Darwin came "to place somewhat more value on the definite and direct action of external conditions," so that by 1869 he requested Carus to make a complete retranslation into German of the fifth edition of the *Origin* because "I have been thus led to alter in many places *a few words;* and unless you go through the whole new edition, one part will not agree with another, which would be a great blemish" (1887–88, 3:109). In the *Variation,* as we tried to show, Darwin made an enormous effort to destroy the image attacked by his critics of the *exclusive* action of natural selection on chance variations. He went so far as to propose a "tentative hypothesis of Pangenesis," which accommodated the inheritance of acquired characteristics including experience and learning.

FREUD AND THE INHERITANCE
OF ACQUIRED CHARACTERISTICS

As we have already traced above, the inheritance of acquired characteristics was not completely rejected by biologists until 1930. Freud apparently was not aware of the change until 1938, when Jones called to his attention the change resulting in "the present attitude of biological science, which refuses to hear of the inheritance of acquired characters by succeeding generations." Until then Freud had not been "clearly aware of my audacity in neglecting" to make a "distinction between . . . an inherited tradition" and "one transmitted by communication" (1939 [1934–38], *SE* 23:110). He acknowledged that "on further reflection I must admit that I have behaved for a long time as though the inheritance of memory-traces of the experience of our ancestors, independently of direct communication and of the influence of education by the setting of an example, were established beyond question" (23:99).

Faced at the very end of his life with this change in biological thought from that familiar to him from Darwin's writings and from his university training in evolutionary biology (to be discussed in part II), Freud felt that he could not "do without this factor in biological evolution." He needed it to bridge the gulf between individual and group psychology. He had used it for this purpose in *Totem and Taboo* (1913) and in *Group Psychology and the Analysis of the Ego* (1921) apparently without objection from anyone. "If we assume the survival of these memory-traces in the archaic heritage, we have bridged the gulf between individual and group psychology: We can deal with peoples as we do with an individual neurotic." Without it "we shall not advance a step further along the path we entered on, either in analysis or in group psychology. The audacity cannot be avoided."

And so, in spite of appeals from his colleagues, Freud continued in *Moses and Monotheism* with the line of thought with which he had begun this book as lectures in Vienna in 1934 until he completed it as a refugee from Hitler in London in 1938. The strongest evidence he could offer in support of "the presence of memory-traces in the archaic heritage" was "the residual phenomena of the work of analysis which call for a phylogenetic derivation" (23:100). He supported his contention with a paragraph that has associations with Darwin's theory of descent, which in Freud's view "tore down the barrier that had been arrogantly set up between man and beast" (1925, *SE* 19:221). By assuming the presence of memory traces in the archaic heritage, "we are diminishing the gulf which earlier periods of human arrogance had torn too wide apart between mankind and the animals." This passage also reveals Freud's acceptance of animal instinct as defined and treated by Darwin in *The Expression of the Emotions in Man and Animals:* "If any explanation is to be found of what are called the instincts [*instinkt*] of animals, which allow them to behave from the first in a new situation in life as though it were an old and familiar one—if any explanation at all is to be found of this instinctive life of animals, it can only be that they bring the experiences of their species with them into their own new existence—that is, that they have preserved memories of what was experienced by their ancestors. The position in the human animal would not at bottom be different. His own archaic heritage corresponds to the instincts of animals even though it is different in its compass and contents" (*SE* 23:100).

5

"Ontogeny Recapitulates Phylogeny"

The seductive biological concept that "ontogeny recapitulates phylogeny" was not dependent upon the acceptance of the inheritance of acquired characteristics and so, despite repeated attacks, it survived in embryological textbooks beyond both the Lamarckian view and Freud's lifetime. However, Freud's acceptance of the views developed by Darwin in the *Variation* and reiterated in all Darwin's later works of the inheritance of acquired characteristics, including the mental ones, made it possible for Freud to apply to human psychology the recapitulation theory frequently attributed to Haeckel but reinstated in modern biology by Darwin in chapter 13 of the original *Origin* "as the explanation of the wide difference in many classes between the embryo and the adult animal, and of the close resemblance of the embryos within the same class" (1888, 1:88–89). Stephen J. Gould, professor of geology at Harvard, recalls being taught it as "Haeckel's doctrine . . . fifty years after it had been abandoned by science" (1977, p. 1). Fascinated by this "currently unpopular" subject, he went on to write a whole book on the subject (*Ontogeny and Phylogeny* [1977]).[1]

The subject was considered by Gould's colleagues in the latter part of the twentieth century no more to be mentioned publicly than sex had been in medical circles one hundred years earlier, when Freud studied with Charcot at the Salpêtrière in Paris. In the clinic Charcot had never mentioned sex. Nor had any of Freud's professors at the University of Vienna.

Yet to Freud's amazement, at an evening reception at Charcot's home, he heard the famous man exclaim to a colleague, Professor Brouardel, about a young couple: "*Mais dans des cas pareil c'est toujours* la chose génitale, *toujours . . . toujours . . . tourjours*" ("But in this sort of case it's always a question of the genitals—always, always, always," trans. by ed.). Similarly, in Vienna professor of gynecology Rudolf Chrobak, "perhaps the most eminent of all our Viennese physicians," had referred to Freud an impotent man's still virgin wife whose anxiety was incurable because, as he confided to Freud, "the sole prescription . . . is familiar enough to us but we cannot order it:

'R$_x$ Penis normalis
        dosim
    repetatur!'"   (Freud 1914, *SE* 14:14–15)

Chrobak later denied it. So did Breuer deny the comment he had made to Freud after their chance encounter with a patient's husband: "These things are always '*secrets d'alcôve*'" ('secrets of the marriage-bed')" (14:13–14).

Gould describes his similarly "curious experience" with more than twenty of his colleagues: "I tell a colleague that I am writing a book about parallels between ontogeny and phylogeny. He takes me aside, makes sure that no one is looking, checks for bugging devices, and admits in markedly lowered voice: 'You know, just between you, me, and that wall, I think that there really is something to it after all'" (1977, pp. 1–2).

FREUD'S APPLICATIONS

In 1913 Freud wrote: "In the last few years psychoanalytic writers," Abraham, Sabina Spielrein, and Jung, "have been aware that the principle 'ontogeny is a repetition of phylogeny' must be applicable to mental life" (1913 [1912–13], *SE* 13:184). That year in *Totem and Taboo* Freud developed his most famous and controversial application of this theory to the Oedipus complex as the ontogenetic recapitulation of an actual occurrence in the development of civilization at the period of Darwin's primal horde. In 1915 he tried unsuccessfully to extend the application of the recapitulation theory to his work on the neuroses. *A Phylogenetic Fantasy* (1987 [1915]) met a fate similar to Freud's unsuccessful 1895 attempt to apply neurophysiology in the "Project for a Scientific Psychology." Failing to pass the censorship of their author's judgment, they each survived among the papers of the particular colleague with whom Freud was sharing his thoughts at the time and were published posthumously more than half a century later.

But Freud did not reject the recapitulation theory itself. He used it quite frequently in the following years, even adding it to the 1919 edition of the *Interpretation of Dreams* (1900): "Dreaming is on the whole an example of regression to the dreamer's earliest condition, a revival of his childhood. . . . Behind this childhood of the individual we are promised a picture of a phylogenetic childhood—a picture of the human race, of which the individual's development is in fact an abbreviated recapitulation influenced by the chance circumstances of life" (*SE* 5:548). A year before, he had been "reading about Darwinism without any real aim" (1965, p. 268).

Freud usually used the recapitulation theory to refer to recapitulation of events in the history of the human race, that is, cultural history: "All the old cultural levels—those of the Middle Ages, of the Stone Age, even of animistic prehistory—are still alive in the great masses" (1960, December 9, 1928, "Letter to Richard S. Dyer-Bennett, p. 384). He pointed out parallels in the thinking of children and of primitive man. For instance, "there is a great deal of resemblance between the relations of children and of primitive man towards animals" (1913 [1912–13], *SE* 13:126). The "piece of arrogance" of civilized man in denying animals the possession of reason and attributing to himself an immortal soul and "a divine descent which permitted him to break the bond of community between him and the animal kingdom . . . is still foreign to children, just as it is to primitive and primaeval man. It is the result of the later, more pretentious stage of development. At the level of totemism primitive man had no repugnance to tracing his descent from an animal ancestor. In myths, which contain the precipitate of this ancient attitude of mind, the gods take animal shapes, and in the art of earliest times they are portrayed with animals' heads." As for children, "a child can see no difference between his own nature and that of animals. He is not astonished at animals thinking and talking in fairytales; he will transfer an emotion of fear which he feels for his human father onto a dog or a horse, without intending any derogation of his father by it. Not until he is grown up does he become so far estranged from animals as to use their names in vilification of human beings" (1917, *SE* 17:140).

Freud also applied the recapitulation theory to man's animal origins, traces of which he was convinced remained in man's mental and physical structure. His discovery of "an early efflorescence [of sexual life] which comes to an end at about the fifth year and is followed by what is known as the period of latency (till puberty) . . . leads us to suppose that the human race is descended from a species of animal which reached sexual maturity in five years" (1939 [1934–38], *SE* 23:74–75). In the *Introductory Lectures* (1916–17) Freud told his audience that "each individual somehow recapitulated in an abbreviated form the entire development of the human race" (*SE* 15:199). The incestuous love affairs of childhood "pass away because their time is over, because the children have entered upon a new phase of development in which they are compelled to recapitulate from the history of mankind the repression of an incestuous object-choice, just as at an earlier stage they were obliged to effect an object-choice of that very sort" (1919, *SE* 17:188).

For Freud, as he cautions his reader, "thoughts like these, which emphasize the hereditary, phylogenetically acquired factor in mental life, . . . are only admissible when psycho-analysis strictly observes the correct order of precedence, and, after forcing its way through the strata of what has been acquired by the individual, comes at last upon traces of what has been inherited" (1918, *SE* 17:121). Observing this procedure, Freud found a "phylogenetically inherited schemata . . . concerned with the business of 'placing' the impressions derived from actual experience." But, "wherever experiences fail to fit in with the hereditary schema, they become remodelled in the imagination" (17:119). The unconscious is a storehouse of the archaic heritage and from it children with their fantasies "simply fill in the gaps in their individual truth with prehistoric truth." It seemed to Freud that the fantasies told to him in analysis—"the seduction of children, the inflaming of sexual excitement by observing parental intercourse, the threat of castration (or rather castration itself)—were once real occurrences in the primaeval times of the human family" (1917, *SE* 16:371). The same conditions which originally necessitated the inherited schema usually recur in the life of the individual and partly veil this phylogenetic point of view.

But "wherever experiences fail to fit in with the hereditary schema . . . we are often able to see the schema triumphing over the experience of the individual" (1918, *SE* 17:119). In the case of the "Wolf Man" the little boy's father became the castrator although in reality the threats of castration in his life had come from the women who tended him, his mother and his nurse: "At this point the boy had to fit into a phylogenetic pattern, and he did so, although his personal experiences may not have agreed with it. Although the threats or hints of castration that had come his way had emanated from women, this could not hold up the final result for long. In spite of everything it was his father from whom in the end he came to fear castration. In this respect heredity triumphed over accidental experience; in man's prehistory it was unquestionably the father who practiced castration as a punishment and who later softened it down into circumcision" (17:86).

Freud found the phylogenetic origin of the libido more obvious than that of the ego. Nevertheless, in one of the 1917 lectures he stated that the recapitulation theory applied to the course of development of the ego as well as of the libido, "for both of them are at bottom heritages, abbreviated recapitulations of the development which all mankind has passed through from its primaeval days over long periods of time" (1917, *SE* 16:354). As early as 1905 Freud had given some indication of what the heritage of the ego might be: "It is during [the] period of total or only partial latency that are built up the mental forces which are later to impede the course of the sexual instinct and, like dams, restrict its flow—disgust, feelings of shame and the claims of aesthetic and moral ideals. One gets an impression from civilized children that the construction of these dams is a product of education, and no doubt education has much to do with it. But in reality this development is organically determined and fixed by heredity, and it can occasionally occur without any help at all from education" (1905, *SE* 7:177–78).

After Freud began to develop his ego psychology in 1915, he implied increasingly that there were intrinsic maturational factors in ego development. In a footnote to *Group Psychology and the Analysis of the Ego* (1921), Freud referred to "the ego's nucleus, which comprises the 'archaic heritage' of the human mind" (1921, *SE* 18:75). Nevertheless, except for a single posthumous reference to an "undifferentiated ego-id," Freud always defined the ego as experientially differentiated from the id, which contained *all* that was inherited. In *An Outline of Psycho-Analysis*, written in 1938 and published posthumously in 1940, Freud wrote: "We may picture an initial state as one in which the total available energy of Eros, which henceforward we shall speak of as 'libido,' is present in the still undifferentiated ego-id and serves to neutralize the destructive tendencies which are simultaneously present" (*SE* 23:149). An "undifferentiated ego-id" was firmly established as a concept in psychoanalysis in 1946 by Freud's followers Heinz Hartmann, Ernst Kris, and Rudolph Loewenstein, which brought it into line with the above footnote to *Group Psychology* and with Freud's 1917 statement that both the ego and the libido "are at bottom heritages, abbreviated recapitulations of the development which all mankind has passed through from its primaeval days over long periods of time" (*SE* 16:354).

Darwin had placed the great authority of his name behind the application of the historical or genetical explanation to the discredited parallelism of the embryological and paleontological records. The resulting law of recapitulation that Darwin thus reinstated Freud applied in *Totem and Taboo* to the parallelisms he saw in mythology, ethnological material, and the Oedipus complex to reconstruct what he considered the "actual" killing of the father by "Darwin's primal horde" and the consequent guilt and repression of incest. Freud later applied the idea of parallelism or recapitulation in *Group Psychology and the Analysis of the Ego* (1921) to bridge the gap between individual and group psychology and in *Moses and Monotheism* to reconstruct the origin not only of the Jewish religion but of man's belief in, and acceptance of, monotheism.

The primal horde theory of *Totem and Taboo* based on a hypothesis by Darwin in *The Descent of Man* is Freud's most extensive and best known application of both the recapitulation theory originating in chapter 13 of Darwin's *Origin* and of the neo-Lamarckism developed and expanded by Darwin in *The Variation of Animals and Plants under Domestication*. It will be discussed in the next chapter. Here we will only call attention to Freud's conclusion in *Moses and Monotheism* of his summary of his primal horde theory that "the ambivalent emotional attitude of the sons to their father," after they had destroyed his power by killing him, "remained in force during the whole of later development" (*SE* 23:130–31). "The later development" that Freud is referring to here is of course the later development of all mankind and not just the development of the sons involved in the particular killing of the particular father. In fact, Freud thought the killings may have been repeated in different groups, thus providing the repetition that Darwin and others considered a necessary factor for the inheritance of experience or learning.

DARWIN'S ROLE IN REVIVING RECAPITULATION

Darwin recalled in his "Autobiography" that "hardly any point gave me so much satisfaction when I was at work on the 'Origin'" (1887 [1876–82], p. 125) as the explanation "by descent with modification" of the embryological observations made thirty years earlier by von Baer of "the very general, but not universal difference in structure between the embryo and the adult" and of "embryos of different species within the same class, generally but not universally resembling each other" (1950 [1859], pp. 375–76). The recapitulation theory also explains "the supposed law" of Agassiz, as Darwin calls it, that ancient forms of life resemble the embryonic stages of recent forms. Darwin believed that where, as is usual, the embryonic form does not have to gain its own living it is not as subject to modification as the adult form. Therefore, the embryo remains "the animal in the less modified state; and in so far it reveals the structure of its progenitor" (p. 381). Progenitors had been disallowed within science since Geoffrey St. Hilaire's defeat at the hands of the great Cuvier at the French Academy of Science in 1832; expressions of descent or recapitulation were left in disrepute to the *Naturphilosophes* until Darwin.[1]

The early evolutionists, like Johann Friedrick Meckel and Lorenz Oken, had considered that they had as conclusive evidence for the descent of existing from earlier species the embryological observations of the French anatomist Étienne Renaud Augustin Serres, which supported parallelism. Serres thought he had observed in the development of the chick embryo a series of changing shapes of various organs and parts that were replicas of the corresponding parts in the adult stage of its ancestors and that appeared in the temporal order corresponding to the relative antiquity of the ancestral class. He went so far as to claim that "a man becomes a man only after passing through transitional stages of organization in which he is similar first to a fish, then to a reptile, then to birds and mammals." This parallelism was destroyed in 1828 by the infinitely superior observations of von Baer, which helped transform the embryology of *Naturphilosophie* into modern laboratory embryology.

In the first volume of his *Über Entwicklungsgeschichte der Thiere: Beobachtung und Reflexion (On Animal Development: Observation and Reflexion* 1828) von Baer violently attacked Serres's "generally accepted conception" of parallelism as "not based upon accurate observation" (1:157). Von Baer reported in extraordinary detail his own observations, which failed to support Serres's claim. In the fetal stages of the chick von Baer found only vague resemblances to more ancient types of organisms and then not in the order in which according to the geological evidence the supposed ancestors succeeded one another. These vague coincidences did not, in von Baer's opinion, support parallelism but were the inevitable consequence of the law of embryonic development, that development proceeds from the general to the specific. According to von Baer, "When one observes the progress of the formation" of the embryo, "what first of all leaps at the eye is that there is gradually taking place a transition from something homogeneous and general to something heterogeneous and special" (1:153).

Von Baer never accepted the evolutionary interpretation put upon his embryological observations by Darwin. Until Darwin, von Baer's *Entwicklungsgeschichte* of 1828 had effectively stopped talk about recapitulation among scientists. Von Baer's careful work in his *Entwicklungsgeschichte* had, long before Darwin's *Origin*, demonstrated that the developing chick, for example, was at a very early stage a vertebrate and did not recapitulate the organization of a polyp, a worm, or a mollusc; any recapitulation that did occur was only recapitulation of single organs and never the complete organization of other adult forms. After Darwin, von Baer discovered that talk of recapitulation was starting up again. In an 1876 essay von Baer wrote: "My opposition to the view of recapitulation received fairly general recognition. Johannes Müller, who in the first edition of his physiology had adopted the doctrine of Meckel and Oken, deleted it from the second edition. In general nothing was heard of it for a long while. Only most recently it is cropping up again here and there, yet without serious foundation" (2:243). Johannes Müller, although a vitalist, was the highly respected teacher of Freud's Professor Brücke and of Brücke's friends Helmholtz, Ludwig, and Du Bois-Reymond, who had joined in a vow against vitalism.

Darwin, who usually was scrupulously careful about examining the observational evidence of earlier specialists whose work was relevant to his hypothesis, failed to give von Baer's *Entwicklungsgeschichte* careful consideration. The enigma of Darwin's looking upon the leading facts in embryology as "second in importance to none in natural history" (Darwin, 1950 [1859], p. 382) and at the same time neglecting von Baer's great work is fully elucidated by Jane Oppenheimer in "An Embryological Enigma in the *Origin of Species*" (1959). Oppenheimer called attention to a Freudian slip on Darwin's part in attributing von Baer's ideas on embryological resemblances to Louis Agassiz. Although in his notes Darwin had correctly ascribed the passage to von Baer, Darwin did not mention von Baer until the third edition of the *Origin*. In the first two editions he left uncorrected the passage in which he used Agassiz's name in place of von Baer's: "The embryos, also, of distant animals within the same class are often strikingly similar: a better proof of this cannot be given than a circumstance mentioned by Agassiz [*sic*], namely, that having forgotten to ticket the embryo of some vertebrate animal, he cannot now tell whether it be that of a mammal, a bird, or a reptile" (1959 [1859], pp. 372–73; 1860 [1859], pp. 438–39).

Although Agassiz could never support recapitulation and is well-known for the strong attack upon Darwin that he mounted from the traditional point of view of species as distinct and immutable creations, he at least put the considerable weight of his authority behind parallelism, which in the hands of evolutionary thinkers like Darwin became recapitulation. Von Baer's *Entwicklungsgeschichte*, as we have seen above, attacked parallelism itself. Perhaps, Darwin avoided thinking too much about von Baer's book, or perhaps had not even read it carefully because of his difficulty with the German language. Or perhaps because it might have required him to give up one of the proofs of evolution. Had Darwin renounced or modified the "embryonic-recapitulation argument . . . his successors would doubtless have done the same. But as he neither abandoned nor emended it, that argument in its original form held its place in biology for almost a century" (Lovejoy 1959, p. 442).

In 1857 Darwin wrote to Gray that "embryology leads me to an enormous and frightful range" (1888, 1:478). Darwin was surprised and disappointed that "no notice of this point [recapitulation] was taken . . . in the early reviews of the 'Origin.'" Notice, however, was taken of it by a young zoologist in Brazil, Fritz Müller-Desterro, whose *Für Darwin* was mentioned above, and in a few years Darwin found that "several reviewers have given the whole credit to Fritz Müller and Haeckel." With his usual modesty Darwin conceded in his "Autobiography" that they "undoubtedly have worked it out much more fully, and in some respects more correctly than I did. I had materials for a whole chapter on the subject, and I ought to have made the discussion longer; for it is clear that I failed to impress my readers; and he who succeeds in doing so deserves, in my opinion, all the credit" (1887, pp. 88–89). As we have seen, in the long run the credit for recapitulation accrued to Darwin's greater name.

Fritz Müller, like Haeckel and Brücke a pupil of Johannes Müller, published in 1862 a small but important book, *Für Darwin* (*For Darwin*). Haeckel includes it in the list of forty-eight "works referred to in the text" of the *History of Creation*, "the study of which is recommended to the Reader" (1876 [1868], 2:371). As with Darwin's *Variation*, Freud could have learned of Fritz Müller's most important contributions not only from Haeckel's popularizations but also in studying zoology with Claus. In Claus's textbook *Grundzüge der Zoologie* both the Darwin and the Müller works play significant parts. However, from what we know of Freud's reading habits, he may have read two such important and current books for himself. Müller's book, once John Murray had undertaken to publish it in English for Darwin, was the only book by another author listed along with Darwin's own titles at the front of all English editions of Darwin that Freud bought. If Freud had read Müller, he would also have learned of the significance of Claus's work as support for Darwin's theory; it would have added to his eagerness to study with Claus when he entered the university, where he immediately signed up for Claus's elective on "Darwin and Biology."

Fritz Müller in *Für Darwin* stated that he was applying and extending the views expressed by Darwin in the *Origin*, particularly in chapter 13. Chapter by chapter in the *Origin* Darwin had taken up the problems that had assailed him and that he anticipated his critics would raise. Chapter by chapter he was able to provide answers. He reserved for last the discussion of problems that he had not as yet solved to his own satisfaction. Among them was the question of the parallelism of the embryological and paleontological records. Agassiz considered that science had revealed that God had used the same pattern in both cases. Darwin wrote that "Agassiz insists that ancient animals resemble to a certain extent the embryos of recent animals of the same class; or that the geological succession of extinct forms is in some degree parallel to the embryological development of recent forms." Darwin was aware that this doctrine of Agassiz accorded well with the theory of natural selection. In chapter 13 Darwin attempted to show that "the adult differs from its embryo, owing to variations supervening at a not early age, and being inherited at a corresponding age. This process, while it leaves the embryo almost unaltered, continually adds, in the course of successive generations, more and more differences to the adult. Thus the embryo comes to be left as a sort of picture, preserved by nature, of the ancient and less modified condition of each animal."

Perhaps Darwin's pet view was overlooked by his critics and friends because with his typical caution Darwin conceded that "he must follow Pictet," the Swiss zoologist-paleontologist, "and Huxley in thinking that the truth of this doctrine is very far from proved. . . . This view may be true, and yet it may never be capable of full proof" because "it would be vain to look for animals having the common embryological character of the Vertebrata, until beds far beneath the lowest Silurian strata are discovered—a discovery of which the chance is very small." However, he did "fully expect to see it hereafter confirmed, at least in regard to subordinate groups, which have branched off from each other within comparatively recent times" (pp. 286–87).

Fritz Müller's work was credited by Haeckel, Claus, and other writers of the day with providing the confirmation Darwin predicted. Darwin himself considered it important enough to arrange for a translation into English by W. S. Dallas, "an excellent and busy translator" as he assured Müller, and publication in 1869 at his (Darwin's) expense by his publisher John Murray, who "would not undertake it on his own risk" (Darwin 1887–88, 3:87). It was called more fully *Facts and Arguments for Darwin*. By 1872 Darwin felt that the evidence for recapitulation was sufficient for him to withdraw his reservations and to revise for the sixth and final edition of the *Origin* the passage cited above containing his earlier reservations: "Agassiz and several other highly competent judges insist that ancient animals resemble to a certain extent the embryos of recent animals belonging to the same classes; and that the geological succession of extinct forms is nearly parallel with the embryological development of existing forms. This view accords admirably well with our theory" (1902 [1859], 2:120).

Darwin, who had established that the sessile barnacles were Crustacea and published other valuable work on the Cirrepedes, indicated the value of the Crustacea for shedding light on the question of parallelism. Müller not only had Darwin's work and his own rich harvest of the Brazilian waters to observe directly but also the work on the intermediate forms of Crustacea, the Copepoda, by the man who was to become Freud's zoology professor. Müller utilized Carl Claus's work on the missing "connecting intermediate forms which would have permitted us to refer the regions of the body and the limbs of the larvae to those of the adult animals." Claus's "comprehensive and careful investigations . . . have filled up this deficiency in our knowledge and rendered the section of the Copepoda one of the best known in the whole class." From "the abundance" of Claus's "valuable materials" Müller selected "only those which are indispensable for the comprehension of the development of the Crustacea in general, because, in what relates to the Copepoda in particular, the facts have already been placed in the proper light by the representation of their most recent investigator [Carl Claus] and must appear to any one whose eyes are open, as important evidence in favour of the Darwinian theory" (Müller 1869 [1864], p. 85).

The Copepoda include "wonderfully deformed" parasites and also species living in a free state both in fresh waters and in "far more multifarious forms" (p. 84) in the sea. Claus had found that all the free Copepoda that he investigated emerged as nauplius broods, a fact long known in the freshwater *Cyclopes* and observed by Nordmann in "several parasitic Crustacea, which had previously passed, almost universally, as worms." Claus traced the development of the nauplius broods of the free-living Copepoda through their various stages to the adult forms, thus filling the lacuna of "the connecting intermediate forms which would have permitted us to refer the region of the body and the limbs of the larvae to those of the adult animal." Although the forms of the nauplius broods of the Copepoda studied by Claus are extremely various "sometimes compressed laterally, sometimes flat,—sometimes elongated, sometimes oval, sometimes round or even broader than long, and so forth," they all "have, at the earliest period, three paris of limbs (the future antennae and mandible), the anterior with a single, and the two following ones with a double series of joints, or branchiae. The unpaired eye, labrum, and mouth, already occupy their permanent positions. The posterior portion, which is usually short and destitute of limbs, bears two terminal setae, between which the anus is situated" (pp. 85–86).

According to Müller, "*the primitive history of a species will be preserved in its developmental history the more perfectly, the longer the series of young states through which it passes by uniform steps*" (p. 121). Claus's studies had revealed such a series for the free Copepoda; and for some of the parasitic ones as well; through the various molts of the early stages the larva of the free Copoepoda continues like a nauplius, its progress consisting essentially in the extension of the body and the sprouting forth of new limbs. Müller continued the description of the larval changes with a quotation from Claus: "The following stage already displays a fourth pair of extremities, the future maxillae." The next three new pairs of limbs (the maxillipedes and the two anterior pairs of natatory feet) do not change the nauplius nature of the larvae, for the three anterior pairs of limbs represent rowing feet. It is only at the next molt that "it is converted into the youngest *Cyclops*-like state, when it resembles the adult animal in the structure of the antennae and buccal organs, although the number of limbs and body-segments is still much less" (p. 86) than in the adult.

Here variations provide living examples of a developmental stage that may be the final adult form in one animal but from which others continue to progress or even, as in some parasitic forms, regress. According to Müller, "in the Cyclopedae the posterior antennae have lost their secondary branch, and the mandibles have completely thrown off the previously existing natatory feet, while in the other families these appendages persist, more or less altered." Most significant as evidence for the recapitulation theory are the variations in development at this stage, which Müller quotes from Claus: "Beyond this stage of free development, many forms of the parasitic Copepoda, such as *Lernanthropus* and *Chondracanthus*, do not pass, as they do not acquire the third and fourth pairs of limbs, nor does a separation of the fifth thoracic segment from the abdomen take place; others (*Achtheres*) even fall to a lower grade by the subsequent loss of the two pairs of natatory feet. But all free Copepoda, and most of the parasitic Crustacea, pass through a longer or shorter series of stages of development, in which the limbs acquire a higher degree of division into joints in continuous sequence, the posterior pairs of feet are developed, and the last thoracic segment and the different abdominal segments are successively separated from the common terminal portion" (p. 87).

From his own experience Müller provided a simple example "well adapted to open the eyes of many who, perhaps, would rather not see" of how "in the short period of a few weeks or months, the changing forms of the embryo and larvae will pass before us, a more or less complete and more or less true picture of the transformations through which the species, in the course of untold thousands of years, has struggled up to its present state." In describing the development of the tubicolar annelids, Müller reported that "three years ago I found on the walls of one of my glasses some small worm-tubes (fig. 65), the inhabitants of which bore three pairs of barbate branchial filaments, and had no operculum. According to this we should have been obliged to refer them to the genus *Protula*. A few days afterwards one of the branchial filaments had become thickened at the extremity into a clavate operculum (fig. 66), when the animal reminded me, by the barbate opercular peduncle, of the genus *Filograna*, only that the latter possess two opercula. In three days more, during which a new pair of branchial filaments had sprouted forth, the opercular peduncle had lost its lateral filaments (fig. 67), and the worms had become *Serpulae*" (pp. 112–13).

Claus's work on the Copepoda also provided an example for Müller of the tendency toward direct development, that is, the straightening out of development. Where the conditions of existence are as changed as in the parasites, it becomes particularly desirable for the young to acquire the advantages of the adult form as soon as possible. In the developmental history of some of the parasitic Crustacea, for example *Achtheres percarum*, the entire series of nauplius stages described above that are passed through by the free Copepoda are "completely overleapt." Although this group quits "the egg like the rest in a Nauplius-like form, inasmuch as the plump, oval, astomatous body bears two pairs of simple rowing feet, and behind these, as traces of the third pair, two inflations furnished each with a long seta," underneath this nauplius skin which is burst within a few hours is a very different larva which, according to Claus, "agrees in the segmentation of the body and in the development of the extremities with the first *Cyclops*-stage" (p. 88).

Similar traces of a transition toward direct development cited by Müller are "the egg-like larva of Cryptophialus . . . the *Nauplius*-envelope of the embryos of *Mysis* and the maggot-like larva of *Ligia*, etc." (p. 133). As a consequence of this tendency toward direct development as well as the possibility of variations intervening in early as well as final stages of development, the record is rarely as clearly preserved as in the development of the Copepoda. Nevertheless, Müller was able to find and trace "in the section of the higher Crustacea (Malacostraca)" as furnishing "the truest and most complete indications of its primitive history" the development of a prawn "from the Nauplius through states analogous to Zoëa and *Mysis* to the form of a Macrurous Crustacean" (p. 122). Concluding his study of the genealogy of the Crustacea with a discussion of their evolution, Müller stated: "We may see, without further discussion, how the representation given by Claus of the development of the Copepoda may pass almost word for word as the primitive history of these animals" (p. 133). Freud was later to make the controversial assumption that the psychosexual development he found in children, particularly the Oedipus complex, could pass for the primitive history of mankind or, in Darwin's words, had "come to be left as a sort of picture, preserved by nature, of the ancient . . . condition of" (1950 [1859], p. 287) man.

Müller established for the Crustacea the relationship between individual development and the primitive history of its group but, as may already have become clear, it was not the oversimplified "ontogeny repeats phylogeny" inaccurately attributed today to Haeckel or to Haeckel's biogenetic law. Müller found that "the historical record preserved in developmental history is gradually EFFACED as the development strikes into a constantly straighter course from egg to the perfect animal, and it is frequently SOPHISTICATED by the struggle for existence which the free-living larvae have to undergo" (p. 114).

In 1864 both Darwin and Müller were cautious about assuming common ancestry outside a proved group. Müller concluded by recommending for further examination "the supposition that the Insecta had for their common ancestor a Zoëa," an early larval form of certain decapodal Crustacea, "which raised itself into a life on land." He could find no bridges from the nauplius to the "nearer provinces of the Myriopoda and Arachnida" (p. 140). Haeckel with his belief in monism was less cautious. When in 1862 he succeeded in producing a genealogy for the Radiolaria, he immediately went on to trace the series of man's ancestors in his *Generelle Morphologie* of 1866. In 1869 in a monograph on the Medusae Haeckel proposed the controversial gastrea theory, in which he assumed from the presence of the two-layered gastrula stage in the embryonic development of numerous multicellular animals that all multicellular animals must pass through such a stage and therefore that the first stable form of multicellular animal, which he called a gastrea, must have resembled this two-layered gastrula stage.

Nevertheless, the simplest formulation of the recapitulation theory or theory of parallelism, which even Haeckel subscribed to, was that "ontogeny is a brief and imperfect recapitulation of phylogeny" (1905 [1903], 1:xxi). And this approximates the form in which we find it stated by Freud: "The prehistory in which the dream-work leads us back is of two kinds— on the one hand, into the individual's prehistory, his childhood, and on the other, in so far as each individual somehow recapitulates in *an abbreviated* form the entire development of the human race, into phylogenetic prehistory too" (1900, *SE* 5:548; 1916 [1915–16], *SE* 15:199 italics added).

RECAPITULATION AND THE INHERITANCE OF ACQUIRED CHARACTERISTICS

Recapitulation and the inheritance of acquired characteristics, both rejected by today's biologists, were not regarded by all biologists as necessarily mutually dependent, although in 1917, in the period when the inheritance of acquired characteristics was losing ground, the embryologist E. W. MacBride once again revived the theory of recapitulation in support of Lamarckism in his article "Recapitulation as a Proof of the Inheritance of Acquired Characters." Belief in the recapitulation theory did not, as Freud thought, depend on the inheritance of acquired characters and so it survived beyond the demise of neo-Lamarckism. Fritz Müller, who "demonstrated with clear examples that in their individual development animals repeat the history of their race" (Krause 1885, p. 150), had throughout his *Für Darwin* reasoned from his observations completely upon the basis of natural selection and without recourse to the inheritance of acquired characteristics. Weismann, even after enunciating his theory of the continuity of the germ plasm, wrote that "the ontogeny arises from the phylogeny by a condensation of its stages" (1904 [1902]).

Those of Freud's followers who were critical of his neo-Lamarckian explanations did not fault him for his application of the recapitulation theory, except as he based it on the inheritance of acquired characteristics; some even made use of it themselves. Ernst Kris, for instance, who for the BBC centennial observance of Freud's birthday wrote in 1956 that "Freud's Lamarckian propensities much regretted by many of us are the 'dated' part of his views" (p. 632), was at the same time stimulating the interest of his co-researchers in psychoanalytic child development at the Yale Child Study Center with the statement that "ontogeny repeats phylogeny" (S. Ritvo, personal communication, 1954).

In 1930, when Ronald Aylmer Fisher's *The Genetical Theory of Natural Selection* put an end to biologists' consideration of the inheritance of acquired characteristics, Gavin de Beer still found it necessary to plead, "If only the recapitulationists would abandon the assertion that that which is repeated is the *adult* condition of the ancestor, there would be no reason to disagree with them" (p. 120). It was the repetition of the adult condition of the ancestor that—in disregard of von Baer—Darwin, Müller, Haeckel, and Freud all thought was to be found repeated in the development of the embryo, larva, or child.

Emanuel Rádl, tracing *The History of Biological Theories* in the Lamarck centennial year of 1909, just after the Darwin semicentennial, held Darwin responsible for making von Baer famous for the very theory that von Baer had always opposed, the repetition of the adult form by the embryo. Others held the German embryologist Oskar Hertwig, developer with his brother Richard von Hertwig of the germ-layer theory, responsible for lending weight to the theory by erroneously calling "von Baer a guarantor ('*Gewährs-mann*') of the idea of parallelism" (Meyer 1935, 10:388). Von Baer compared embryos with embryos and established as his disregarded fourth law that "fundamentally the embryo of a higher animal form never resembles the adult of another animal form, but only its embryo" (1826, p. 224, trans. in Russell 1916, pp. 125–26). Haeckel is accused of suppressing this law in pushing his own theory.

But whether it bore the name of Darwin, Müller, Haeckel, or von Baer, the recapitulation theory as Freud understood it, despite many attacks through the years, had been revived as a consequence of Darwin's support, finding its way into and holding its place in embryology and in elementary textbooks of biology until the end of Freud's life. At the time of Freud's death I was being taught it in embryology at a college highly regarded for its sciences, especially zoology. It was often treated as one of the most important biological generalizations. It had become for "those charged with the responsibility of expounding the law of evolution . . . a familiar maxim, easily learned, and a convenient skeleton on which to hang the discrete data of embryology"; it was "with a sigh of regret" that in the 1930s and 1940s those biologists "reared in the phylogenetic tradition" (Shumway 1932, 7:98) anticipated its passing.

All that was left of it in biological thought in 1959, one hundred years after the *Origin* and twenty years after Freud's death, is revealed in a statement by Ernst Mayr in the article "Agassiz, Darwin, and Evolution," in which he deplored "the great number of biologists left who to this very day believe that there must be a close correlation between ontogeny and phylogeny because both deal with processes occurring in the time dimension." According to Mayr, "the complex difference between the two phenomena becomes most apparent if expressed in terms of the information theory: ontogeny is the decoding of coded information, phylogeny is the creating of ever new codes of information and the survival of the most successful ones" (1959, 13:181).

This is post-Freudian thinking. Freud's life and writings belong to the century following Darwin's revival of the recapitulation theory. With Darwin's great name behind it, and occasionally even von Baer's great name falsely appended to it, the recapitulation theory survived a century of criticisms directed from time to time at differing aspects of the theory.

Before we move on to Freud's use of Darwin's primal horde theory, it may be interesting to look over Freud's shoulder as his imagination plays freely with the theory of recapitulation in the recently discovered *Phylogenetic Fantasy*. It proved a fantasy that in the end could not withstand his critical thinking; Freud consigned it to the wastebasket. A *Phylogenetic Fantasy* survives in a 1915 draft Freud sent to his colleagual friend in Hungary, Sándor Ferenczi, with permission to "throw it away or keep it" (1987 [1915], p. xvi). Fortunately, Ferenczi chose to keep it with other Freud correspondence, where in 1983 Ilsa Grubrich-Simitis found it while preparing the Freud–Ferenczi correspondence for publication.

From November 1914 until the summer of 1915 Freud was working on a series of twelve papers for a book he hoped would "clarify and carry deeper the theoretical assumptions on which a psychoanalytic system could be founded" (1917 [1915], *SE* 14:222n). Six papers have never been found.

Five others were realized as classic metapsychological papers basic to psychoanalytic theory. Published promptly in 1915 were "Instincts and their Vicissitudes," "Repression," and "The Unconscious" and, two years later, "Mourning and Melancholia" and "A Metapsychological Supplement to the Theory of Dreams." Freud could well afford to throw away *A Phylogenetic Fantasy* and its six unsuccessful siblings as a less prolific mind might have been reluctant to do. Darwin, endowed with an equally prolific theorizing capacity, repeatedly said that it was important to know when to give up an inquiry.

A Phylogenetic Fantasy reveals Freud attempting to apply the recapitulation theory as far as his imagination would take him. Darwin's son Francis reported that his father "often said that no one could be a good observer unless he was an active theorizer." Francis's description of his father's theorizing propensities also describes Freud's, as it probably does the hidden workings of other great scientific minds: "It was as though he were charged with theorizing power ready to flow into any channel on the slightest disturbance, so that no fact, however small, could avoid releasing a stream of theory, and thus the fact became magnified into importance. In this way it naturally happened that many untenable theories occurred to him; but fortunately his richness of imagination was equalled by his power of judging and condemning the thoughts that occurred to him" (1887–88, 1:49).

Many nonscientists have a distorted image of the road to scientific discovery because until the Freudian era it was not seemly to acknowledge any errors, failed efforts, or foolish ideas on the part of great men, whether scientists or patriots. Great men were preserved as models of perfection. Darwin privately referred to his "foolish experiments," such as having one of his sons play the flute to his plants to determine whether plants respond. Today, as scientists are once again testing plants' reactions to sound waves, Darwin does not seem as foolish as he might have to himself and his contemporaries. It is appropriate that Freud's closest associates, Princess Marie Bonaparte, Anna Freud, and Ernst Kris, only eleven years after his death and in disregard of his wish for its destruction, pioneered by publishing Freud's failed "Project" (1895) for the insights it provided into the workings of the scientific mind. Modern scientists, like the Nobel Prize winning geneticist James Watson in his *Double Helix* (1968), now themselves publicly reveal their human foibles for a more realistic view of the scientist at work. The trend may have gone too far. We are assailed by academic adventurers seeking easy fame from exposing the weaknesses, true or fabricated, of great men without troubling to integrate their findings into the larger picture of a whole human being. The Freudian revolution may not be solely responsible. The Greeks, too, had their "dwarves who saw so far because they stood on the shoulder of giants," an aphorism that Newton had modestly applied to himself and to which Freud countered, when a colleague mentioned it to him, "Yes, but the louse in the astronomer's hair does not see a thing" (Sterba 1982, p. 120).

Freud had called his draft "Overview of the Transference Neurosis." He started by trying to synthesize the transference neuroses, anxiety, conversion-hysteria, and obsessional neuroses. He found that their "most important distinguishing characteristic . . . would only become evident by contrast" (1987 (1915), p. 10) with the narcissistic neuroses of dementia praecox (today's schizophrenia), paranoia, and melancholia-mania. In detailing "comparisons between the way people with transference neuroses are able to establish and maintain relationships, and the way those with narcissistic neuroses have difficulty maintaining a firm grasp on their interpersonal relationships and on reality" (ibid., editor's "preface," p. ix), Freud's discussion of the acquisition of neuroses eventually led him to the factor of disposition. In an era of the recapitulation theory disposition, insofar as it is constitutional, has to have been acquired in "still earlier prehistory" than the individual's prehistory "because one can justifiably claim that the inherited dispositions are residues of the acquisition of our ancestors" (ibid., p. 10). With the recapitulation theory it was "still legitimate to assume that the neuroses must also bear witness to the history of the mental development of mankind" (p. 11). But "how much the phylogenetic disposition can contribute to the understandings of all the neuroses cannot yet be estimated" (p. 10).

It is difficult today when we no longer believe in recapitulation to understand how Freud could have hoped to gain any insights for psychoanalysis by projecting his psychoanalytic findings onto man's prehistory. Perhaps, it was the satisfaction Darwin described of "an astonishing number of isolated facts" being "connected and rendered intelligible." In a fashion similar to Freud here Darwin had continued to hope his "well-abused hypothesis of Pangenesis" would accomplish this "if anyone should hereafter be led to make observations by which some such hypothesis could be established" (1958 [1876–82], p. 130). As an already established theory, recapitulation opened such a vista for Freud. Understanding the neuroses "would naturally be much easier if the developmental history of the ego were given to

us somewhere else," that is, in phylogeny, "instead of our having to proceed in the opposite direction" (1987 [1915], p. 11).

Based on his 1915 understanding of the customary time of onset of the
neuroses, which he later found to be mistaken, Freud thought a series
existed "to which one can attach various far-reaching ideas." He still
thought that only the transference neuroses arose in childhood: "Anxiety
hysteria, almost without precondition, is the earliest, closely followed by
conversion hysteria (from about the fourth year); somewhat later in pre-
puberty (9–10) obsessional neurosis." The narcissistic neuroses seemed to
continue this time series unbroken: "Dementia praecox in classic form is
[an] illness of the puberty years, paranoia approaches the mature years,
and melancholia-mania the same time period, otherwise not specifiable."

When considering libidinal dispositions, Freud saw another series running in the opposite direction. In general terms only, "the later the neurosis appears, the earlier the phase of the libido to which it must regress
. . . conversion hysteria is directed against primacy of the genitals, obsessional neurosis against the sadistic preliminary stage, all three transference neuroses against complete development of the libido." Freud's
time series, starting with the transference neuroses, continues with the
narcissistic neuroses unbroken into puberty and adulthood: "anxiety hysteria—conversion hysteria—obsessional neurosis—dementia praecox—
paranoia—melancholia." Arising later, the narcissistic neuroses regress
even further than the transference neuroses "to phases before the finding
of object."[2]

But the three narcissistic neuroses did not follow one another in proper
inverse order as the transference neuroses had. Dementia praecox, which
Freud thought "in classic form" was an "illness of the puberty years, . . .
regresses as far as auto-eroticism," although "it unquestionably appears
earlier than paranoia." Paranoia "approaches the mature years" in the
onset but regresses only "as far as narcissistic identification with the object." Melancholia-mania, also of adult onset, "permit(s) no certain ranking
with respect to time." Freud concluded from this that the development of
the libido was not the sole determinant of "the time sequence of the neuroses" (p. 12).

Thanks to the recapitulation theory Freud could identify a third series,
"which is really concurrent with the time sequence of the neuroses," a phylogenetic series. The recapitulation theory encouraged not only Freud but
his colleagues Fritz Wittels and Ferenczi to imagine scenarios for man's

prehistoric ancestors. Friz Wittels (1912) "first expressed the idea that the primal human animal passed its existence in a thoroughly rich milieu that satisfied all needs." A "rich milieu satisfying all needs" sounds like uterine existence or a newborn at the breast. But Freud, obviously never having tried full-time care of infants without benefit of an extended family or auxiliary help and under modern bottle-feeding conditions, identified the all-satisfying milieu with early infancy and found support for it in "echoes . . . retained in the myth of the primaeval paradise." He also speculated that under these idyllic conditions primal man may have "overcome the periodicity of the libido" found in other mammals, which continued to interest him long after his association with Fliess.

According to Ferenczi (1913), primal humans developed under "the influence of the geological fate of the earth." By the Ice Age there was a human race and "the exigencies of the Ice Age in particular gave it the stimulus for the development of civilization" (Freud, 1988 [1915], p. 13). The transference neuroses, arising in childhood, Freud fitted ingeniously into the onset and exigencies of the Ice Age, at the end of which "the human race had disintegrated into individual hordes that were dominated by a strong and wise brutal man as father" (pp. 15–16). Freud had already developed this theme in *Totem and Taboo* from "Darwin's theories of the earliest state of human society" (*SE* 13:141), as we shall see in the next chapter.

Freud attempted, in more detail than we have room for here, to complete "a program envisioned by Ferenczi [1913, p. 236] 'to bring the neurotic types of regression into harmony with the stages of human phylogeny'" (p. 16).[3] He found the temptation "great to recognize in the three dispositions to anxiety hysteria, conversion hysteria, and obsessional neuroses regressions to phases that the whole human race had to go through at some time from the beginning to the end of the Ice Age, so that at that time all human beings were the way only some of them are today." He acknowledged that regression is not the only contributor to neurosis; in addition characteristics continue to be acquired and inherited as Freud had learned many years earlier from Haeckel, so "the pictures naturally cannot coincide completely" (p. 13).

It is impressive how many details from the neuroses Freud could draw into his phylogenetic reconstructions. Anxiety hysteria is the earliest in Freud's time series. In the phylogenetic series mankind became "generally *anxious*" when the "hitherto friendly outside world which bestowed every

94

satisfaction, transformed itself" with the approach of the Ice Age "into a mass of threatening perils." The privations imposed by "the encroaching Ice Age" provided "good reason for realistic anxiety about everything new"; and so, in infantile anxiety, the child "is generally inclined to be fearful of anything new," and "when satisfaction is denied, the child transfers object libido into realistic anxiety about strangers." Anxiety hysteria regresses to this stage.

As food eventually became insufficient to permit an increase in their number, primal humans "must have been subjected to the conflict between self-preservation and desire to procreate, which finds its expression in most of the typical cases of hysteria." Freud could visualize for this period a situation that "obviously corresponds to the conditions of conversion hysteria." The obligation to limit reproduction felt by Freud's middle-class patients was once a real necessity imposed by the impending Ice Age and "promoted a certain regression to the phase of the libido before the primacy of the genitals, . . . perverse satisfactions that did not lead to the propagation of children" (p. 15). More concerned than men about the consequences of sexual intercourse—infanticide for Ice Age mothers—women were more severely affected, as was brought home to Freud in his practice.

"Obsessional neurosis recapitulates the characteristics" of mankind's next phase, which "primarily affected the male." Surviving unchanged in obsessional neuroses are "the overemphasis on thinking, the enormous energy that returns in the compulsion, the omnipotence of thoughts, the inclination to inviolable laws" (p. 16). After learning to "degrade his sexual activity to an earlier phase" by regression, "actuating his intelligence became paramount" for primal man so he could "investigate" and "understand the hostile world somewhat" and "master it with inventions. His beginnings of language seemed magic and his thoughts omnipotent." His world view was animistic "with magical trappings" (p. 15). Some characteristics are recapitulated by neurotics in a negative way due to reaction formation.

It was a brutal period. The "egoistically jealous and inconsiderate nature" he hypothesized for the dominant male of the primal horde Freud thought may have arisen as an adaptation to the severe Ice Age. "Against the brutal impulses that want to replace love life" arise "the resistance of later developments which from the libidinal conflict finally saps the life energy of the individual and . . . leaves [over] as compulsion only the impulses that have been displaced to trivialities." Once valuable for the development of civilization, this type "perishes in its return from the demands of love life." So too does the "grandiose type of the primal father himself" perish "from the familial relationships he created for himself" (p. 16).

In *Totem and Taboo* Freud had published his speculations about Darwin's primal horde and the killing of the father. In *The Phylogenetic Fantasy* he developed two acts leading to the final parricidal act, identified each with one of the narcissistic dispositions, and placed them all in the post–Ice Age, when lessening exigencies reduced the need for the protection of the jealous, dominating brutal father. In *Totem and Taboo* the father had driven the sons out at puberty: "Ψ A experiences admonish us, however, to substitute another, more gruesome solution—namely, that he robs them of their manhood—after which they are able to stay . . . as harmless laborers." Dementia praecox recapitulates the "extinguishing of the libido and a standstill in individual development" caused in the primal sons by castration. Freud points out that youthful sufferers behave as though castrated and that "self-castrations are not uncommon." Dementia praecox, "especially as hebephrenia, leads to giving up every love-object, degeneration of all sublimations, and return to auto-erotism." Only the degenerative or regressive features belong in the phylogenetic pictures. The almost more noticeable "speech alterations and hallucinatory storms . . . represent restitutive attempts, the numerous efforts to regain the object" (1987 [1915], p. 17).

As castrates, the sons cannot pass on the resultant characteristics or experiences. It remains for the youngest son of the aging father, "thanks to the intercession of the mother," to elude their fate and succeed the father. But Freud did not explain how the youngest son, not a castrate himself, can acquire for transmission the reactions of his castrated brothers. Is knowledge of the fate of his older brothers and fear of it for himself sufficient for the more fortunate younger son to go through the same "vicissitudes of the male sex and . . . propagate them as dispositions?" Women, too, do not experience or even fear castration. Yet they suffer equally with men when it comes to dementia praecox, paranoia, and melancholia. Freud's imagination failed him when it came to "the vicissitudes of women in these primeval times"; there may be "conditions of life not yet recognized." Freud turned to "human bisexuality" to be "spared the grossest difficulty" of recapitulation in women of exclusively male prehistoric experience.

Awareness of unresolved problems protected Freud from the temptation to place "the phylogenetic disposition above everything else. . . . There remains room for new acquisitions" (p. 20) and unknown influences. Gould's solution to the enigma of male nipples might serve here: the differentiation of the sexes from the same common form.

In the second act of the primal horde drama the sons avoid castration by fleeing. Freud, only twenty years after the famous jailing for homosexuality of his contemporary Oscar Wilde, unabashedly assigns a highly significant role to homosexuality as fundamental to man's development of social feelings that became the basis for every later society. This second act of the primal horde drama is the possible source for "the long-sought hereditary disposition of homosexuality." In learning to take upon themselves the struggle for survival—a Darwinian idea basic to the entire endeavor of the *Fantasy*—the brothers lived together as allies; "in ⟨paranoia⟩ secret alliances are not lacking and the persecutor plays a tremendous role." Living together "had to bring social feelings to the fore and could have been built upon homosexual sexual satisfaction." The social feelings "sublimated from homosexuality became mankind's lasting possession" (p. 18). Paranoia is a defense against the return of homosexuality. In trying "to ward off homosexuality, which was the basis for the organization of brothers," paranoia "must drive the victim out of society and destroy his social sublimations." Alternation of depression and elation is characteristic of melancholia-mania.

The primal horde ended with the brother clan overpowering and killing the primal father. The "triumph over his death" is followed by "mourning over the fact that they all still revered him as a model" (p. 20) and identified with him. Such identification Freud had already established in a more successful metapsychological paper of that year, his just completed "Mourning and Melancholia" (1917 [1915]), "as the prerequisite for the melancholic mechanism" (p. 21).

A Phylogenetic Fantasy, as we have seen, rested heavily not only on the recapitulation theory but also on Darwin's "struggle for existence" and his primal horde theory. Although Freud threw away *A Phylogenetic Fantasy*, he believed at the time that it was only the beginning, not the end, of understanding of the phylogenetic factor. He had applied it confidently the year before to his understanding of the "Infantile Neurosis" (1918 [1914]) of the "Wolf Man," where, as we have seen, the patient feared castration by his father although the threats had come from mother and governess.

97

Freud saw no need in 1918 to expurgate the phylogenetic considerations when publishing the case. However faulty the theory, Freud's observations were correct. Darwin had been sure that one could do no harm to science with a false theory but only with false observations; there were always plenty of people eager to correct a false theory. Falsified observations are not as readily recognizable. Experiments as well as direct observations are hard to repeat and seldom are.

6

Freud's Use of
Darwin's Primal Horde
Hypothesis

> Many authors regard a primordial state of
> promiscuity as highly unlikely. I myself, in all
> modesty favour a different hypothesis in regard
> to the primordial period—Darwin's.
> Freud letter to Jung, May 14, 1912

In his last completed[1] book *Moses and Monotheism* (1939) [1934–38] Freud summarized the primal horde theory he had based on a hypothesis from Darwin's *Descent of Man:* "In 1912 I attempted, in my *Totem and Taboo*, to reconstruct the ancient situation. . . . In doing so I made use of some theoretical ideas put forward by Darwin, Atkinson and particularly by Robertson Smith, and combined them with the findings and indications derived from psychoanalysis. From Darwin I borrowed the hypothesis that human beings originally lived in small hordes, each of which was under the despotic rule of an older male who appropriated all the females and castigated or disposed of the younger males, including his sons." To Darwin's small horde hypothesis Freud added Atkinson's "idea that this patriarchal system ended in a rebellion by the sons, who banded together against their father, overcame him and devoured him in common." Robertson Smith's totem theory provided Freud with the assumption that the father-horde gave place to the totemic brother-clan. "In order to be able to live in peace with one another, the victorious brothers renounced the women on whose account they had, after all, killed their father, and instituted exogamy. The power of fathers was broken and the families were organized as a matriarchy" (*SE* 23:130–31).

Freud's speculations in *Totem and Taboo* on Darwin's primal horde theory, repeated in "Thoughts for the Times on War and Death" (1915) and in *Group Psychology* (1921), belong to the period when Freud was introducing the concepts of narcissism and of an ego ideal in his paper "On Narcissism: An Introduction" (1914). In this last-named paper, in "Mourning and Melancholia" (1917 [1915]), and in chapter 11 of *Group Psychology* (1921) Freud was giving much consideration to the "critical agency" that led to the hypothesis of the superego in *The Ego and the Id* (1923) and a fresh assessment of the sense of guilt. In "Thoughts for the Times on War and Death" Freud referred to "the obscure sense of guilt to which mankind has been subject since prehistoric times and which in some religions has been condensed into the doctrine of primal guilt, or original sin." He went on to say that "in my book *Totem and Taboo* (1912–13) I have, following clues given by Robertson Smith, Atkinson and Charles Darwin, tried to guess the nature of this primal guilt." He believed, too, that the "Christian doctrine of today enables us to deduce it. If the Son of God was obliged to sacrifice his life to redeem mankind from original sin, then by the law of talion, the requital of like by like, that sin must have been a killing, a murder. Nothing else could call for the sacrifice of a life for its expiation. And the original sin was an offense against God the Father, the primal crime of mankind must have been a parricide, the killing of the primal father of the primitive human horde, whose mnemic image was later transfigured into a deity" (*SE* 14:292–93).

It is significant that, in coming across a universal sense of guilt not further traceable to events in the lives of individuals, Freud was not willing to accept it as a given but proceeded beyond the limits of his field to seek its origin still further back in the history of mankind; and further, that when he did, "Darwin's theories of the earliest state of human society" (1913 [1912–13], *SE* 13:141) should play the same role for Freud as Malthus's population theory had for Darwin, something already known which when recalled helped fit all the other pieces together. As Freud described it in his "Autobiography," his "starting-point was the striking correspondence between the two taboo-ordinances of totemism (not to kill the totem and not to have sexual relations with any woman of the same totem-clan) and the two elements of the Oedipus complex (getting rid of the father and

100

taking the mother to wife)." Helpful were "two facts from psycho-analysis, a lucky observation of a child made by Ferenczi [1913] . . . and the analysis of early animal-phobias in children, which so often showed that the animal was a substitute for the father . . . on to which the fear of the father derived from the Oedipus complex had been displaced."

Freud needed little more to be able to "recognize the killing of the father as the nucleus of totemism and the starting-point in the formation of religion." He found the "missing element" in W. Robertson Smith's introduction of the "so-called 'totem meal' as an essential part of the totemic religion." Freud's recollection continued: "When I further took into account Darwin's conjecture that men originally lived in hordes, each under the domination of a single powerful, violent and jealous male, there rose before me out of all these components the following hypothesis, or, I would rather say, vision." The horde that Freud envisions in his primal horde theory was not the "very large and unorganized mass of people," usually brought to mind by the word, but a "more or less organized group of limited size—that Atkinson (1903) terms the 'cyclopean family'" (1925 [1924], *SE* 20:67–68).

In making use in *Totem and Taboo* of "Darwin's theories of the earliest state of human society" Freud was aware that "this earliest state of society has never been an object of observation. The most primitive kind of organization that we actually come across—and one that is in force to this day in certain tribes—consists of bands of males; these bands are composed of members with equal rights and are subject to the restrictions of the totemic system, including inheritance through the mother" (1912–13, *SE* 13:141), although, as Freud states, "Atkinson . . . pointed out that the conditions which Darwin assumed to prevail in the primal horde may easily be observed in herds of wild oxen and horses and regularly lead to the killing of the father of the herd" (13:142).

The hypothetical "historic" episode that Freud reconstructed of the killing of the primal father bridges the gap between the most primitive society that can be observed and what Freud referred to as "Darwin's primal horde." We have already noted Freud's use of this primal horde concept in *Totem and Taboo*, in *Moses and Monotheism*, in Freud's "investigations into the 'unconscious sense of guilt,'" and in his "attempts at forming a closer connection between social psychology and the psychology of the individual." In his "Autobiography" Freud added that he also made "use of the idea of an archaic heritage from the 'primal horde' epoch of mankind's development in explaining susceptibility to hypnosis" (*SE* 20:69). He did so in *Group Psychology and the Analysis of the Ego* by describing hypnosis as "a group of two." In the chapter "The Group and the Primal Horde" Freud wrote: "The uncanny and coercive characteristics of group formation, which are shown in the phenomena of suggestion that accompany them, may therefore with justice be traced back to the fact of their origin from the primal horde. The leader of the group is still the dreaded primal father; the group still wishes to be governed by unrestricted force; it has an extreme passion for authority; in Le Bon's phrase, it has a thirst for obedience. The primal father is the group ideal. Hypnosis has a good claim to being described as a group of two. There remains as a definition for suggestion: a conviction which is not based upon perception and reasoning but upon an erotic tie" (*SE* 18:127–28).

In the preface to his translation of Bernheim's *De la suggestion et de ses application à la Thérapeutique* (1888–89) Freud had already expressed his skepticism of Bernheim's view that "all hypnotic phenomena are to be traced to the factor of suggestion, which is not itself capable of further explanation." Utilizing the primal horde theory more than thirty years later, Freud came "to the conclusion that suggestion is a partial manifestation of the state of hypnosis, and that hypnosis is solidly founded upon a predisposition which has survived in the unconscious from the early history of the human family" (18:128n). The hypnotist's measures "awaken in the subject a portion of his archaic heritage which had also made him compliant towards his parents and which had experienced an individual re-animation in his relation to his father." It awakens "the idea of a paramount and dangerous personality, towards whom only a passive-masochistic attitude is possible, to whom one's will has to be surrendered; . . . In some such way as this . . . we can picture the relation of the individual member of the primal horde to the primal father" (18:127).

Freud's use of Darwin's primal horde conjecture belongs to a period shortly before Freud's investigation of Lamarck's evolutionary work in 1915 and his references to the biological blow to man's narcissism from "Darwin and his collaborators and forerunners" in 1917. Reference to Darwin's primal horde began some years earlier in 1912–13 in *Totem and Taboo* with a long quotation from Darwin's *Descent of Man* and a reference to Darwin's *The Variation of Animals and Plants under Domestication*.

7

"The Biological Fact that Inbreeding is Detrimental to the Species"

When Freud presented his primal horde theory for the first time in 1913, he quoted at length from volume 2 of Darwin's *Descent of Man* (1871). He started by acknowledging that his "attempt" was "based upon a hypothesis of Charles Darwin's upon the social state of primitive men. Darwin deduced from the habits of the higher apes that men, too, originally lived in comparatively small groups or hordes within which the jealousy of the oldest and strongest male prevented sexual promiscuity." He then quoted Darwin:

"We may indeed conclude from what we know of the jealousy of all male quadrupeds, armed, as many of them are, with special weapons for battling with their rivals, that promiscuous intercourse in a state of nature is extremely improbable. . . . Therefore, if we look far enough back in the stream of time, . . . judging from the social habits of man as he now exists . . . the most probable view is that primaeval man aboriginally lived in small communities, each with as many wives as he could support and obtain, whom he would have jealously guarded against all other men. Or he may have lived with several wives by himself, like the Gorilla; for all the natives 'agree that but one adult male is seen in a band; when the young male grows up, a contest takes place for mastery, and the strongest, by killing and driving out the others, establishes himself as the head of the community.' (Dr. Savage, in *Boston Journal of Nat. Hist.*, vol. v, 1845–7, p. 423.) The younger males, being thus expelled and wandering about, would, when at last successful in finding a partner, prevent too close inter-breeding within the limits of the same family" (Darwin, 1871, 2, 362 f.). (*SE* 13:125).

This lengthy quotation from Darwin follows Freud's thorough but unsuccessful attempt to find for the origin of man's horror of incest other explanations, some of which involved "the biological fact that inbreeding is detrimental to the species" (p. 123). The question of what is or might be "detrimental to the species" is in itself Darwinian. Starting with a suggestion by Andrew Knight that "with all hermaphrodites two individuals, either occasionally or habitually, concur for the reproduction of their kind" (1950 [1859], p. 82), Darwin devoted much thought and effort to finding in the breeding habits and reproductive systems of plants and animals one of the answers to the question he had raised of what is harmful and what is beneficial to the species. The importance for Darwin of the effect of interbreeding is evidenced by the place he made for it in the quick condensed resumé of his life's work that appeared as the first edition of *On the Origin:* "I have collected so large a body of facts showing, in accordance with the almost universal belief of breeders, that with animals and plants a cross between different varieties, or between individuals of the same variety but of another strain, gives vigour and fertility to the offspring, and on the other hand, that *close* interbreeding diminishes vigour and fertility, that these facts alone incline me to believe that it is a general law of nature (utterly ignorant though we be of the meaning of the law) that no organic being self-fertilizes itself for an eternity of generations; but that a cross with another individual is occasionally—perhaps at very long intervals—indispensable. On the belief that this is a law of nature, we can understand several large classes of facts" (p. 83).

On the Various Contrivances by which Foreign and British Orchids are Fertilized by Insects (1862), Darwin's first book after the *Origin*, has as its full title *and on the Good Effects of Intercrossing*. At the end of 1871 Darwin notified Haeckel that he hoped "to publish next summer the results of my long-continued experiments on the wonderful advantages derived from crossing" (1903, 1:335). *The Expression of Emotions* published in 1872 is obviously not the work referred to. But in 1876 Darwin published a book devoted entirely to *The Effects of Cross and Self-Fertilization in the Vegetable Kingdom*, which I found in Freud's library in the 1876 edition inscribed "6/9/81," three months before Freud's report to the Vienna Academy of Sciences on his histological research in Brücke's Physiological Institute, "On the Structure of the Nerve Fibers and Nerve Cells in the

River Crab" ("Über den Bau den Nervenfasern und Nervenzellen beim Flusskrebs" December 15, 1881).

Asa Gray, in an 1875 *New York Tribune* article on the question "Do varieties wear out, or tend to wear out?" reprinted in his *Darwiniana: Essays and Reviews Pertaining to Darwinism* (1876), recalled that "the result of a prolonged and rather lively discussion of the topic about forty years ago in England . . . was, if we rightly remember, that the nays had the best of the argument" (p. 338). But since then "a presumption has been raised under which the evidence would take a bias the other way. There is now in the minds of scientific men some reason to expect that certain varieties would die out in the long run" (p. 339). Darwin had brought the observations of breeders to the attention of scientists. According to Gray, "After all—apart from speculative analogies—the only evidences we possess which indicate a tendency in species to die out, are those to which Mr. Darwin has called attention. There are, first, the observed deterioration which results, at least in animals, from continued breeding in and in, which may possibly be resolvable into cumulative heritable disease; and, secondly, what may possibly be termed the sedulous and elaborate pains everywhere taken in Nature to prevent close breeding." As a botanist Asa Gray could provide evidence about such "arrangements which are particularly prominent in plants, the greater number of which bear hermaphrodite blossoms. The importance of this may be inferred from the universality, variety, and practical perfection of the arrangements which secure in the end; and the inference may fairly be drawn that this is the physiological import of sexes" (p. 354).

In *The Variation of Animals and Plants under Domestication* (1868) from which Freud also quoted in *Totem and Taboo*, Darwin had a whole chapter "On the Good Effects of Crossing, and on the Evil Effects of Close Interbreeding" (2:92–126). In it Darwin extended the discussion to "the effects of close interbreeding in the case of man" (2:102) and to the "curious problem" of the "origin of his [man's] abhorrence of incestuous marriages" (2:103). Darwin might have had a strong personal interest in this subject; he, like his older sister, had entered into a consanguineous marriage with a Wedgwood first cousin. Darwin's "curious problem" of man's abhorrence of incest is central to the subject of Freud's *Totem and Taboo;* Freud discussed it just before quoting from Darwin's *The Descent of Man.* Although Freud did not enter into a consanguineous marriage like Darwin, the Freud family had proposed one for him with his niece Pauline Freud, daughter of his older half-brother Emmanuel. Pauline was born at about the same time as her uncle Sigmund, who recalled joining her slightly older brother John in treating "the little girl cruelly, and one may assume that this included some erotic component—whether manifest or not" (Jones, 1:11). It was to encourage such a marriage and a possible business career with Pauline's father that Freud visited with his half-brothers in Manchester upon finishing *Gymnasium*.

ABHORRENCE OF INCEST

Although Darwin rejected the idea that man's abhorrence of incest is innate, Freud reported that E. Westermarck in *The Origin and Development of the Moral Ideas* (1906–08) utilized Darwin's thinking about the evils of too close interbreeding to support the argument for "an innate aversion to sexual intercourse between persons living very closely together from early youth" (Westermarck, 2:36 in Freud 1913 [1912–13], *SE* 13:123). Freud, like Darwin, rejected the idea that man's abhorrence of incest is innate. He found it "very remarkable that Westermarck should consider that this innate aversion to sexual intercourse with those with whom one has been intimate in childhood is also the equivalent in psychical terms of the biological fact that inbreeding is detrimental to the species" (pp. 122–23). According to Freud, "A biological instinct of the kind suggested would scarcely have gone so far astray in its psychological expression that, instead of applying to blood-relatives (intercourse with whom might be injurious to reproduction), it affected persons who were totally innocuous in this respect, merely because they shared a common home" (p. 123).

Darwin had dismissed the idea of an innate abhorrence with the simple statement that "it has been clearly shown by Mr. Huth that there is no instinctive feeling in man against incest any more than in gregarious animals" (1868, 2:103–04). Apparently this was not sufficiently convincing for everyone, as evidenced by Westermarck. Freud answered Westermarck with a cogent psychological argument made by J. G. Frazer in *Totemism and Exogamy* (1910): "It is not easy to see why any deep human instinct should need to be reinforced by law." And then Freud added to "these excellent arguments of Frazer's," that "the findings of psychoanalysis make the hypothesis of an innate aversion to incestuous intercourse totally untenable." On the contrary, "the earliest sexual excitations of youthful human beings are invariably of an incestuous character" and "such impulses when repressed play a part that can scarcely be over-estimated as motive forces of neuroses in later life" (13:123–24).

Having like Darwin rejected the possibility that the abhorrence of incest might be innate, Freud viewed the problem as Darwin had in terms of how "these prohibitions arose during early and barbarous times" (Darwin 1868, 2:103). In doing so, Freud, once again like Darwin, rejected the suggestion that these prohibitions arose from observations of the detrimental results of too close inbreeding, either human or animal. For Freud "everything that we know of contemporary savages makes it highly improbable that their most remote ancestors were already concerned with the question of preserving their later progeny from injury." He found it "almost absurd to attribute to such improvident creatures motives of hygiene and eugenics to which consideration is scarcely paid in our own present-day civilization" (13:124). He supported this in a footnote with an observation from Darwin's *Variation:* "Darwin [1875, 2, 127] writes of savages that they 'are not likely to reflect on distant evils to their progeny'" (13:124 n. 2). Darwin in his short discussion of incest also mentioned "some anomalies in the prohibitions not extending equally to the relations on the male and female side" (1868, 2:1). Freud discussed these anomalies at some length in *Totem and Taboo* as offering significant support for his hypothesis of the killing of the father in Darwin's primal horde.

Although the relationship between the human abhorrence of incest and the evils of too close interbreeding called attention to by Darwin was discussed by both Darwin and Freud, it did not prove very fruitful for either of them. Darwin concluded his discussion in the *Variation* by saying: "Although there seems to be no strong inherited feeling in mankind against incest, it seems possible that men during primeval times may have been more excited by strange females than by those with whom they habitually lived; in the same manner as according to Mr. Cupples (*Descent of Man*, 2nd. edit. p. 524), male deerhounds are inclined towards strange females, while the females prefer dogs with whom they have associated. If any such feeling formerly existed in man, this would have led to a preference for marriages beyond the nearest kin, and might have been strengthened by the offspring of such marriages surviving in greater numbers, as analogy would lead us to believe would have occurred." Darwin continued with consideration of consanguinity, with which he had good reason to be concerned, as already noted. "Whether consanguineous marriages, such as are permitted in civilised nations, and which would not be considered as close interbreeding in the case of our domesticated animals, cause any injury will never be known with certainty until a census is taken with this object in view. My son, George Darwin," with equal cause for interest, "has done what is possible at present by a statistical investigation, and he has come to the conclusion, from his own researches and those of Dr. Mitchell, that the evidence as to any evil thus caused is conflicting, but on the whole points to the evil being very small" (2:104).

According to Freud not much more was known on this point forty years later when he wrote in *Totem and Taboo* that "not only must the prohibition against incest be older than any domestication of animals which have enabled men to observe the effects of in-breeding upon racial characters, but even today the detrimental results of in-breeding are not established with certainty and cannot easily be demonstrated in man" (13:124). After a discussion of the literature, from which we have here selected only the parts relevant to our topic, Freud found he must concur with Frazer's statement of 1910 that "'thus the ultimate origin of exogamy, and with it of the law of incest—since exogamy was devised to prevent incest—remains a problem nearly as dark as ever' (Frazer, 1910, I, 165)" (13:125n). Freud pessimistically concluded his discussion of what is already known about the origin of the incest taboo: "It might have been expected that here again we should have before us a choice between sociological, biological and psychological explanations. (In this connection the psychological motives should perhaps be regarded as representing biological forces.) Nevertheless, at the end of our inquiry, we can only subscribe to Frazer's resigned conclusion. We are ignorant of the origin of the horror of incest and cannot even tell in what direction to look for it. None of the solutions of the enigma that have been proposed seems satisfactory" (13:124–25). Freud follows this pessimistic conclusion with a dramatic pause.

DARWIN AND THE HISTORICAL APPROACH

After the pause Freud started anew with an approach that is even more basically Darwinian—the historical approach: "I must, however, mention one other attempt at solving it. It is of a kind quite different from any that we have so far considered, and might be described as 'historical.' This attempt is based upon a hypothesis of Charles Darwin's" (13:125). It is noteworthy that Freud places the word "historical" in quotations and associates its application with Darwin. Darwin, following Lyell's example in *The Principles of Geology* (1830), had succeeded in extending the scientific validity of the "historical" approach from geology to biology—from the inorganic to the organic world. For Freud one of the most continuously useful concepts from biology was the historical approach proclaimed by Darwin in the *Origin:* "When we no longer look at an organic being as a savage looks at a ship, as at something wholly beyond his comprehension; when we regard *every production of nature as one which has had a history;* when we contemplate every complex structure and instinct as the summing up of many contrivances, each useful to the possessor, nearly in the same way as when we look at any great mechanical invention as the summing up of the labour, the experience, the reason, and even the blunders of numerous workmen; when we thus view each organic being, how far more interesting—I speak from experience—will the study of natural history become!" (p. 411; italics added).

Freud's very first scientific efforts were in natural history under Carl Claus. Perhaps he was inspired to the study of natural history by Darwin's words as well as by Haeckel's popularizations of Darwin. He seized the opportunity at the University of Vienna Medical School, which we will examine in the next section, to work under the aegis of a scientist thoroughly dedicated to teaching Darwin's approach to biology, an approach that Darwin, himself, predicted would be of even greater value for psychology: "In the distant future I see open fields for far more important researches. Psychology will be based on a new foundation, that of the necessary acquirement of each mental power and capacity by gradation" (p. 413).

Part Two
Darwinian Teaching and Science during Freud's Medical School Training: (1873–1882)

What is known as medical education appears to me to be an arduous and circuitous way of approaching the profession of analysis. No doubt it offers an analyst much that is indispensable to him. But it burdens him with too much else of which he can never make use, and there is a danger of its diverting his interest and his whole mode of thought from the understanding of psychical phenomena. A scheme of training for analysts has still to be created. It must include elements from the mental sciences, from psychology, as well as from anatomy, *biology and the study of evolution.*

Sigmund Freud,
"Postscript to the Question of Lay Analysis"
[italics added]

111

8

"In Many of Us the Path to the Sciences Led Only Through Our Teachers"

$$\mathbf{D}$$arwinism was at its zenith when Freud entered the medical faculty at the University of Vienna. Symbolically, its last great opponent, Louis Agassiz, died that very year, 1873. In Europe, controversy over the main thrust of Darwin's theory, evolution versus creation, had ended a few years earlier.[1] The cautious Darwin, who followed with great interest the reception of his theory on the Continent, had published in 1871 the statement made by one of his early popularizers, Karl Vogt, in his address as president of the National Institution of Geneva (1869), that "personne, en Europe au moins, n'ose plus soutenir la création indépendante et de toutes pièces, des espèces" ("nobody, at least in Europe, any longer dares to uphold the independent and sudden creation of species" [1:i]).

More significantly for this study, the very year in which Freud enrolled at the University of Vienna Carl Claus was brought from Göttingen to modernize the zoology department, which at that time meant bringing it into line with the new paradigm being established in biology by Darwin's work. Consequently, although Freud himself never met Darwin during the almost twenty-six years that their lives overlapped (May 1856–April 1882), he did have the opportunity at the University of Vienna of studying and working with a man who had shortly before been received by Darwin

Chapter title is from Sigmund Freud, "Some Reflections on Schoolboy Psychology."

at his home in Down. In 1871 while in London for marriage to his English second wife, Rose Warder, Claus had availed himself of the opportunity through the kind offices of Darwin's colleague and neighbor Sir John Lubbock and his wife, not only to be their house guest at High Elms but also to visit Down "wo der berühmte Begründer der Selectionslehre Ch. Darwin auf seinem Landgute wohnte" ("where the famous founder of the selection theory, Ch. Darwin, lived on his estate"). Claus found unforgettable "how Lubbock's charming wife arranged for [me] to visit at the home of Darwin, for whom it was already difficult" at sixty-two "because of bodily pain to be affable with foreign scholars, but who nevertheless met with special attention and kindliness those younger German scientists who had tested his doctrine without prejudice and had enthusiastically embraced it" (1899, p. 18). Freud quickly took advantage of the opportunity presented by Claus's arrival at Vienna to try to satisfy the great expectations aroused by Darwin's theories. Freud recalled from this period of his life "my first contacts with the sciences, among which it seemed open to me to choose to which of them I should dedicate what were no doubt my inestimable services" (1914, *SE* 13:241).

His first semester, the winter term of 1873–74, Freud dutifully enrolled in the classes expected of a regular medical student, anatomy and chemistry. But "asked what" his "greatest wish might be" he "would have answered: a laboratory and free time"—a wish Claus would twice grant him while he was still a medical student—"or a ship on the ocean with all the instruments the researcher needs" ("Letter to Eduard Silberstein Sept. 1875" in Gay 1988, p. 26), to be another Darwin on the *Beagle*, perhaps. Darwin's *A Naturalist's Journal of Researches into the Natural History and Geology of Countries Visited during a Voyage Around the World*, known today simply as *The Voyage of the Beagle*, had appeared in Victor Carus's excellent German translation the year that Freud recalled these early wishes in his letter of September 1875 to his friend Edward Silberstein. But with his love of English authors, he had no doubt read it avidly in the original while still in *Gymnasium*. We know that while still in *Gymnasium* he chose to attend a public lecture by Carl Brühl, which was on comparative anatomy, a subject of public interest because of Darwin's theory. Freud was still interested enough in Darwin's *Voyage of the Beagle* after he became a physician to obtain and inscribe "Dr. Sigm Freud 2/XI 81" in *Reise eines Naturforschers um die Welt*, volume 1 of *Darwins Gesammelte Werke* (*Collected Works of Charles Darwin*) translated by Victor Carus. The second semester (summer term 1874), still inspired by

Darwin's *Voyage of the Beagle,* Freud added as electives Claus's course on "Biology and Darwinism" as well as Brücke's lectures "On the Physiology of Voice and Language" to the regular twenty-eight-hour-a-week medical program in anatomy, chemistry, microscopy, biology, and mineralogy.

The third semester (winter term 1874–75) he added Brentano's reading seminar in philosophy to the twenty-eight-hour-a-week medical program of anatomical dissection, zoology, physics, and physiology. At this period physiologists were separating only certain aspects of psychology from philosophy for scientific investigation; for the most part psychology, which was Freud's primary interest, was still considered part of the study of philosophy. Franz Brentano, famous for his act-psychology, is known also for his efforts to establish psychology as a separate science. Nevertheless, Brentano, unlike Claus, Brücke, and Meynert, seems to have played no significant role in the transmission of Darwin's influence to Freud. We know that at least one of Brentano's pupils and followers, Baron Christian von Ehrenfels, a contemporary of Freud at the University of Vienna who introduced the term *Gestalt* into psychology, became thoroughly convinced of the adequacy of the Darwinian explanation of moral values, but as for himself, "Brentano, according to Kraus," in his 1876 *Was für ein Philosoph manchmal Epoche macht*, "never accepted the evolutionary explanation, although he never definitely opposed it in his published work" (Eaton 1930, p. 327). According to Freud's most recent biographer, Peter Gay, Brentano, an ex-priest, "believed in God and respected Darwin at the same time" (1988, p. 29). Although Brentano may have recommended and upheld the genetic approach, he himself never succeeded in being more than descriptive.

By the fourth semester (summer term of 1875) Freud deserted the medical program to pursue his own preferences. He switched from "zoology for medical students" to fifteen hours of zoology proper with Claus. In Brücke's courses he found no need for change. Brücke's Institute of Physiology was the center of basic research in biology, including biochemistry and biophysics. Although Brücke's classes and laboratory courses were considered part of the medical curriculum, little attention was given to any medical application of the research done there. In addition Freud took two physics courses, one more than the medical curriculum required, and a course with Brentano on Aristotle as well as continuing with Brentano's reading seminar.

After two years at the medical school he confided to his friend Eduard Silberstein in the letter of September 1875, "I now have more than one ideal. To the theoretical one of my earlier years a practical one has now been added." He was after all nineteen. "Now I vacillate about whether I should not rather say: a large hospital and plenty of money, to curtail some of the evils which befall our bodies, or to remove them from the world" (p. 26). But even as he was writing this, his actions in the fifth semester or third year (1875–76) completed his shift from medicine to biology. He spent most of his time on advanced work in Claus's Institute of Zoology and Comparative Anatomy. He took a course in plant physiology, worked in Brücke's physiology laboratory, enrolled in the seminars and classes on nerve physiology and spectral analysis given by Brücke's assistants Exner and Fleischl, and continued with philosophy.

During the summer he resumed anatomic dissections. March and September he worked on his first research assignment in the Marine Zoological Station established by Claus at Trieste in 1875. Claus aided and honored Freud with one of the earliest grants. He renewed the grant and himself presented Freud's maiden scientific effort at the March 15, 1877, meeting of the Vienna Royal Academy of Science. The academy published in its April *Bulletin* Freud's "Beobachtungen über Gestaltung und feineren Bau der als Hoden beschriebenen Lappenorgane des Aals" ("Observations on the formation and more delicate structure of the lobe-shaped organs of the eel, described as testicles").

Nevertheless, Freud considered himself lacking in talent as a zoologist: "I was compelled, moreover, during my first years at the University, to make the discovery that the peculiarities and limitations of my gifts denied me all success in many of the departments of science into which my youthful eagerness had plunged me." A mystery persists around Freud's denial of his recognized successes under Claus. Apparently Claus did not provide the model Freud sought. "At length, in Ernst Brücke's physiological laboratory, I found rest and full satisfaction—and men, too, whom I could respect and take as my models: the great Brücke himself, and his assistants, Sigmund Exner and Ernst Fleischl von Marxow" (1925, *SE* 20:8).

The seventh semester, or beginning of the fourth year (autumn 1876), Freud became a *famulus* (research student) in Brücke's Institute of Physiology, where he remained until 1882; from May 1881 as demonstrator, he did ontogenetic and phylogenetic studies on the histology of the nervous system. Although Freud's work in Brücke's laboratory "Über den Ursprung der hinteren Nervenwurzeln im Rückenmarke von Ammocoetes (Petromyzon Planeri)" (On the origin of the posterior nerve roots in the spinal cord of the ammocoetes) was subsequent to his research with Claus,

Brücke was the first to present to the Vienna Academy of Science a paper by Freud (January 4, 1877). It was published in the January 1877 *Bulletin*. Both papers appeared before Freud was twenty-one. Darwin could have received these *Bulletins* as an honorary foreign member of the academy.

Freud recalled in his *Autobiographical Study* that "the various branches of medicine proper, apart from psychiatry, had no attraction for me" (20:10). The psychiatry lectures given by Meynert took note of Darwin's *The Expression of the Emotions in Man and Animals*, a work referred to twice by Freud in his earliest psychological writings, *The Studies on Hysteria* (1893–95). The appendix to Meynert's *Psychiatrie* is deeply indebted to Darwin's *Expression of the Emotions*. The introduction and appendix contain Meynart's criticism of Darwin's definition of "instinct as inherited learning." According to Amacher, in "The Ideological Wellsprings of Psychoanalysis" (Ritvo 1970), inasmuch as Brücke and his assistant Exner subscribed to Meynart's neurophysiological views, they too would have rejected Darwin's definition of instinct as inherited learning without having any question about the action of inheritance through use and disuse in other instances. Freud continued his recollection of this period: "I was decidedly negligent in pursuing my medical studies, and it was not until 1881 that I took my somewhat belated degree as Doctor of Medicine" (1925, 20:10).

Until 1882, when the desire to marry finally forced Freud to reappraise his financial situation more realistically and renounce a career in science on which he was well launched, Freud's expectations lay not in the practice of medicine but in the sciences, which at that time still had their home in the medical school. On leaving the medical school Freud was able to continue his scientific endeavors for three more years (autumn 1882 to autumn 1885) in Meynert's laboratory for cerebral anatomy.

9

Carl Claus and
the New Darwinian
Biology

We must consider Darwin's work on the origin
of species as the very foundation of a new epoch
of the biological sciences.
Carl Claus, "Lamarck als Begründer der
Descendenzlehre"

BIOGRAPHICAL INFORMATION

Because Carl Claus has been neglected in studies of other aspects of
psychoanalytic history but is of special prominence in the study of Darwin's influence on Freud and because biographical material about Claus is
not generally available, particularly to the English reader, it is included
here in some detail. Freud was strangely silent about Carl Claus, thus
misleading historians of psychoanalysis into overlooking him. Carl Claus
was born at Kassel, Germany, January 2, 1835, to Heinrich Claus, assay-
master like his father before him, and to his wife Charlotte, daughter of
the legation councillor Johann Conrad Richter. Claus was stimulated by
his natural science teachers at the Kassel Gymnasium to collect as a hobby
all sorts of natural objects. He started with a herbarium because of the
number and varieties of forms that flowers offered, followed by a large and
valuable collection of minerals. Finally he was attracted to the biology of
insects, especially the Lepidoptera and their metamorphoses. Insects

offer an abundance of transitional variations. A passionate interest in insects, especially beetles, played an important role for both Darwin and Wallace in their independent discoveries of the origin of species by natural selection.

Although intended by his mother to continue her family's tradition in jurisprudence, Claus pursued his youthful interest by matriculating in medicine and natural science at the Landes-Universität at Marburg on Easter 1854. Two years later he transferred to Giessen at the suggestion of Professor Leuckart, who, as mentioned above, became one of the earliest scientists to respond favorably to Darwin's theory. The plethora of botanical and inverteberate specimens with closely related variations revealed the inadequacies in traditional systems of classification. Their observations prepared botanists such as Hooker and Asa Gray and invertebrate zoologists such as Huxley, Haeckel, Fritz Müller, and Claus to be more quickly receptive to, and enthusiastic about, Darwin's theory than the vertebrate zoologists, physiologists, or scientists outside the biological field whose data did not require a new theory.

In his *Autobiographie* (1899) Claus recalled Leuckart's influence with enthusiasm: "I must recall as the greatest good luck and of the highest significance for my further course of instruction that I became acquainted with Professor R. Leuckart, who at the time [1856] held a chair at Giessen and was at the onset of the heyday of his creative and working power, and that I was stimulated by him in the most friendly fashion to pursue the study of zoology under his direction" (pp. 9–10). Claus studied zoology, comparative anatomy, and *Entwicklungsgeschichte* (the term then for development, probably metamorphosis and embryology) at Giessen with Leuckart, who is credited among other things with finding out the "evolutional process [life cycle] in two well-known human parasites, *Taenia solium* and *T. saginata*, and in the liver-fluke which is fatal to domestic animals. *Trichinae* first became known through Leuckart" (Nordenskiöld, p. 422), who produced an important textbook on human parasites. Leuckart attempted to explain "indirect metamorphoses, in which both processes of reduction and new development take place, as the result of the necessity which the simply organized larva, hatched at an early stage of development, laboured under of acquiring special arrangements for its protection and nourishment." Leuckart's explanation appeared to Claus "an important factor for the full understanding of these remarkable processes, but still is by no means an explanation of them. It is only by the aid of the Darwinian principles and the theory of descent that we can get nearer to an explanation. According to this theory, the form and structure of larvae are to be considered in relation to the development of the race, *i.e.* phylogeny, and are to be derived from the various phases of structure through which the larval stages would correspond to the primitive, and the older, on the other hand, to the more advanced and more highly organized animals, which have appeared later in the history of the race" (1884, 1:122).

While studying with Leuckart, Claus began his observations of the Entomostraca, particularly the *Cyclops*. The value of Claus's work on the Copepoda as support for Darwin's theory was publicized by Fritz Müller in his *Für Darwin* in 1864. That same year Claus, as a poor struggling professor of zoology at Marburg with a growing family to support, resolved "to write a textbook which, in accordance with the modern state of zoology, would do justice to the genetic point of view rather than treating the latter in the usual and antiquated way and which in the event of my carrying it through successfully could bring a welcome addition to my income which at that time was rather scanty" (1899, p. 16).

By 1866 he was able to publish the first part of his textbook, *Grundzüge der Zoologie* (known after the fourth edition as *Lehrbuch der Zoologie*), reflecting the profound changes in biology created by Darwin. He had already called attention to some of the theoretical implications, such as for the distinction between the plant and animal kingdoms. In an 1863 work *On the Borderland of Animal and Vegetable Life* (*Über die Grenze des thierischen und pflänzlichen Lebens*) he pointed out that these two kingdoms must flow unbroken into each other but that the old division was nevertheless still useful. He incorporated such theoretical subjects into the General Part of the textbook. He also incorporated the contributions of Fritz Müller's *Für Darwin*, which he discussed that year in a lecture on the characteristics of the species and variations of "The Copepoda-Fauna of Nice: . . . 'in the Darwinian Sense'" (Die Copepodenfauna von Nizza: Ein Beitrag zur Characteristik der Arten und deren Abänderungen "im sinne Darwins").

Ten years later, when Freud was in the midst of work with him, Claus continued to discuss Müller's *Für Darwin* at length in new editions of his textbook and in his *Studies for the Investigation of the Genealogical Foundations of the Crustacean System: A Contribution to the Theory of Evolution* (*Untersuchungen zur Erforschung der Genealogischen Gründlage des Crustaceen-Systems: Ein Beitrag zur Descendenzlehre* [1876]). He concluded the General Part of the textbook with a discussion of the "Meaning of the System," which consists primarily of the "Theory of Descent Based on Natural Selection (Darwinism)" and "Evidence in Favour of the Theory of Descent."

The second part of the textbook appeared in 1868. Claus was proved correct in his assessment of the financial potential of a textbook that presented zoology from the then modern genetic or Darwinian viewpoint. There were ten editions, as *Grundzüge* or *Lehrbuch*, during Claus's lifetime and translations into many other languages. It continued to be re-edited and published after his death in 1899 and was eventually used in England to meet the need expressed earlier by Darwin in a letter of November 5 [1864] appealing to Huxley to write such a work: "I have been asked more than a dozen times to recommend something for a beginner and could only think of Carpenter's Zoology" (1887, 3:3).

Carpenter's *Zoology*, the best available to Darwin in 1864 when Claus also recognized the need and set out to capitalize on it, assumed without discussion the permanent creation of species and began with man in the traditional fashion referred to by Lamarck as "the usual direction from the most perfect to the most imperfect animals" (1914 [1809], p. viii). Darwin was "sure that a striking Treatise would do real service to science by educating naturalists" (1887, 3:3). In 1884 Adam Sedgwick of Trinity College, Cambridge, "undertook the translation of Professor Claus' excellent 'Lehrbuch der Zoologie' with a view of supplying the want, which has long been felt by teachers as well as students in this country, of a good elementary text-book of Zoology. Professor Claus' works on zoology are already well known in this country; and I think it will be generally admitted that they take the first place amongst the zoological text-books of the present day" (Sedgwick "Preface" to Claus 1884, 1:3).[1]

On his death the *Proceedings of the Linnean Society of London* (October 1899) memorialized Claus "as a pioneer-investigator of the Crustacea and a foremost student of the Coelenterata" and "as the writer of a text-book which, unlike most German works of its kind, was something more than a mere compilation and had a freshness and originality peculiarly its own." It noted that "his 'Grundzüge der Zoologie,' perhaps the most generally known of all German text-books on that subject, appeared in 1868 and rapidly passed through four editions, with subdivision into two volumes. Prompted by its success he meanwhile produced (1880) a 'Kleines Lehrbuch,'" a short textbook, "thus leading up to the successive editions of his famous 'Lehrbuch' (1883–1897)," which at the time of his death had become "a work close upon 1000 pages, perhaps more universally in vogue than any zoological text-book extant." In Sedgwick's translation it crossed the Atlantic; copies were bought by university libraries including Yale, Princeton, and Chicago. Claus "is said to have considered the development of these books his favorite occupation" and, asserts the Linnean Society memorial, it "cannot be denied that they have been among the most useful aids in the popularization of Zoology during the last 30 years."

Of the many editions of Claus's textbook, I have been fortunate in obtaining the two that span the period when Freud was studying and doing research with Claus. The second edition (1873 [1872]) would have been in use by Claus's pupils when Freud began his studies in 1873. Claus's thinking and concerns during Freud's period of training are revealed in additions Claus was preparing for his third edition (1876).[1] Among them were current objections to Darwin's theory. Another concern of Claus's when Freud was with him was the recent attack by Haeckel treating Claus as an anti-Darwinist because of the conservative nature of Claus's support for Darwin. Claus's first publication at Vienna, "Cuvier's Typology and Haeckel's so-called Gastraea Theory" (Cuviers Typenlehre und E. Häckel's sogenannte Gastraea-Theorie [1875]), was in response. Freud probably heard the argument that year as part of Claus's lectures on "Biology and Darwinism." The animosity subsided after Darwin's death or at least by Claus's two 1888 lectures to the *Wissenschaftlichen* (Science) Club in Vienna, "Lamarck als Begründer der Descendenzlehr" (Lamarck as Founder of the Descent Theory) and "Über die Wertschätzung der natürlichen Zuchtwahl als Erklärungsprincip" (On the Value of Natural Selection as an Explanatory Principle).

In addition to the new editions of his textbook, Claus averaged more than four publications a year from 1857 to 1895.[2] In its *Proceedings* of October 1899 the Linnean Society of London, to which Darwin and Wallace had made the first startling announcement in 1858, acknowledged Claus's many other contributions: "Of the numerous new genera and species he described, of his revolutionary classifications, his elaborate studies of the morphology of all parts of the Crustacean skeleton, of his fascinating work upon anatomy and histology of the heart and internal organs of certain microscopic forms, and of the importance of that upon the larval nervous system, it is but necessary to remind the trained zoologist, to whom everything he wrote came as a relief, a bright inspiration, which rendered clearer some involved corner in the mighty maze of Crustacean life." The memorial testifies that "in his addresses, books, and published essays" Claus "declared himself a firm upholder of the Darwinian doctrine of Descent, while he held special views of his own upon the part played by the organism in 'Selection'" (pp. 48–50).

Claus had an opportunity to evaluate Darwin's contributions in a two-page memorial to Darwin in the *Vienna Medical Journal* (April 1882). The credibility of his encomiums to Darwin's theory is enhanced by his scrupulous inclusion of what he saw as its limitations. "It was surely Darwin's selection theory which snapped the fetters of a false fundamental doctrine which until then dominated biology. . . . The dogma of the immutability of species, of repeated total life-destroying catastrophes, of fixed creations in successive spurts which for many long decades held the biological sciences in rigid bonds . . . appeared through Darwin's teaching . . . to have been fundamentally destroyed and disposed of for all time. . . . An even greater advance was gained" from Darwin's work "for the understanding of the unity (*Einheit*) of the inorganic and the organic in the material world; with the help of the selection theory it became possible to explain by a mechanical cause the harmony of the biological order which had previously been thought to be teleological and to attribute to necessity what earlier had been considered to have been arranged purposefully by a wise Providence." Even if it did not itself attain the mechanical laws of matter and energy for the understanding of the organization and functioning of organisms, Darwin's "selection theory brought it a vital step closer." It provided a "ray of hope" for the mechanical explanations of life. As a consequence of Darwin's work "a large series of phenomena which previously could be interpreted or understood only teleologically appeared attributable to causes and causal relationships operating according to necessity and brought closer to a mechanical physical explanation."

Claus declared that "twenty-three years ago in his epochmaking work on the *Origin of Species*" Darwin had performed "a great scientific feat when . . . with the quiet certainty and dignity of a methodical, exemplary treatment as well as the utilization of an astoundingly comprehensive mechanism of sharply significant observations and convincing facts," he "elevated the descent theory expressed long before by men like Lamarck and Geoffrey St. Hilaire" and "through genealogical reconstruction raised the until now misunderstood system of organisms to a natural system, from natural description to natural history" (1882, p. 513). Freud performed a strikingly similar feat when he transformed psychiatry from classification and description of mental illnesses into reconstruction of the developmental history of such illnesses. The need in psychiatry was recognized in the period after Darwin's *Expressions of the Emotions* by Meynert, whose 1884 *Psychiatrie* calls for "the establishment of a *natural* system of classification" to replace the old "artificial types of mental diseases" (p. vii). In 1888, following the impact of Weismann's publication of the germ-plasm theory, Claus addressed the Vienna Science Club on the question of "Lamarck as Founder of the Descent Theory" (Lamarck als Begründer der Descendezlehre). He did so entirely in terms of Darwin's theory. He followed it the same year with two consecutive lectures "On the Evaluation of Natural Selection as an Explanatory Principle" (Über die Wertschätzung der natürlichen Zuchtwahl als Erklärungsprincip).

Claus may have mellowed in later years and earned the words of his English memorialist: "During the 23 years he held office his Laboratory was the scene of a ceaseless activity, a centre of attraction to zoologists of all nations. . . . He retired into private life in 1896, distinguished as an investigator, and *by the student beloved*" (p. 48; italics added) but not by Freud. Freud was attracted to Claus's laboratory but seemed to have experienced some unrevealed disappointment. There is a curious absence of Claus's name in Freud's recollections even where the references are to the period of Freud's work with him. Only once, in listing his researches on an application for the title of professor, did Freud mention "the name of the teacher who suggested the work, and one cannot help detecting a lot of resentment against him." Freud "gave such a disparaging version of this piece of work as almost to insinuate that it had been a futile and pointless one. . . . In the circumstances no one could well have done better, but Freud was much more dissatisfied with his inconclusive results than was his chief. An ambitious youth must have hoped for a task where some brilliant and original discovery would be made" (Jones 1953, 1:38).

Claus's writings reveal him as a sharply critical man, a trait that may have contributed to Freud's sense of inadequacy in relation to zoology despite the recognition he achieved before the age of twenty-one. Claus's life was beset with personal difficulties, particularly the early loss of three wives. The consequent concern for his own children left him little interest in the personal problems of his students in contrast to the older Brücke, whose fatherly interest and advice meant much to Freud. Brücke had suffered the loss of a son who was a promising medical student and took a fatherly attitude toward his students.

CONTROVERSY WITH HAECKEL AND
THE QUESTION OF GRADATION

In an era when supporters and opponents were misinterpreting aspects of Darwin's theory, when even Huxley disagreed with Darwin about gradation and Haeckel exaggerated claims for Darwin's theory, Claus's transmission of Darwin's views are impressively accurate and clear-headed. Like Darwin, Claus recognized the great amount of work required to overcome the current limitations and difficulties in the theory and its applications. Like Darwin he was willing to labor first at the slow accretion of the necessary observations before publishing any claims.

Although Claus's scientific skepticism led him to positions consistent with Darwin's modest, cautious ones, Haeckel was not satisfied. Controversy between Claus and Haeckel erupted as Freud came under Claus's tutelage. The public exchange between these two supporters of Darwin dramatized for Freud the choice of styles by which a great scientific revolution like Darwin's might be pursued. Attracted to science by Haeckel's extravagant style, Freud later learned that solid advances could be realized by Claus's cautious one. The difference in their manner of support for Darwin probably contributed to Freud's recollection: "When, in 1873, I first joined the University, I experienced some appreciable disappointments." After the exuberant promises of Haeckel's popularizations of Darwin, Freud was inducted by the rigorously disciplined Claus, not only into scientific skepticism but also into the slow, tedious reality of research. Freud had not yet "grasped the importance of observation as one of the best means of gratifying" his curiosity. One wonders how much gratification he could have derived from dissecting four hundred eels for the "lobe-shaped organ, described as the testicle," especially as he "was moved by a sort of curiosity which was, however, directed more towards human concerns than towards natural objects" (1925 [1924], *SE* 20:9).

Claus and Haeckel disregarded their differences as long as they were joined in combating the creationists. In his early work on the Copepoda Claus had with his characteristic caution "refrained from drawing conclusions on the basis of the relatively sparse and somewhat scattered observations," whereas "in the meantime Ernst Haeckel in his 'Contribution to the Knowledge of the *Corycaeiden*' had come out even more definitely in the same sense, convincing himself on the basis of comparative measurements of the variability of species" (1866, pp. 2–3). In "Copepoda of Nice: A Contribution to the Character of Species and Their Varieties 'in the Darwinian Sense'" (*Die Copepodenfauna von Nizza: Ein Beitrag zur Charac-teristik der Arten und deren Abänderungen "im sinne Darwins"* [1866]) Claus brought together in detail the evidence from his plentiful observations of the Copepoda of Nice, Messina, and Helgoland in support of a system of classification based on Darwin's theory of evolution by gradual variation, with natural selection accounting for the missing links. In 1866 he cited Haeckel at length in support of the variability of species.

When the battle over the mutability of species subsided, Claus referred to Haeckel as "the most exaggerated hyper-Darwinist." In the October 1870 preface to the second edition of his *Text-Book* Claus anticipated Haeckel's criticism, confident that his own "more thoroughgoing treatment of the General Part, especially that of the doctrine of transmutation and of selection (Darwin) will, hopefully, be all the more welcome to the younger public because I tried to give as objective a presentation as possible. I do not think anybody but the most exaggerated hyper-Darwinist will blame me for having treated the Special Part not according to family trees and family tables but in the until now customary fashion according to wider and narrower circles" (1872 [1866–68], 1: vi).

The year Freud elected Claus's lectures on "Biology and Darwinism" Haeckel openly attacked Claus. In proposing the "Gastraea Theory" (Die Gastrea-theorie, die phylogenetische classification des Thierreichs und der Keimblatter, [1874]) Haeckel quoted extensively from the second edition of Claus's *Text-Book*, particularly in reference to Cuvier's typology, as an example of "the most striking refutation of Darwin's heresy and the strongest proof against the truth of the doctrine of evolution" (Haeckel 1874, p. 47, quoted in Claus 1875, p. 6). One of Haeckel's admirers pointed out that in his relations with Rudolf Virchow and Du Bois-Reymond, whose skeptical temper dominated Berlin, Haeckel, "the ardent evolutionist and opponent of Catholicism, was impatient of a reserve that he felt to be an anachronism in science and an effective support of reactionary ideas" (McCabe, "Introduction" to Haeckel 1906, p. 9).

Undoubtedly, Claus was hurt at being classed by "the philosopher of Jena" with the anti-Darwinians, for he regarded himself as a strong supporter of Darwin. And so did Darwin. "Anyone who knows the *Text-Book of Zoology* and my other works realizes that I consider Darwin's doctrine as essentially correct and that, insofar as an objective, unprejudiced treatment permits, I strongly support it. But, and this I value particularly, he will also bear witness that I refrain from any premature, precipitate eagerness, that I have not permitted myself to rush into wild speculations which we consider to be nothing more than a new edition of Natural Philosophy, and which we reject all the more definitely as alien to the essence of true science, the greater the sense of infallibility with which they are pronounced" (1875, p. 6). In Claus's opinion there was not yet enough material on which to establish genealogical tables as Haeckel would have him do and as Haeckel himself was doing. "While we admire the bold speculations of E. Haeckel's genealogical attempts, it must be admitted that at present there is room for innumerable possibilities in detail, and that subjective judgment holds a more conspicuous place than objective certainty of fact" (1884, 1:150). When Freud was with him, Claus was contributing "objective certainty of fact" to the theory of evolution by careful *Studies for the Investigation of the Genealogical Basis of the Crustacean-System, (Untersüchungen zur Erforschung der Genealogischen Grundlage des Crustaceen-Systems: Ein Beitrag zur Descendenzlehre* [1876]), which he "dedicated to Darwin with heartfelt admiration."

Although Claus believed that "almost invariably, if conducted in an objective, unprejudiced spirit, systematic works which surveyed a larger number of series of forms led not only to the elimination of the concept of a sharp demarcation line between the narrower and wider categories of the system, but also resulted in making the concept of species less rigid in the Darwinian sense" (1875, p. 3). Haeckel in his 1874 article on the gastraea theory included Claus and his *Text-Book* in the charge that modern zoologists had more and more accepted the view "of the entirely independent character and the inherent 'structural plan'" of the animal types. In his first publication at Vienna Claus tried to answer Haeckel's charge that "the modern zoologists, indeed, attempted to define the independent and entirely unique character of the four new types (protozoa, coelenterata, echinoderms, worms) and to distinguish each one of them as an isolated structural unit with a particular structural plan just like the three retained older types (arthropods, molluscs, vertebrates) of Baer and Cuvier." In support of this charge Haeckel had used as his example "Claus who, for instance, in the newest edition of his Zoology (1872, p. 41) designates the theory of types as 'the most significant progress of science since Aristotle and as the foundation of the natural system'" (1874, quoted in Claus 1875, p. 6). Freud could have known from studying Claus's *Text-Book*, although Claus does not take the trouble to point it out, that Haeckel had quoted Claus out of context. It was in the course of providing a "Historical Review" that Claus had evaluated Cuvier's accomplishments.

Even before evolutionary studies had made much headway, Claus had in

1863 expressed the need to modify the concept of types established by Cuvier in 1812.[3] By the time Freud became his pupil, Claus was teaching that in regard to plants and animals "the question has to be discussed, whether there are any absolute distinctive characters which sharply separate the one kingdom from the other. . . . With the progress of experience, the conviction is forced upon us that the traditional conception of animals and plants needs, so far as science is concerned, to be modified" (1884, 1:15). Freud later became convinced "with the progress of experience" of a similar need to make modifications in the traditional conception of neuroses.

When Freud was studying with him, Claus "relied for support for the modified view of Cuvier's concept of types on the conformity between the developmental forms of various types and pointed, especially, to the larvae of Amphioxus, Ascidia and Coelenterata as significant for the genetic connection between various types" (1875, p. 5). Claus himself pointed out that "even between animal groups of distinct types, transition-forms were discovered" (p. 3). Breuer and Freud in the theoretical portion of the *Studies on Hysteria* wrote that "between the extremes of these two forms [*dispositional* hysteria and *psychically acquired* hysteria] we must assume the existence of a series of cases within which the liability to dissociation in the subject and the affective magnitude of the trauma vary inversely" (1893, *SE* 2:13). They do not explain why the assumption of a series must be made for hysteria. (For evaluation of the role of Darwin and others in Freud's assumption of gradualism see the section "Conclusion on the Gradual Change of Species" in chapter 2).

Like Darwin, Claus was thoroughly convinced of development by gradation starting from the inorganic. Not only organisms and species develop gradually but also organs. For instance, the vegetative organs, that is, the organs of nourishment, "gradually and in the most intimate connection with the progressive development of the animal function attain a higher and more complicated structure" (1884, 1:52). Like Darwin, whose biology he was teaching, and Freud, who was his pupil, Claus assumed that even psychical life and instincts have developed by gradation, although as Claus acknowledged, "In what manner the irritability of the lower protaplasmic organisms leads by gradual transitions and intermediate steps to the first affection of sensation and consciousness is as completely hidden from us as are the nature and essence of the psychical processes which we know are dependent on the movement of matter" (1:93).

For Claus the knowledge of gradation and the existence of transitional types do not destroy the usefulness of the idea of groups and types. "Just as the transitional forms between animals and plants cannot abolish the distinction between these two most important conceptions of the organic kingdom, so the existence of such transitional forms do not in any way affect the value of the idea of groups and types as the chief divisions of the animal system, but only renders it probable that the different groups have developed from a similar or common starting-point" (1:138). Unlike many of those who apply Freud's findings without careful study, Freud was aware that his now famous psychosexual stages in human development did not in reality exist as distinct stages but were, as Claus had said of Cuvier's types, convenient divisions for the study of what was actually a continuum from a common starting point. In one of the *Introductory Lectures* Freud reminded his audience that "we are picturing every such [sexual] trend as a current which has been continuous since the beginning of life but which we have divided up, to some extent artificially, into separate successive advances" (1917 [1916–17], *SE* 16:340).

Freud's propensity for thinking in terms of gradations and a continuum and his awareness that sharp classifications, as Claus had pointed out about Cuvier's types, may have no reality but can nevertheless be useful concepts are evidenced also in his structural models (fig. 1a and b). Freud himself never drew a sharp line of demarcation between the id and the ego or between the ego and the superego. He derived one from the other. He regarded the ego as developing from the id under the "exigencies of life" and the superego developing out of the ego. For Freud there was always a continuum stretching back through the individual's development and the development of the human race to the development of life itself from the inorganic. He was very ingenious in working out the ways in which one type of behavior might be derived from another, one mental process from a more primitive, one structure from an earlier. He derived the secondary process from the primary process, the higher mental functionings from the reflex arc, the pleasure principle from the constancy principle, as well as the ego from the id, the superego from the ego. In *Instincts and Their Vicissitudes* (1915) Freud showed how masochism can be derived from aggression by the turning around of the aggression from the external world onto the self. In 1920 in *Beyond the Pleasure Principle* he reconsidered the possibility that masochism might be primary, the death instinct of the organism; then aggression would be the turning of masochism from the self onto the external world.

In light of the errors of Ernst Haeckel and Anton Dohrn, which Claus

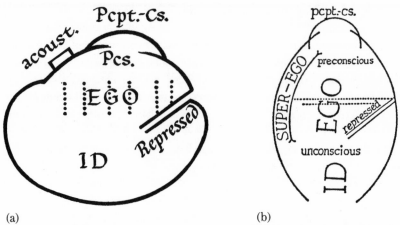

(a)   (b)

Fig. 1. Freud's structural model of the mind. (a) Earliest diagram showing that "the ego is not sharply separated from the id" and that "the repressed merges into the id as well" (*The Ego and the Id*, 1923, *SE* 19:24). (b) "Unassuming sketch" of ten years later for the lay public portraying "the structural relations of the mental personality" (lecture 31 of *New Introductory Lectures on Psycho-Analysis*, 1933 [1932]a, *SE* 22:78).

attributed to the "flight of imagination which is not held back by compre-hensive detailed studies and an objective critical method of comparison," Claus "began to realize fully the uncertainties and dangers inherent in every attempt at trying to solve even the most modest question" (1876, p. vi). Claus issued these warnings the year Freud attempted research for the first time. Claus along with Brücke may be responsible for the exces-sive caution Freud later exercised when his researches in Brücke's insti-tute on the *Petromyzon* (1878) and "On the structure of the nerve fibers and nerve cells of the fresh water (river) crayfish" (1882) led him to antici-pate (1884 [1882]) but not publish the neurone theory.

In undertaking *Studies for the Investigation of the Genealogical Foun-dation of the Crustacean System* (1876), Claus "had no illusions in regard to the difficulties inherent" in attempting to establish genealogical founda-tions, and probably permitted Freud none about his research either. We can hear the words of the experienced scientist: "Numerous examples had taught me how easily, when one treats such questions, the imagination might lead to rash and unfounded speculations, which, thereupon, were proclaimed with the greatest assurance as the results of true scientific re-search; I have, therefore, tried to apply the principles of the theory of evolution objectively and cautiously, and, in contrast to the certainty which lies in the proof of fact, I have rarely ascribed a higher value than that of greater or lesser probability or possibilty to the deductions" (p. v). Freud's writings, too, for those who pay attention to his signposts ("speculation," "interesting line of thought," "hypothesis," "theory," or "principle") "rarely ascribe a higher value than that of greater or lesser probability or possibility to the deductions . . . in contrast to the certainty which lies in the proof of fact." Darwin also distinguished between fact and theory, cautioning that false observations not false theories are harmful to science.

The harsh criticism Freud might expect from Claus if he gave in to his imagination were amply evident in print in 1874. Claus may have gone even further in his lectures. Claus criticized Haeckel's methodology in well-measured words before condemning: "Reading the few sentences E. Haeckel brings forward for the foundation of his pedigree, everybody who has studied the organization and the development of the Crustacea at all carefully must necessarily understand that as summary a method as Haeckel uses for establishing, without any thorough knowledge, a pedigree of the Crustaceans does not only not bear any fruit but that by such methods one basically only propagates wrong ideas about the mutual relations between the groups of Crustaceans." Claus then went on to denounce as "fictitious" Haeckel's results. "Essentially, we can say, this author's fictitious pedigree amounts to nothing but the well-known classification of the crabs which derives the crab directly from Nauplius and Zoea. . . . Haeckel's pedigree represents, in his own style, a transformation of the well-known, by using Fr. Müller's discovery" (pp. v–vi).

THE PROBLEM OF NATURAL SELECTION

Claus was critical of Haeckel and Weismann for claiming that natural selection is the only principle necessary to explain evolution. Even in his Darwin obituary (1882, p. 515) Claus vigorously opposed as "an excessive exaggeration" (*"eine masslose Übertreibung"*) Haeckel's comparison of Darwin to Newton. He added this objection cautiously as "eine etwas starke Übertreibung" (*"a somewhat strong exaggeration"*; Claus's italics) to the second edition of the *Text-Book* (1872, 1:53), in which he anticipated Haeckel's criticism. After Haeckel's attack Claus felt free to drop the softening *"etwas"* from new editions, including Sedgwick's 1884 translation, and to emphasize the strength of his objection with italics: "It is clearly *a great exaggeration* when enthusiastic supporters of the Darwinian theory"—

131

here Claus directs the reader in a footnote to "compare E. Haeckel, *Natürliche Schopfungsgeschichte.* 4 Auflage. Berlin. 1873, pag. 23, 25 etc."—"say that it ranks as equal to the gravitational theory of Newton, because 'it is founded upon a single law, a single effective cause, namely, upon the interaction of adaptation and heredity.' They overlook the fact that we have here only to do with the proof of a mechanical and causal connection between series of biological phenomena, and not in the remotest degree with a physical explanation" (1884, 1:147).

Claus agreed with Haeckel that Darwin's theory was based on the interaction of adaptation and heredity. But "we must certainly admit that Darwin's selection theory, although supported by what we know of biological processes and of the operation of the laws of nature, is very far from discovering the final causes and physical connection of the phenomena of adaptation and heredity, since it is unable to explain why such or such a variation should appear as the necessary consequence of a change in the vital conditions, and how it is that the manifold and wonderful phenomena of heredity are a function of organised matter." In the absence of an understanding of the complicated phenomena of heredity "even if we are justified in connecting the phenomena of adaptation with the processes of nourishment, and in conceiving heredity as a physiological function of the organism, we still stand and regard these phenomena as the 'savage who sees a ship for the first time,'" a quotation from Darwin's *Origin* that needed no identification.

Claus thought that inheritance through use and disuse came closer than natural selection to being a physico-chemical explanation. "While the complicated phenomena of heredity remain completely unintelligible, we are only in a position to explain in general terms certain modifications of organs, on physical grounds, by the altered conditions of metabolism. It is only rarely—as in the case of the operation of use and disuse—that we are able more directly to relate the development or the atrophy of organs to the increase or decrease in their nutritive activity, *i.e.*, to give a chemico-physical explanation" (1884, 1:147). Claus stressed in a footnote that "it is clearly a misuse of the word 'Law' to represent the numerous partially opposed and limiting phenomena of heredity as so many 'laws of heredity,' as Haeckel does" (1:147n).

Claus thought that "the effect of natural selection presupposes an already prevailing variety in structure and mode of living of organisms, such as the exclusive occurrence of few and very simply formed species, however numerous, in uniform environments cannot offer." Therefore, "the most difficult question in the entire theory of evolution, to which only a very incomplete answer can be supplied," is that "in the beginning there could be but few species of simple single-cell protophyte and protozoic organisms consisting or protoplasm and sarcode. In view of the limited competition and the stability of the environment, there would have been no levers anywhere on the earth's surface to compel the creation of useful changes."

Claus recognized that spontaneous generation would be helpful with both the Helmholtzian and the Darwinian viewpoints, which he (and later Freud) espoused. "The existence of the *generatio oequivoca* would offer a very important service to our contention for the physico-chemical explanation; *it even appears to be a necessary postulate in order to explain the first appearance of organisms*" (1876 [1866–68], 1:95, Claus's italics). Nevertheless, Claus declared that "in the present state of our knowledge" there is no evidence for spontaneous generation even in the simplest and lowest form of life, "although very recently some investigators (Pouchet) have been led by results of remarkable but equivocal experiments to the opposite view" (1884, 1:10). "According to our present knowledge, cells always originate from pre-existing cells" (1:30). Claus's position on spontaneous generation resembled that communicated by Darwin in letters to his German supporters, Carus in 1866 and Haeckel in 1873, that "if it could be proved true this would be most important to us" ("Letter 193 to Victor Carus Nov. 21st, 1866," 1903, 1:273) but "as for myself I cannot believe in spontaneous generation" ("Letter to Haeckel September 25, 1873," 1887–88, 3:180). For Lamarck, at an earlier stage of science, spontaneous generation was constantly in operation creating lowly organisms, each destined to evolve into higher and higher forms.

"Entirely justified" for Claus was "Nägeli's question whether it is at all conceivable 1) that the whole complicated organisation of the highest plants and animals developed gradually from imperfection solely through purposeful adaptation; 2) that the microscopic single-cell plant after innumerable generations became a phanerogamic plant solely through its fight for existence; or 3) to cite animals, that the amoeba became a polyp, the planula a vertebrate" (1876, 1:85–86). Claus felt that "Nägeli's subsequent considerations" in his *Entstehung und Begriff der naturhistorischen Art (The Origin and Concept of Natural Species*, 1865) "contained no wholly correct reply" (1:86). Attempts to fill the gap, which Claus concurred with Nägeli in finding in Darwin's theory of natural selection, "so far all lack a true and positive basis and contain nothing but circumscriptions of unexplained conditions." At the top of such worthless attempts Claus placed "Nägeli's *perfection theory*, which postulates that individual changes occur not randomly nor uniformly in all directions, but preferentially . . . guided, not by supernatural intervention, but by a tendency inherent in the organism toward perfection" (1:89).

Claus acknowledged the probability of the direct influence of external conditions of life in the creation of variations, a view consistent with Darwin's. "Variations in coloring occur very frequently in most classes of animals; they are usually estimated as of very little value; in all probability they are caused by the direct influence of the exterior conditions of life, of the medium, of the temperature, of nutrition. The differences in the size of the bodies are more important; they are mainly caused by natural selection and influenced by exterior conditions of life and nutrition" (1866, p. 4). According to Claus, Darwin "recognizes in the alteration of the vital conditions and the mode of nourishment the primary cause of slight modifications of structure. But it is only *natural selection which accumulates those alterations, so that they become appreciable to us* and constitute a variation which is evident to our senses. It is exactly upon the intimate connection of direct physical action with the consequences of natural selection that the strength of the Darwinian theory rests" (1884, 1:148). The italics are Claus's.

In the 1876 German edition of his *Text-Book* Claus had also italicized that Darwin "recognizes *in the alteration of the vital conditions and the mode of nourishment the primary cause of slight modifications of structure.*" It becomes evident from Claus's third edition of the *Text-Book* that Darwin as well as Claus had been assuming up to now that the variations upon which natural selection operates are the consequences of unknown physical causes in the environment. In 1876 Claus reported that "recently we have heard this important concession from Darwin himself as follows: 'In the past I have underestimated the frequency and significance of modifications occurring as a result of spontaneous variability.'" Claus hastened to add that as a consequence of this concession on Darwin's part, "the effect of natural selection is not changed in the least, especially since it is impossible in any other way to explain the countless contrivances in nature which are based on purposeful adaptation" (1876, 1:85).

Claus felt that "much leeway remains here for subjective evaluation and individual judgment" because "the advantages of life preservation of a specialization of organization combined with division of labor as a consequence of the effect of natural selection can by no means be ruled out." He concluded that "whether one attributes a greater or smaller influence to natural selection becomes a matter purely of *belief*" (1:88). Claus continued to conclude the General Part of his *Text-Book* with the same evaluation of Darwin's selection theory as he had in the second and third editions, which spanned the period of Freud's work with him. "However well grounded we admit the theory of selection to be, we cannot accept it as in itself sufficient to explain the complicated and involved metamorphoses which have taken place in organisms in the course of immeasurable time. If the theory of repeated acts of creation be rejected and the process of natural development be established in its place, there is still the first appearances of organisms to be accounted for, and especially the definite course which the evolution of the complicated and more highly developed organisms has taken has to be explained. In the many wonderful phenomena of the organic world, amongst others in the origin of Man in the diluvial or tertiary period, we have a riddle the solution of which must remain for future investigators" (1884, 1:179).

"OBJECTIONS TO DARWIN" (1876)

With increased interest in Darwin's theory came an increase also in misunderstandings and objections that multiplied and required attention in the period in which Freud was studying with Claus. In the preface to the third edition (January 1876) Claus indicated that in spite of his intention to abbreviate the systematic details with which he started to revise this work, the actual result was "an expansion of the General Part since I had to take into account numerous writings and works of recent date, particularly those in the field of Evolution, in which there had occurred such an enrichment of available material that in certain sections it became necessary not only to completely rework but also to increase the text" (1876, 1:v). Discussion of objections to Darwin's theory required an additional ten pages. As a student Freud was introduced to the confusions and misunderstandings surrounding the early stages of Darwin's theory. The knowledge could have been reassuring to Freud when his own theory encountered similar difficulties. Late in life when, as Freud described himself, he had regressed to "the cultural problems which had fascinated me long before" (1935, *SE* 20:72), he used Darwin's theory as an example of the fate of such scientific theories (1939, *SE* 23:66–67; see epigraph above).

Some criticisms of Darwin's theory Claus regarded as misapprehensions in need of correction. In the second edition of the *Text-Book* Claus had already taken the Swiss entomologist Oswald Heer to task for assuming that Darwin's theory claimed that gradual changes were *consistently* occurring. In arguing against Darwin's evolution by gradualism and in favor of jumps, Heer cited the mummified Egyptian mammals as evidence that since the beginning of human history the presently existing species had not changed. Heer did not take this as proof that species did not change but rather that they changed suddenly. Claus claimed that Darwin recognized that there were long periods of stability in which no changes occurred but that when changes did occur, they occurred gradually. Claus challenged the author of *Die tertiäre Flora der Schweiz, sowie Die Urwelt der Schweiz* (1865) "with Fawzett's question 'whether because Mt. Blanc and the other Alpine mountains have had exactly the same height for three thousand years as today, mountains never previously had been gradually raised'" (1872, 1:94n). Claus claimed that "Heer misinterprets Darwin," that "Darwin's teaching nowhere asserts what Heer ascribes to it—an uninterrupted, steady advance in the evolution of species. On the contrary, Darwin's theory actually agrees with Heer in the sense that the period in which species remain unchanged are infinitely greater than the periods during which through natural selection new varieties and species are developed. According to Darwin, nothing can be achieved until non-advantageous variations occur which certainly only take place with a gradual change in the environment" (1:94).

Another misapprehension with regard to Darwin's theory that Claus sought to correct was in relation to the role of "chance" in Darwin's theory. "Darwin has been unjustly reproached with having left chance to play a considerable part in his attempt to account for the origin of varieties, with having accounted for everything by the struggle for existence, and with having given too little prominence to the direct influence of physical action on the mutation of forms." As Claus rightly pointed out, "Darwin says himself that the expression 'chance,' which he often uses to explain the presence of any small alteration, is a totally incorrect expression, and is only used to express our complete ignorance of the physical reasons for such particular variation" (1884, 1:148).

Claus was very harsh with claims like those of Heer that "the instincts are not learned, but inborn, placed there by the Creator, which is best demonstrated by the fact of their constancy" (Heer 1865, p. 601). For Claus the constancy of instincts is not a "fact," for "how do we know with such certainty that the instinctual drives are not capable of development?" Furthermore, "That Heer arrives at this belief proves only how little he is inclined to use the great span of time which reaches beyond the Floods" (1872, 1:94 n. 1). The scientific breakthrough by geologists of the limitations of biblical time on the age of the world was so recent that not all scientists had adapted to it, even when they did accept it. Darwin was quite an old man when he discovered that 4004 B.C., Archbishop Ussher's dating of the creation, was not in the Bible. But the release of science from this constraint did not immediately open up the great span of 4.6 billion years acceptable to today's scientists. The physicists, led by Helmholtz and the great Lord Kelvin, could prove in the days before the discovery of radioactivity that the Earth could not have been warm enough to sustain life for the length of time required by the evolutionists.

As in the discussion of Heer, Claus often resorted to knowledge from, or analogies with, geology to meet opposition to Darwin's claims. Modern geology, Freud would have learned from Claus, if he did not already know it from his own voracious reading, also supports the idea of "a gradual process of development." On the advice of his geologist friend and professor, the "sagacious Henslow," Darwin "had brought with" him on the *Beagle* the just published "first volume of Lyell's *Principles of Geology*, which [he] studied attentively." He recalled that "this book was of the highest service to me in many ways." Henslow, who like all other geologists believed at that time in successive cataclysms, had admonished Darwin "on no account to accept the views therein advocated," but the very first place Darwin examined, St. Jago in the Cape Verde Islands, showed him "clearly the wonderful superiority of Lyell's manner of treating geology," that is, on the "principle that the past must be explained by the present, unless good cause can be shown to the contrary; and the fact that so far as our knowledge of the past history of life on our globe goes, no such cause can be shown" (1958 [1876–82], p. 77).

Freud knew the relationship of Lyell's work to Darwin's. Just before entering the university, in a letter to his friend Silberstein August 6, 1873, Freud placed Lyell between Huxley and Darwin among the English scientists whose writings "would always keep him a partisan of their nation" (in Gay 1988, p. 31). He started with Tyndall, the Irish physicist, geologist, and microbiologist who had studied glaciers with Huxley. In the 1870's, from his powerful position as Faraday's successor to superintendent at the Royal Institution of Great Britain, John Tyndall was delivering the deathblow to spontaneous generation with scientifically irrefutable demonstrations (1870–76) that optically pure air, moteless and germless, was incapable of putrefaction. Freud brought back with him to England sixty

137

years later Tyndall's 1876 "The forms of water in clouds and rivers: Ice and glaciers," signed "Sigm Freud 24/08/78." After Darwin Freud named Thomson—either Charles Wylie, the Scottish marine biologist who had just published the oceanographic classic *The Depths of the Sea* (1872), describing his discoveries on two deep-sea biological and depth-sounding expeditions off Scotland (1868–69) and in the Mediterranean (1870) of a wide variety of many previously unknown invertebrate forms at some 650 fathoms; or the Scottish mathematician and physicist William, better known today as Kelvin after receiving the Baronetcy of Largs in 1892 for his scientific achievements and the instrumentation that made possible the laying of the Atlantic cable in 1867.

After 1844, from his studies of heat, Kelvin considered Lyell's Uniformitarianism untenable, even more so after 1852 as a consequence of the second law of thermodynamics. In 1862 Kelvin attacked Lyell's assertion that an absolute geochronology is not useful and probably not attainable. Kelvin calculated that the sun "has not illuminated the earth for 100,000,000 years, and almost [certainly for not more than] 500,000,000 years," a period more helpful for evolutionists than biblical time, if only Kelvin had not also pointed out that the Uniformitarianist geologists' assumption of the central heat of the earth to account for volcanic action and other geological processes involving thermal variations meant that for a long period the surface of the earth had been the scene of violent and abrupt changes unsuited to Darwinian evolution. Kelvin's acceptance of the dynamical theory of heat and his subsequent reformulation of the axiom of thermodynamics led to a thirty-year controversy that the geologists could not win against the physicists until Becquerel's 1896 discovery of radioactivity in uranium made possible the work of the Curies, for which the three received the 1903 Noble Prize in Physics.

Freud ended his list with Lockyer, the astronomical physicist who with the newly developing spectroscopy had in 1868 made the bold identification of a line in the spectrum of the sun's atmosphere as a new element, helium, probably nonexistent on earth and just published *Contributions to Solar Physics* (1873), a subject as we saw that was the hope and despair of Uniformitarians and evolutionists. Shortly before, Lockyer had helped found *Nature*, a magazine hospitable to evolutionary writers; in 1900 he published *Inorganic Evolution*. Along with these active modern scientists Freud, who as a young man could well be excited by the latest scientific achievements, found Lyell's forty-year-old *Principles of Geology* still inspiring.

Darwin was able to study and test Lyell's *Principles* with his own observations. He used it to make important contributions to geology, particularly *On the Formation of Coral Reefs* (1842), before extending it to understanding the origin of species; Darwin was secretary of the Geological Society 1838–41. He was in close association with Sir Charles Lyell when he heard from Alfred Russell Wallace and realized that the younger scientist seeking his advice had made the same discovery. Lyell joined Darwin's friends Huxley and Hooker in urging Darwin to prepare a shortened version and in arranging an amicable arrangement for the two men to announce together at a meeting of the Linnean society.

Claus did not hedge in declaring that "Lyell has proved in a convincing way on geological grounds that there were not sudden revolutions extending over the whole surface of the earth, but that changes took place slowly." The paradigm in geology that Lyell contested was the catastrophic. The only disagreement until Lyell had been over the nature of that catastrophe. Geologists divided into two camps, the vulcanists and the neptunists. Was it a volcano that suddenly engulfed the world? Or the Floods? Claus expounded Lyell's revolutionary view that "the past history of the earth consists essentially of a *gradual* process of development, in which the numerous forces which may be *observed in action at the present day* have, by their long continued operation, had an enormous effect in transforming the earth's surface" (1884, 1:166, italics added). Earlier in the *Text-Book* Claus had already pointed out that "the variability of species, the origin of new species from previous ancestral forms in the course of ages, has become, accordingly, since the time of Lyell, a necessary postulate of geology in order to explain naturally the differences of animals and plants in successive periods without the supposition of repeated acts of creation" (1:144). Necessary as Lyell's geology made this postulate, Claus felt that "a more securely grounded theory based upon a firmer standpoint was needed in order to give more force to the Transmutation hypothesis which had remained disregarded; and this service was effected by the English naturalist, Charles Darwin, who employed a mass of scientific material to found a theory of the origin and mutation of species." Darwin's "theory, which is closely connected with the views of Lamarck and Geoffrey St. Hilaire and in harmony with Lyell's doctrines, has received an almost universal recognition, not only on account of the simplicity of its principle, but also because of the objective and convincing way in which his genius expounded it" (1:144–45).

Like Darwin, Claus rejected evolution by mutation or large jumps. He wrote in the second and third editions of his *Grundzüge* about Kölliker's "*Über die Darwin'sche Schöpfungstheorie*" (*On the Darwinian Creation Theory* [1864]) that "we are not in a position to present any significant probability for the jumps which Kölliker assumes on grounds of the alternation of generations." Claus "can hardly find any other explanation for the origin of heterogamy than the gradual and slow advantageous adaptation of organization to significantly deviating living conditions and that only the final product would suddenly and in apparent discontinuity . . . be appropriately a species or race" (1872, 1:95–96). Claus's footnote here reveals that both Claus and Kölliker were uncritically utilizing recapitulation in arriving at their differing points of view about evolution whether by gradation or leaps. "Surely there is much better ground for the idea of conceiving of alternation of generations in analogy with development by metamorphosis as recapitulation of a slow and gradual process of species development than for the idea of a sudden jump" (1:95n).

In the second edition Claus devoted much space to a discussion of Wagner's *Die Darwin'sche Theorie und das Migrationsgesetz der Organismen* (1866). Claus elevated August Weismann's "just arguments" in 1868 against Wagner's position from a footnote in the second edition to the text itself in the next edition. For Claus, "however important the influence of this spatial isolation may be on the existence of varieties and species, it does not follow as recently M. Wagner in his *Darwinian Theory and the Law of Migration of Organisms* believes that it is a *necessary* requirement for the *success of natural selection*" (1872, 1:80). Wagner had focused on one point made by Darwin in his theory and had come to see it as all important. Freud was to have a similar experience with some of the followers of his own theory. Otto Rank, for instance, with *The Trauma of Birth* (1924) attempted to construct about a concept introduced by Freud in 1909 and reemphasized in *The Ego and the Id* (1923) "an entirely new theory that repudiated the Oedipus complex and postulated radical new changes in theory and technique" (Eisenstein, p. 46). Claus agreed that in answering Wagner, "Weismann argues with justice that even the migration of a single pair across a barrier which is difficult to pass does not constitute complete separation from the original species since among the offspring of this new pair only a few will have the beginnings of a useful property while most of their offspring will be wholly identical with the original form. Only in the second or third generation does the influence of changed conditions of life which favor the variation become valid for the migrating colonists and at this time, the conditions change from a majority of the unchanged individuals identical to the original species to an equal number of variants" (1884, 1:81).

In 1870 Wagner abandoned Darwinism in an article "Über den Einfluss der geographischen Isolierung und Colonienbildung auf die morphologischen Veränderungen der Organismen" (On the Influence of Geographical Isolation and Colony-Building on the Morphological Changes of Organisms). Claus noted in the third edition of *Grundzüge* that "more recently, M. Wagner after it became clear to him that 'The Law of Migration' contained within itself the negation of the principle of natural selection abandoned *Darwinism* completely without at the same time finding a new point of view to support the untenable teaching of species creation through separation and colony building and without postulating any kind of clarifying principle for transmutation in lieu of the process of natural selection" (1875, trans. 1884, 1:83). Claus referred his readers to Weismann's "Über den Einfluss der Isolierung auf die Artbildung" (1872, On the Influence of Isolation on the Development of Species) to see "how little this one-sided migration teaching which has been emancipated from Darwinism can stand up" (1:83n1). This fate of a complex theory was therefore familiar to Freud when aspects of his theory were "emancipated" from their psychoanalytic base. As Neal Miller of the Rockefeller Institute points out, psychologists today are unaware of their indebtedness to Freud for the parts of his work that they have adopted as their own. They only acknowledge and attack as Freud's the aspects that they either disagree with or misunderstand, unaware of having "emancipated" any of Freud's teaching from its base in his theory (personal communication December 17, 1971).

Claus regarded as valid some of the criticisms of "the fundamental arguments of the Darwinian theory of selection and transmutation theory founded upon it." Claus's persistence in pursuing Darwinian biology while openly recognizing these criticisms could have fortified Freud when his own theory encountered the same or similar criticisms: "The theory is based on postulates which cannot be submitted to direct inquiry" and "further, plants and animals which are under the influence of natural selection are entirely inaccessible to the experiments of man. . . . The action of natural selection, in Darwin's sense, is therefore in general incapable of direct proof, and even for the origin of varieties can only be illustrated and rendered probable by hypothetical examples" (1884, 1:150–51).

Like astronomy, queen of the sciences until the eighteenth century, neither evolutionary biology nor psychoanalysis is an experimental science. All three are dependent upon the accumulation and interpretation of observable data without opportunity for experimental manipulation. For over twenty centuries astronomy advanced by observing and hypothesizing without being able to manipulate a single variable for experimental purposes. Unable to vary the positions, orbits, velocity, density, or composition of a single heavenly body, astronomy was still a science. Darwin, too, had to rely on what he could find in nature. Until modern genetics, which evolved from his theory, man could not experiment with making one species out of another. Freud could not have missed this affinity, of astronomy, evolutionary biology, and psychoanalysis, coincidental as it might have been, when he singled out these particular sciences "to describe how the universal narcissism of men, their self-love, has up to the present suffered three severe blows from the researches of science" (1917, *SE* 17:139).

Claus readily acknowledged the validity of such criticisms: "When the fundamental arguments of the Darwinian theory of selection and the transmutation theory founded upon it are submitted to criticism, it is soon apparent that direct proof by investigation is now, and perhaps, always will be impossible" (1884, 1:150). Nevertheless, Claus devoted a major portion of his efforts to Darwinian theory because against these valid arguments he saw that "we must set the fact that there is a great probability in favour of the correctness of the theories of descent and transmutation of species, which have never received better support than from the natural selection theory of Darwin; and that this probability is supported not only by the whole weight of morphological evidence but also by the testimony of Paleontology and of geographical distribution" (1:151). Claus, of course, did not neglect to provide his students with "the morphological evidence" and "the testimony of Paleontology and of geographical distribution." In the third edition Claus added that "the results, too, of embryology, i.e., individual development from the egg to completed form, to which for decades modern science has been wont to look for the key to the understanding of taxonomy and of comparative anatomy, fit entirely into the premises and conclusions of Darwin's *doctrines of selection and descent*" (1876, 1:95).

By the third edition Claus took note that Bronn and Broca as well as Nägeli "emphasize that many characteristics lend no usefulness at all to their owners and could therefore not have been generated by natural selection nor even influenced by it" (1:85). Claus countered with Darwin's work, particularly *The Various Contrivances by which Orchids are Fertilized by Insects*, which as we noted in part I Freud acquired a few years later in 1879. "With respect to the supposed usefulness of various parts of the body, Darwin appropriately points out that even in the higher and best known animals many forms exist which are so highly developed that no one doubts their importance, even though it has not yet been discovered at all or only very recently. With respect to plants he refers to the strange structural peculiarities of orchid blossoms, whose differences, even a few years ago, were considered to be purely morphologic. Darwin's intensive investigations have recently proved that these peculiarities are of greatest importance to fertilization by means of insects, and they have probably been achieved through natural selection. Furthermore, it is now known that the different lengths of stamina and pistil, as well as their arrangement in dimorphic and trimorphic plants are of essential use" (1:86).

Freud applied to the understanding of hysterics the idea that apparently meaningless symptoms were serving a psychological need or had done so in the past. Freud had learned from Claus that "it would be rash to claim," as Nägeli does, that "the so-called 'morphologic characteristics' which now seem useless and hence *appear* unimportant for the struggle for survival were of absolutely no value even at the time of their occurrence" (1:87). Freud paid attention to such seemingly meaningless phenomena as parapraxes and dreams and found their psychological value, their meaning often derived from the past. Claus taught that "Darwin rightly countered" Nägeli's argument "by observing that we are only inadequately or not at all informed about the usefulness of many characteristics, and that which in fact does not now convey any advantage may have been useful in the past and under other conditions" (1:85).

Claus took Nägeli to task for assuming from Darwin's theory that indifferent characteristics must be variable and that useful ones must be constant. According to Claus, "Indifferent peculiarities, too, can become so confirmed through heredity over the course of innumerable generations, that they may be taken as absolutely constant; that is particularly true for those which determine the systematic categories of higher orders. On the other hand, useful characteristics need not yet have attained the limit of usefulness which they convey to the organism; especially under changed living conditions they might become still much more useful."

Nägeli's *Entstehung und Begriff der Naturhistorischen Art*, already noted by Claus in the second edition, was published in 1865. In 1872 two other "scholars, unanimous in their acceptance of evolution theory inasmuch as like Darwin they trace back their kinship of species to a common origin," each produced a book attributing evolution to "determinately directed variation" or internal causes. These attempts did not fill the gap Claus credited Nägeli with rightly recognizing in natural selection but not filling. "One soon finds out that Nägeli, despite his acute and correct recognition of the existing gap, instead of filling it introduces only a phrase. And the acceptance of this phrase is linked to the notion that it yields something like an explanation. In reality, the expressions 'perfection tendency' or 'perfection theory' are only a carry-over of the formerly current and misused phrase *Bildungstrieb* or *nisus formativus* from individual development to phylogeny. The same applies to the doctrine of the 'determinately directed variation' or evolution "from internal causes," as we find them expressed in the writings of Askenasy (*Beiträge zur Kritik der Darwin'schen Lehre*. Leipzig. 1872) and A. Braun (*Über die Bedeutung der Entwicklung in der Naturgeschichte*. Berlin. 1872)" (1:86–87). When in 1888 Claus turned his attention to Lamarck's work, he pointed out in describing Nägeli's theory that "one feels reminded of Lamarck's doctrine, in which the effect of the laws of formation, which correspond to Nägeli's inner causes, provide the explanatory reason for the natural gradation of the animal classes rising from the lower to the higher steps of evolution" (1888b, p. 14).

While some scientists, as we have just seen, were accepting transmutation but not natural selection, other biologists appear to have been accepting natural selection but not the mutability of species. According to Claus, "for some biologists the chief difficulty lies in the assumption that there is an unbridgeable gulf between variety and species. In part they acknowledge the operation of natural selection, even concede that in climatic varieties Darwinism has actually been proved, but they always invoke the concept of species and the limits of the permanency of forms designated thereby—which, so far as can be observed, are never transgressed" (1876, 1:89–90). Claus attributed this misunderstanding to the fact that "proof through direct observation of the transition of one life-form into another is excluded by the selection doctrine itself" (1:90).

The mutability of species is, as Claus pointed out, "the cardinal point of every transmutation theory, however differently we may visualize how mutation has occurred; whether we accord to natural selection a critical influence or only the importance of a corrective; or whether we refute its effect altogether and substitute for an explanation general phrases, such as mutation from inner causes, of sudden or spasmodic change of forms; new species have to form from old ones if there is any justification at all to the descent or transmutation theory" (1:91).

Claus could therefore answer those who might still be reluctant to give up the old idea of the immutability of species with a lengthy quotation from a "pertinent discussion" by Nägeli, with whom, as we have just seen, Claus disagreed about Darwin's theory in other respects.

"Artificially bred races behave similarly to real species; they have an analogous range of forms and an analogous stability; they, too, show a reduced fertility when producing bastards; and the bastards, like those of the species, have strange forms which can arise in no other way. Nor can the races occurring in nature be rigorously and sharply distinguished from species. The only absolute hallmark of species, their immutability, is sacrificed in practice even by those who accept it in theory: they talk of in-between forms, of the transition of one species into another, of their degeneration, of genuine or typical, and of deviant forms of a species, or of better and worse species. Although these characterizations are wholly adapted to reality, they only fit into the theory of transmutability. The concept of species in the hitherto accepted taxonomy was rooted in the realm of faith; it was inaccessible to scientific perception or to proof by facts; it was the toy ball of individual judgement, of tact, or of caprice. For future taxonomy it will be a scientific category for which definite characteristics will be observable in nature and verifiable by experiment" (1:90–91).

For the transmutationists it was clear, no matter what else they disagreed about, that "the closeness of kinship and not some unknown plan of creation forms the invisible bond which links the organisms in different stages of similarity" (1:92). There also seemed to be agreement, or at least no disagreement requiring discussion, about inheritance through use and disuse. Everyone seems to have accepted it no matter what else they disagreed about.

LAMARCK

In Freud's day, if one judges from Claus's *Grundzüge*, Claus did not attribute much significance to Lamarck. In discussing "The Meaning of the System" in the *Grundzüge*, Claus mentioned that "in the year 1809, Lamark [*sic*] in his 'Philosophie Zoologique,' broached the theory of the descent of species from one another. He referred the gradual alterations in some degree to changing conditions of life but mainly to use and disuse" (trans. 1884, 1:44). In the second and third editions Claus went on to comment about Lamarck that "the manner and form of his attempts at clarification obviously are not based on a strongly developed and well thought-out theory but for the most part on rather general rough appearances

145

which in some cases seem almost laughable while in other cases, although possible, in no instance could they ever be proven." As examples of Lamarck's rough or unprovable cases Claus cited "the long tongues of the woodpecker and anteater which are supposed to have originated from the habit of these animals of hauling their food out of narrow and deep crevices," "the neck of the giraffe which has become long thanks to the constant stretching to the crown of higher trees," and "the webs between the toes formed as the result of the attempts to swim of many animals forced to live in the water" (1876, 1:69). In the third edition of the *Grundzüge* Claus concluded his short discussion of Lamarck's work by saying that Lamarck, "in addition to adaptation, placed the greatest emphasis for the explanation of the descent theory on inheritance to which he attributed, step-wise, the continuous changes of similar characteristics (*Aehnlichkeits-abstufungen*). The origin of the simplest organisms he explained by way of spontaneous generation (*Urzeugung*), and he assumed that to start with only the simplest and lowest animals and plants existed" (1:69–70).

Except for the reference in *Grundzüge* to Lamarck, Claus himself appears from his publications to have neglected Lamarck in favor of Darwin until 1888, when for the first time he considered that it might "seem in place to have a close look at Lamarck's doctrines, all the more since, in the short reports, they have been either praised in an exaggerated way or else underestimated in their value and received only casual mention" (p. 7). He was addressing a lecture to the Vienna Academy of Sciences on "Lamarck als Begründer der Descendenzlehre" (Lamarck as Founder of the Descent Theory). According to Claus, as well as Haeckel and Weismann, "Lamarck's doctrine had in his lifetime already fallen into oblivion, from which it was only rescued when Darwin's work received the attention of natural scientists" (p. 26).

Inheritance through use and disuse, unlike natural selection, posed no problems for Claus until August Weismann's publications of *Über die Continuität des Keimplasmas als Grundlage einer Theorie der Vererbung (On the Continuity of the Germplasm as the Basis for a Theory of Heredity* [1885]) and of *Die Bedeutung der sexuellen Fortpflanzung für die Selectionstheorie (The Significance of Sexual Reproduction for the Selection Theory* [1886]). By then Freud had ceased to be involved with either Claus or biological questions. Weismann's work forced Claus, apparently for the first time, to examine the question of inheritance through use and disuse, which he had been assuming as an accepted principle, just as his pupil Freud was to do to the end of his life.

Thus challenged, Claus called upon the authority of both Lamarck and Darwin for the inheritance of acquired characteristics, which he felt was essential to the operation of natural selection and transmutation. "Lamarck as well as Darwin presumed that there was no doubt as to the inheritance of acquired characteristics; they made ample use of this theory in explaining transformation as a result of the influence of external causes. Darwin modified this theory by ascribing great influence also to the indirect effect of changes in living conditions on the reproductive system." Without the inheritance of acquired characteristics, Claus thought Darwin's theory would become dependent on the "inner orthogenetic drive towards perfection," which natural selection presumably replaced. "Should one answer the question of the inheritance of acquired characteristics negatively, not only Lamarck's explanatory principle would be annihilated but it would endanger Darwin's doctrine of natural selection in such a way as to make it necessary to derive the variability necessary for selection entirely from inner causes which changed the quality of the germ plasm" (1888b, p. 211).

The view of the inheritance through use and disuse as essential for the operation of natural selection that Claus expressed clearly here is implicit throughout his earlier works. Claus did not have to defend the idea of the inheritance of acquired characteristics while Freud was with him. When it was challenged, Claus pointed to Darwin's work and called attention particularly to *The Variation of Animals and Plants under Domestication* (1873), the first edition of which we now know Freud purchased shortly after starting practice. "Darwin himself in his later work on the variations in animals, in contradiction to his former negative attitude toward Lamarckism, admits the great importance of the use and non-use for the stronger or weaker structure and achievement of the organs and recognizes the useful effect of functional adaptation and thus recognizes a principle which is capable, in many cases, without the help of selection of explaining the origin of the purposeful in a direct manner" (p. 30).

In reaction at first to the "unchanging heredity" of the creationists and later carried over into opposition to the "inner progressive principle" of Nägeli and his followers, Claus—possibly even more than Darwin—emphasized the long neglected environmental factors. Claus regarded Weismann's germ-plasm theory as a return to internal forces. However, as Weismann "concedes the possibility of explaining the origin of climatic varieties and other phenomena of varieties on the basis of changed external conditions," Claus can "not see why in the great number of cases in which the organism reacts more actively by increased or decreased use of the organs, an indirect influence on the structure of the germplasm should not take place, in the same way." For Claus there was an added requirement we have met before in Freud and Darwin: "If only the functional adaptation would have had a continuous effect in a certain direction for a long enough period of time and through many generations." For Claus "the greatest difficulty with Weismann's theory would disappear" because "the wealth of acquired characteristics would no longer be excluded from heredity" (pp. 25–26).

Freud learned his views of the inheritance of acquired characteristics from Claus and from the study of Darwinian biology in the era before it became controversial. Nor, having abandoned the study of zoology before this controversy arose, was he aware until the last year of his life that inheritance through use and disuse had been called into question and found wanting. Like Claus, Freud assumed that progress required the inheritance of acquired characteristics. In attempting in *Totem and Taboo* to explain the transmission of the incest taboos as a result of the Oedipal killing of the father by Darwin's tribal horde, Freud explicitly stated that "if each generation were obliged to acquire its attitude to life anew, there would be no progress. . . . A part of the problem seems to be met by the inheritance of psychical dispositions" (*SE* 13:158). A decade later, in "The Dissolution of the Oedipus Complex" (1924), Freud worked out a psychological mechanism that could suffice to answer the problem without involving heredity, that is, superego formation through identification with the parents and their surrogates. Nevertheless, as we saw, Freud continued to use the inheritance of acquired characteristics in his speculations and even to consider it essential to him for certain purposes.

GOETHE AS A "PRECURSOR OF THE TRANSMUTATION THEORY IN GERMANY"

In the earlier edition of the *Grundzüge* (1872) Claus had unabashedly presented Goethe "as a gifted adherent' (*als Geistvoller Anhänger*) of the transmutation theory. He cited Goethe's scientific works on natural history, *The Metamorphosis of Plants*, the vertebrate theory of the brain, and the intermaxillary bone of man, as being "filled with the idea that one could prove the fundamental unity among the manifold appearance" and that in many other places in his writings and works Goethe "spoke about unending metamorphoses and the unity of life." However, Claus did conclude by pointing out that Goethe's "so beautiful and even meaningful phrases remained more spiritual perceptions; they lacked the fundamental requirement of a fully formed theory reinforced by actual facts" (1:50–51). A lengthy footnote indicates that Claus is following Haeckel's estimation of Goethe as an adherent of transmutation. As an example of the important place ascribed to Goethe by Haeckel, Claus quoted in this footnote two verses from Goethe's *Metamorphosis of Animals*.

Perhaps, Claus's disenchantment with Haeckel led him in revising the third edition to treat with more restraint the contribution of Goethe to the transmutation theory. Claus did not eliminate the lengthy footnote or more than a few words of the text in the passage where he quoted Goethe's poetry. However, he modified the sentence "Finally we have to mention Goethe as a gifted adherent of the transmutation theory" (1:50) to "finally, we have to mention Goethe in a certain sense as a precursor of the transmutation theory in Germany" and added "even though one cannot say that he ever envisaged an actual change of form or he ever actually announced such a concept. In his whole manner of observing the things around him, he was more motivated by a mental tying together of coexistent diversities which in his mind's eye not only formed a useful harmony but at the same time constituted 'an endlessly progressing metamorphosis'" (1876, 1:70).

In leading historically up to Darwin's contribution, Claus discussed Goethe after Lamarck and Geoffrey Saint-Hilaire and just before Lyell and Forbes. By Sedgwick's English edition of 1884 the paragraph on Goethe was reduced to a single sentence: "In Germany, Goethe and the natural philosophers Oken and Schelling pronounced in favour of the unity of animal organization, but it must be confessed without taking account in a comprehensive manner of the actual facts" (1:137). Freud used Goethe much as Claus did in the third edition: he quoted Goethe's felicitous words as poetical insight in accord with later scientific findings and not as the source of his evolutionary orientation, as some authors have claimed.

Fritz Müller, Claus's Exemplary
Darwinian Biologist

Claus shared Darwin's high regard for Fritz Müller's *Für Darwin*. Claus presented Müller to his students as a model of the ideal Darwinian biologist. The "rash and unfounded speculations" to which their imaginations had led scientists like Haeckel and Anton Dohrn in their genealogical attempts almost dissuaded Claus from attempting to investigate the genealogical foundations of the crustacean system. Claus viewed the failure of Dohrn's "History of the Family of the Crabs, Based on the Embryological and Paleological Sources" as "mainly due to the way Dohrn treated the material: full of imagination but far beyond the facts of reality." He credited Dohrn with recognizing the need to give up his "obviously too ambitious task. . . . But Fritz Müller's excellent work 'For Darwin' gave back" to Claus "the confidence that progress is possible on a safe route, too, as long as we let our speculations be guided by the rich treasure of factual experience within the narrow limits of what can be achieved," and well-removed from "the delusion that we are capable of reaching the goal in a daring flight; only persistent work can lead us, slowly and gradually, closer to that goal" (1876, p. vi).

Claus commended Müller's method of testing Darwin's theories as leading to important facts and deductions: "Fritz Müller thought that the safest method for examining the truth in Darwin's theories lies in applying it as strictly as possible to the morphologically so protean class of the Crustaceans; he not only acquainted us that way with a series of important facts which could only be understood if we presume the theory of evolution's correctness . . . but furthermore, Müller pointed to numerous peculiarities in the organization and development of the various groups which were perfectly understandable in the light of Darwin's theories, while they remained inexplicable and could not be understood if one excluded Darwin's doctrine. Müller thoroughly compared the history of the evolution of the Crustaceans from the viewpoint of Darwinism and thus succeeded in reaching important general deductions" (pp. vi–vii).

A MOST REMARKABLE DISCOVERY

Within a year of Darwin's publication of the *Origin*, Fritz Müller was able to publish the discovery of the naupliform larvae of the shrimp (*Archiv fur Naturgeschichte* [1860]), which until the insight provided by Darwinian theory he and other scientists had overlooked. Contemplating the application to the Crustacea of the developmental history of organisms proposed by Darwin, Müller concluded that "if the higher and lower Crustacea were at all derivable from common progenitors, the former also must once have passed through Nauplius-like conditions" (1869 [1864], p. 13). After Müller called attention to the naupliform larvae of the shrimp in Brazilian waters, it was found also in the sea near Naples. For this and similar discoveries which followed subsequently, Fritz Müller pointed out that "it may be remarked in passing, science is indebted less to a happy chance than immediately to Darwin's theory. Species of *Penëus* live in the European seas, as well as here" in Brazil and "their *Nauplius*-brood has no doubt repeatedly passed unnoticed through the hands of the numerous naturalists who have investigated those seas, as well as through my own, for it has nothing which could attract particular attention amongst the multifarious and often wonderful *Nauplius*-forms. When I, fancying from the similarity of its movements that it was a young *Penëus-Zoëa*, had for the first time captured such a larva, and on bringing it under the microscope found a *Nauplius* differing *toto coelo* from this *Zoëa*, I might have thrown it aside as being completely foreign to the developmental series which I was tracing, if the idea of early Naupliform stages of the higher Crustacea, which indeed I did not believe to be still extant, had not at the moment vividly occupied my attention" (pp. 17–18).

Müller, "in examining the truth in Darwin's theories," made the even more striking discovery of the existence of two forms of males with a single kind of female: "Now, in our *Tanais*, the young males up to the last change of skin preceding sexual maturity resemble the females, but then

151

they undergo an important metamorphosis. Amongst other things they lose the moveable appendages of the mouth even to those which serve for the maintenance of the respiratory current; their intestine is always found empty, and they appear only to live for love. But what is most remarkable is, that they now appear under two different forms" (p. 20).

It is a very striking finding. It had surprised even Darwin, as we saw above. Claus, too, was impressed with it. He was able to report a similar finding of his own among the Copepoda of Nice: "While the female *Dias Longiremis* from Nice are essentially identical with those from Helgoland in all parts, the male grasping-claw of the Nice form possesses much stronger hooks and processes which apparently provide for a tighter clutch during copulation. One observes here just like in *Orchestia Darwinii* two different males within the same kind, although in places far distant; thus one might explain their deviations very simply as a consequence of natural selection, possibly supported by the differences in the conditions of the localities" (1866, p. 7).

Claus in an earlier work had called attention to the sexual differences in the development of the delicate filaments on the flagellum of the anterior antennae in the Copepoda, which Spence Bates called "auditory cilia." They were more strongly developed in the male, and Müller favored the view of the German zoologist Franz Leydig that they were olfactory organs "as in other cases male animals are not infrequently guided by the scent in their pursuit of ardent females" (p. 20). Freud applied this view of the sexual importance of the olfactory sense in lower animals in one of his evolutionary speculations in *Civilization and its Discontents* (1930 [1929], *SE* 21:99–100).

Also known were the sexual differences in Crustacea with hand-like or cheliform structures. The enlargement of these claws in the male sometimes was of quite disproportionate size, as Müller showed in Melita and as was commonly known in the males of the calling crabs (*Gelasimus*). In the two forms of the male *Tanais* Müller found that "some acquire powerful, long-fingered, and very mobile chelae, and instead of the single olfactory filament of the female, have from 12 to 17 of these organs, which stand two or three together on each joint of the flagellum. The others retain the short thick form of the chelae of the females; but, on the other hand, their antennae are equipped with a far greater number of olfactory filaments, which stand in groups of from five to seven together" (1869 [1864], pp. 20–21).

Müller examined thousands of *Tanais* with the simple lens and many hundreds with the microscope to determine whether two different species with very similar females might be living together; or whether the males, instead of occurring in two sharply defined forms, might not be only variable within very wide limits. But he was unable to find any differences among the females that would indicate the existence of two species; nor was he able to find any intermediate forms between the two kinds of males.

In 1864 most zoologists were, like Agassiz, still supporters of the old school, which regarded "the plan of creation" as the "free conception of an Almighty intellect, matured in the thoughts of the latter before it is manifested in palpable, external forms." For them Müller's discovery could be "merely a matter of curiosity" or "a mere *caprice* of the Creator" (p. 22). But "from the side of Darwin's theory, on the contrary," Müller argued, "this fact acquires meaning and significance." Furthermore, Müller's finding "appears in return to be fitted to throw light upon a question in which Bronn saw 'the first and most material objection against the theory,' namely, how it is possible that from the accumulation in various directions of the smallest variations running out of one another, varieties and species are produced, which stand out from the primary form clearly and sharply like the petiolated leaf of a Dicotyledon, and are not amalgamated with the primary form and with each other like the irregular curled lobes of a foliaceous Lichen" (pp. 22–23).

Darwin's early translator Bronn, as quoted by Müller, seems to have missed the point of natural selection. Bronn objected that "for the support of the Darwinian theory and in order to explain why many species do not coalesce by means of intermediate forms, he would gladly discover some external or internal principle which should compel the variations of each species to advance in *one* direction, instead of merely permitting them in all directions." In spite of Darwin's work the directing force of natural selection upon chance variations seemed to escape scientists like Bronn and Nägeli, the latter as we saw preferring to assume a "perfecting principle" as Lamarck had. Müller saw clearly that the principle that Bronn sought lay "in the fact that actually only a few directions stand open in which the variations are at the same time improvements, and in which therefore they can accumulate and become fixed; while in all others, being either indifferent or injurious, they will go as lightly as they come" (p. 24).

If the best has already been attained by a species in adaptation to its condition of existence, fresh variations would be retrogressions and disappear as they arose. "The lists would remain open to the males under variation, only in respect of their sexual relations. In these they might acquire advantages over their rivals by their being enabled either to seek or to seize the females better. The best smeller would overcome all that were inferior to them in this respect, unless the latter had other advantages, such as more powerful chelae, to oppose them" (p. 23) and vice versa. "In this manner all the intermediate steps less favoured in the development of the olfactory filaments or of the chelae would disappear from the lists, and two sharply defined forms, the best smellers and the best claspers, would remain as the sole adversaries" (pp. 23–24). Müller observed, not without humor, that at the time the best claspers were winning out over the best smellers one hundred to one.

Müller suspected that the occurrence of two kinds of males in a single species might not be rare in animals in which the structure of the males differs widely from that of the females. "But only in those which can be produced in sufficient abundance, will it be possible to arrive at a conviction that we have not before us either two different species, or animals of different ages" (p. 24).

Offering another example from his experience, the shore-hopper (*Orchestia*), Müller pointed out that "the males would be unhesitantly regarded as belonging to two well-marked species if they did not live in the same spot, with undistinguishable females" (p. 26). He indicated that this may be the case for two different kinds of males (*Orchestia telluris* and *sylvicola*) listed in Spence Bates's catalogue, living together in the forests of New Zealand and for which only one form of female is known. "It does not seem to me to be probable that two nearly allied species of these social Amphipoda should occur mixed together under the same conditions of life" (p. 27).

Despite his own belief in the existence of two male forms in a single species and his own discovery of two male forms of *Dias longiremus* geographically distributed, Claus tried to maintain a critical attitude toward Müller's "most remarkable discovery." On the very first page of *The Copepoda of Nice: An Investigation . . . "in Darwin's Sense"* Claus carefully stated that a "scrupulous critique" by "even the most ardent adherent of 'natural selection' . . . might urge consideration of the possibility, touched upon by Müller," that "his most remarkable discovery of two forms of male *Tanais dubius* (?) and two forms of male 'Orchestia Darwinii' with only a single kind of female in each case might in reality in each instance be males of two different species with the females of the less frequent 'smeller' having escaped detection as yet because of their scarcity." For a proper solution to the questions raised by Müller's "remarkable discovery," Claus emphasized the importance of developmental observations. "Only a very thorough comparison of the limbs, and measurement of the parts of the body, and observation furthermore of the development would have enabled us to uncover clearly the differences between the very similar forms" (1866, p. 1).

As a consequence of Darwin's theory, Claus recommended developmental study not only for distinguishing differences between what appear to be very similar forms but also for determining, as Freud did later in the *Three Essays on the Theory of Sexuality* (1905), whether very different forms might not be "forms of development in different stages of growth and age." Thus the smaller claws of Müller's "smellers" might be "those of the younger, though sexually developed male" (p. 2) rather than the characteristic of a different variety. Claus's critical attitude is very much in evidence here even though as he said himself, "I, for my part, entertain no doubts with regard to Müller's statements" (p. 1).

Darwin's significance for Müller's admirable contribution was emphasized by Claus just as it was by Müller himself. Claus was quick to point out that "Müller bases his theories on a number of remarkable facts concerning both external as well as internal structure, concerning the mode of living and development; he bases them on facts which only in the light of Darwin's doctrine stand out in a surprisingly simple and natural relationship while without Darwin they appear a paradox and cannot be explained" (p. 2).

The observation of development emphasized by Claus as a consequence of Darwin's theories proved more useful to Freud in treating hysteria than the popular electrotherapy of Erb, or the "hereditary taint" teaching of Charcot, or his own efforts in "Project for a Scientific Psychology" (1950 [1895]) to apply the neurophysiological approach he had learned from Meynert. In *Three Essays on the Theory of Sexuality* (1905), Freud applied the developmental approach to human sexuality with much the same results as Müller's application of the developmental approach in the Crustacea. Like Müller with the male *Tanais*, Freud found the equally remarkable connection between two distinctive adult forms of sexual behavior, the normal and the perverse. The two male *Tanais* forms arose from a common but different earlier form. Freud recognized that sexual perversions and normal adult sexuality had a common root in infantile sexuality. The developmental approach helped these men recognize the relatedness of forms so different from each other that they had never before been put in the same class. It also helped them to identify properly what had been constantly overlooked. In the case of Müller it was the nauploid form, that is, the infantile form, of the shrimp. For Freud it was the infantile sexuality of mankind.

Müller's findings provide a striking example of how, as a consequence of Darwin's work, zoologists at this time were enabled to recognize the developmental as well as the evolutionary relationship of many hitherto seemingly distinctive forms. Jones, following Bernfeld, pointed out that after Freud left Claus's institute he did not again deal with problems of sexuality in his scientific research until he began to treat hysteria. The question can be raised whether on returning to the problems of sexuality Freud was better prepared by his early zoological training with Claus in Darwinian biology to regard the possibility of developmental relatedness between such diverse forms as, for instance, infantile sucking and both perverse and normal adult seuxal behavior than those physicians who had not pursued evolutionary biology as assiduously as Freud. For example, we know that the contributions made in the nosological tradition of nineteenth-century medicine by Freud's contemporary in psychiatry, Emil Kraeplin, born like Freud in 1856, were more readily adopted by their colleagues in psychiatry during their lifetime than Freud's developmental psychology.

RETROGRESSION

Application of Darwin's developmental approach led Müller, as it had Darwin, to recognition of retrogression. The subject of retrogression is also fully developed in Claus's *Text-Book*. In his work with Claus Freud would have become very knowledgeable about its various forms in the organic world. According to Claus, "while as a general rule the development of the individual is an advance from a simpler and lower organization to one more complex which has become more perfect by a continued division of labour among its parts . . . yet the course of development may, in particular cases, lead to numerous retrogressions, so that we may find the adult animal to be of lower organization than the larva. This phenomenon, which is known as *retrogressive metamorphosis* (*Cirripedia* and *Parasitic Crustacea*), corresponds to the demands of the selection theory, since under more simple conditions of life, where nourishment is more easily obtained (parasitism), degradation and even the loss of parts may be of advantage to the organism" (1884, 1:158).

If Freud was led to read Fritz Müller's *Für Darwin*, as he probably was by the strong emphasis placed on it by Haeckel, Claus, and other writers of the period, he would have become aware that what was regarded as retrogression in the enlightened era of Darwinian biology of the 1870s had only shortly before been looked upon as "degradation" by the creationists. Referring to the parasitic Crustacea, Müller commented that "it would certainly never appear to any one to be a pastime worthy of the Deity, to amuse himself with the contrivance of these marvelous cripplings, and so they were supposed to have fallen by their own fault, like Adam, from their previous state of perfection" (pp. 3–4). Müller preferred to follow Darwin, who wrote in the *Origin* that "in some genera the larvae become developed either into hermaphrodites having the ordinary structure, or into what I have called complemental males: and in the latter the development has assuredly been retrograde; for the male is a mere sack, which lives for a short time, and is destitute of mouth, stomach or other organ of importance, excepting for reproduction" (p. 375).

Similar to the attitude of the creationists in biology was the traditional view in psychiatry of hysteria and sexual perversions as degraded states—a view that Freud encountered and replaced in his developmental psychology with the concept of regression to earlier events or stages of development. In *An Autobiographical Study* Freud recalled that "such occasional sexual activities as it had been impossible to overlook in children were put down as signs of degeneracy or premature depravity or as a curious freak of nature" (*SE* 20:33), terms very similar, as we have just seen, to those ascribed to certain zoological forms by the creationists.

Freud very carefully rechecked the literature after making the bold assertion in the *Three Essays on Sexuality* (1905) that "so far as I know, not a single author has clearly recognized the regular existence of a sexual instinct in childhood" (p. 173). He found that "somatic sexual manifestations from the period before puberty have only attracted attention in connection with phenomena of degeneracy and as indications of degeneracy" (p. 174, n. 2). Even today infantile sexuality is not widely recognized. In the child abuse scare of the late 1980s even mental health workers are ascribing normal sexual curiosity and activity like masturbation to child abuse. Juries are accepting children's fantasies as evidence for convictions except in those rare cases where a defense lawyer or a judge has heard of infantile sexuality and calls for the testimony of a child psychoanalyst, or a psychiatrist who has studied psychosexual development and not simply pharmacological therapy.

Freud's use of regression has been traced to the influence of Hughlings

157

Jackson, whose evolutionary views derived from Spencer, not Darwin.[2] Freud's familiarity with retrogression from Darwinian biology may have helped him to recognize more quickly than others the significance of Jackson's hierarchical theory, which later became one of the models for his psychoanalytic theory. Freud's neurological book *On Aphasia* (1891) utilized Jackson's evolutionary views at a time when Jackson was either unnoticed or "decried as a 'bedlamite theorist'" (Bernfeld 1944, p. 357). According to Smith Ely Jellife, an American neurologist who knew and corresponded with both Freud and Jung, Freud was "the one author who was alive to and who discussed Hughlings Jackson's views and who definitely leveled a strong criticism of the Wernicke–Lichtheim schemes, then much in vogue, in favor of the genetic views that Hughlings Jackson enunciated; particularly on the ideas of the 'dissolution of functions' so ably set forth by Jackson" (pp. 707–08).

"THE DEVELOPMENTAL HISTORY AS PRIMEVAL HISTORY OF THE SPECIES"

Darwin was not alone in succumbing to the tempting idea of recapitulation in the wake of Fritz Müller's findings in *Für Darwin*. The otherwise critical Claus embraced the idea enthusiastically and presented it uncritically throughout his writings as an important consequence of "Darwin's principles and theory of descent." Claus taught Freud from Müller's *Für Darwin*, from his own work, and from the mammalian findings of the Swiss naturalist Ludwig Rütimeyer that it was scientifically justified and rewarding as a consequence of Darwin's theory to assume phylogenetic history from ontogenetic data, which Freud later did unabashedly from his psychoanalytic studies of individual psychology.

In the *Text-Book* Claus taught very explicitly that "according to this theory" that is, Darwin's theory of descent, "the form and structure of larvae are to be considered in relation to the development of the race, *i.e.*, phylogeny, and are to be derived from the various phases of structure through which the larval stages would correspond to the primitive, and the older, on the other hand, to the more highly organized animals which have appeared later in the history of the race. In this sense the developmental processes of the individual constitute a more or less complete recapitulation of the developmental history of the species" (1:122). We saw earlier how Claus's own work on the Copepoda was used by Müller as a clear example of recapitulation in lower animals.

Whether or not Freud ever read Fritz Müller's *Für Darwin*, he would have known its contents from Claus's thorough discussions and lengthy quotations. Claus wrote that "in his excellent book 'For Darwin' Müller proves the genetic affinity of the different groups of Crustaceans by, so to say, making use of the developmental history as primeval history of the species" (1866, p. 1). Müller also found that the recapitulation has been "complicated, however, by secondary variations due to adaptation, which have been acquired in the struggle for existence." Claus designated this second finding as "Fritz Müller's fundamental principle, called by Haeckel the fundamental law of biogenesis" (1884, 1:122).

From Claus's 1876 *Beitrag zur Descendenzlehre* (*Contribution to the Descent Theory*) one may get the impression that Claus is regarding both aspects as Müller's contributions: "Müller thoroughly compared the history of the evolution of Crustaceans from the viewpoint of Darwinism and thus succeeded in reaching important general deductions; they not only shed new, unsuspected light on the value of individual development and its phenomena but we must consider them to be the most significant addition to the doctrine of evolution since the time of Darwin. Comparing the orders and genera which the races must have gone through with the development of the individuals, Müller came to the conclusion that the historical development of the species is mirrored in the individual developmental history. In a short period, 'the changing forms of the embryo and larvae will pass before us, a more or less complete and more or less true picture of the transformations through which the species, in the course of untold thousands of years, has struggled up to its present state.' And in the closest connection with this strongly founded idea, Müller laid the foundation for the second, not less important doctrine of the gradual disappearance of the primeval history" (p. vii), which we discussed in the previous section.

Claus advised caution in the application of the second principle of the gradual disappearance of the primeval history but failed to do so for recapitulation itself, which he regarded as "strongly founded." He warned that "while the correctness of Müller's doctrine of the falsification of the primeval historical source seems irrefutable, we should be extremely cautious in its practical use because one is too easily tempted to use the doctrine absolutely as the explanatory principle and to consider the morphological difficulties and the contradictions in the sense of the wished-for solution whereas on the contrary the truth or probability of an adulteration has to be proven in every individual instance by the connection of the facts" (pp. vii–viii).

Striking evidence for recapitulation was available at this time from higher animals. In the second and third editions of the *Grundzüge* Claus discussed at length the living example of recapitulation in mammals revealed by the work of the Swiss paleontologist Ludwig Rütimeyer (1825–95) on the living and fossil cattle of Java and Borneo. In a footnote to his lengthy discussion Claus quotes Rütimeyer's own striking statement about his conclusions "from the skull forms of these Java, Borneo, etc. living cattle: If anywhere today the strong anatomical observations of a living mammal must before our eyes make the deep impression that intermediate forms exist between various species, whether living or fossil, then this occurs in the *Banting*, where we can see realized from young female animals to mature males, even in a single individual in the short period of a few years, all the modifications of the skull step by step which the family of Buffalo from Miocenic *Hemobos* to today's *Bubalus caffer* or the family of horned cattle from the Pliocenic *Bos etruscus* to today's *Taurus* made during a long series of geological periods" (1872, 1:88 n. 1).

Nevertheless, Claus recognized a breakdown in the parallelism between ontogeny and phylogeny: "It is true that the grades of animal structure do not, like those of the developing individual, follow one upon the other in a single continuous series; and the parallel between the developmental gradation of types in the animal kingdom as a whole and the successive conditions of an individual animal breaks down so far as we distinguish in the former, as opposed to the latter, a number of types of animal structure often overlapping, but still, in their higher development, essentially different from each other" (1884, 1:24). However, at the lower level of development "it is a very striking fact that an embryo provided with a central cavity and a body wall composed of only two layers of cells appears in different groups of animals as a freely moveable larva capable of leading an independent life." Coupling this fact with Huxley's pre-Darwinian 1849 comparison[1] of "the two membranes of the body wall of the Medusae with the outer and inner layers of the vertebrate blastoderm," Claus felt that "it was not a great step . . . to arrive at the conclusion that there was a similar phylogenetic origin for the similar larvae of the very different animal types, and to trace back the origin of organs functionally resembling each other to the same primitive structure" (1:117). The tracing back of the origin of symptoms in mental illness to earlier or more primitive stages of development is, of course, one of the striking features of Freud's psychoanalytic psychology.

11

Freud's Research in Brücke's Institute of Physiology and Meynert's Institute of Cerebral Anatomy

Inasmuch as it is known that Freud had shown
unusual ability in his Gymnasium work, that
already he had been a keen reader of Darwin
and of Goethe, and moreover an enthusiastic
evolutionist, it is not surprising that Brücke
should have put him to work on a natural
history study of phylogenetic as well as
ontogenetic significance, and that this
biogenetic viewpoint should have been carried
over into his psychoanalytic formulations.
Smith Ely Jelliffe, "Sigmund Freud as a
Neurologist"

In describing the ideas of the Brücke
institute, in which Freud worked from 1876 to 1882, Jones acknowledged
his indebtedness to the fine research of Siegfried Bernfeld in "Freud's
Earliest Theories and the School of Helmholtz" (1944) and "Freud's Scientific
Beginnings" (1949). Bernfeld's research and Jones's extensive use of it
in his biography of Freud focused attention on the influence in Freud's life
of Ernst Brücke and of the so-called Helmholtz school, of which Brücke

was an important member. In the absence of similar research on Claus some of the Darwinian influence we have just found in examining Claus's work has been attributed to Brücke.

Jones, racing death to complete his pioneer biography of their mentor and colleague Sigmund Freud, incorporated without quotation marks Bernfeld's words that

> very closely connected with this *dynamic* [Helmholtzian] aspect of Brücke's physiology was his evolutionary orientation. Not only is the organism a part of the physical universe but the world of organisms itself is one family. Its apparent diversity is the result of divergent developments which started with the microscopic unicellular "elementary organisms." It includes plants, lower and higher animals, as well as man, from the hordes of the anthropoids to the peak of his contemporary Western civilization. In this evolution of life, no spirits, essences, or entelechies, no superior plans or ultimate purposes are at work. The physical energies alone cause effects somehow. Darwin had shown that there was hope of achieving in a near future some concrete insight into the "How" of evolution. The enthusiasts were convinced that Darwin had shown more than that—in fact had already told the full story. While the skeptics and the enthusiasts fought with each other, the active researchers were busy and happy putting together the family trees of the organisms, closing gaps, rearranging the taxonomic systems of plants and animals according to genetic relationships, discovering transformation series, finding behind the manifest diversities the homologous identities (1949, pp. 172–73; Jones, 1953–57, 1:42).

An examination of the writings of Brücke, of his assistants, Fleischl von Marxow and Sigmund Ritter von Exner, and of the biography of Brücke by his grandson, E. Theo. Brücke, indicates that this paragraph, particularly the last sentence about what the "active researchers" were doing, applies more appropriately to Claus and his zoological pursuits than to Brücke and his physiological interests. Freud, himself, did his evolutionary-oriented research in Brücke's laboratory rather than Claus's. Nevertheless, there is no evidence that Darwinian biology or questions of evolution were of major interest to Brücke and his assistants, as we have seen they were to Claus. The titles of the works published by Brücke when Freud was with him show no relation to evolution theory. Someone may yet, as I was unable to do, find references to Darwin in the writings of Brücke, Exner, and Fleischl von Marxow and their biographers; no one, however, could claim that Darwin and his theory are conspicuous in this material. Brücke's *Vorlesungen über Physiologie* (*Physiology Lectures*) do not in either the first edition (1873–74) or the second "improved" edition (1875) call attention to the theory of evolution as an essential assumption of physiology even as little as Claus did with the Helmholtzian in his *Text-Book of Zoology*, that is, by discussing and subscribing to it even if not actually applying it in any significant way and without working on the problems inherent at that period in its application.

In one of his 1888 lectures Claus contended that no physiologist could have made Darwin's discovery because he would have lacked knowledge of geology. Physiological interests did not necessarily lead to involvement with the problems of evolution. Claus's discussion of plants and animals revolved around the problem of classification and "The Meaning of the System" whereas Brücke's interest was in finding "the true difference between animals and plants," and "to find the true difference between animals and plants, one must study their alimentation, their processes of assimilation, and their mode of growth" (1875 [1873–74], p. 40). These need not involve genealogical or historical relationships, and there is no evidence that they did for Brücke.

In 1867 Brücke had traveled to Paris in August and later that month to London with his oldest son Hans. In England Brücke visited at Folkestone with Henry Bence-Jones, a chemist as well as a physician, who at the end of 1865 had treated Darwin, "dieted him severely, and as he," Darwin "expressed it, 'half starved him to death'" (F. Darwin, ed. 1887, 2:215), a regimen that apparently helped Darwin recover from an illness that had incapacitated him for most of that year. The recovery may have been due more to what Bence-Jones did not do than to what he did do. Bence-Jones omitted the then fashionable treatment by arsenic, which may have been causing Darwin's symptoms, symptoms inordinately prevalent among famous Victorians of the time, as John Winslow convincingly demonstrates in *Darwin's Victorian Malady: Evidence for its Medically Induced Origin* (1971). Perhaps, as a chemist, Bence-Jones had a healthier respect for the dangers inherent in the chemicals being dispensed by his colleagues.

There is no mention by Brücke's grandson-biographer of Darwin, whose fame could not have escaped him when in 1928 he published his grandfather's biography. E. Theo. Brücke reported that the English publication in 1856 of the work on bloodclotting which his grandfather had submitted for the Lister prize had been the starting point for correspondence with his English colleagues, especially Bence-Jones, but that at the end of August when Brücke was in London most of the scientists were away. Darwin as we know was rarely gone from Down. Not only did Brücke not visit him, but there is no indication that he included Darwin among those he would have liked to see; Bence-Jones probably could have arranged a meeting with Darwin had Brücke been interested. In Paris earlier in August Brücke had "become acquainted with the Parisian physiologists and met in very friendly intercourse with Claude Bernard, Quatrefages and Milne Edwards" (E. Theo. Brücke, p. 81), all of whom as we saw above ("Solving the Riddles of the Universe," in chapter 1) were at best indifferent to Darwin's theory.

Brücke's lifelong friends, Helmholtz and particularly the Berlin physiologist Du Bois-Reymond, were perhaps more interested than their French colleagues. Helmholtz was cited by Huxley when he wrote for the *Contemporary Review* (1871) that "in a dozen years the 'Origin of Species' has worked as complete a revolution in Biological Science as the 'Principia' did in Astronomy . . . because, in the words of Helmholtz, it contains 'an essentially new creative thought'" (in Darwin, 1887–88, 3:132).

As early as 1860, as we saw above (chapter 1), Darwin had "heard that Du Bois-Reymond agrees with me" (1887, 2:254). Haeckel found Du Bois-Reymond in substantial agreement "with regard to the explanation of innate ideas by Darwinism, which he has attempted in his address (1870) on 'Leibnitzian Ideas in Modern Science' (vol. i. of the *Collected Addresses*) and again in his address to the Berlin Academy of Sciences in January 1883 on 'Darwin and Copernicus' (vol. ii of the *Collected Addresses*) when Du Bois-Reymond says, 'For me, Darwin is the Copernicus of the organic world . . .' (partly in identical words)" (1903 [1892], p. 97, n. 6), with those Haeckel had used much earlier (see "Copernicus and Darwin," chapter 1). In an 1876 lecture *Darwin versus Galiani* Du Bois-Reymond was as critical as Claus of the too early attempts at genealogical trees. Haeckel could not forgive Du Bois-Reymond for saying that "the genealogical trees of phylogeny are about as much worth as, in the eyes of the historical critic, are those of the Homeric heroes" (Du Bois-Reymond 1876 in Haeckel 1903 [1892], p. 98, n. 6, and in Claus 1882, p. 516). Claus did not regard this statement by Du Bois-Reymond as anti-Darwinian. He quoted it as a fitting conclusion to his Charles Darwin memorial in the *Wiener Medizinische Blätter* (April 27, 1882).

In 1873 Du Bois-Reymond, who was in his sixth year as perpetual secretary of the Berlin Academy of Sciences, successfully proposed Darwin for election as a corresponding member; Darwin's nomination was seconded by Helmholtz, as well as the astronomer Christian Peters, the geologist

Julius Ewald, the botanist Nathaniel Pringsheim, and also by the pathologist and political activist Rudolf Virchow. A few years later in 1877 Virchow made a political attack on Darwin's theory of descent by connecting it with socialism in an address at the Munich meeting of German naturalists and physicians published in London by John Murray as *Freedom of Science in the Modern State*. The cast of characters attacking or supporting Darwin and the grounds for attack and support were very fluid during the early years of the theory.

In the 1860s the physiology of what has become known in psychoanalytic literature as the Helmholtz school was the most modern, far-reaching, and exciting part of German university teaching. In Freud's day, although past its peak, it was still very active and famous. It had started in the early 1840s with the friendship of Du Bois-Reymond and Brücke, joined shortly afterward by Helmholtz and Karl Ludwig, who, as professor and head of the Physiological Institute at the University of Leipzig, would pioneer the study of physiology as related to the physical sciences and to improvement in laboratory methods and apparatus. They formed a little private club that they enlarged in 1845 to the Berliner Physicalische Gesellschaft (Berlin Physical Society). Its members were mostly young students of Johannes Müller united in their determination to destroy their teacher's fundamental belief, vitalism. It was before this group, with the purpose of giving a sound foundation to the new physiology, that on July 23, 1847, Helmholtz read his famous paper on the principle of the conservation of energy.

Leipzig's famous professor of physiology and anatomy Johannes Müller did not seem to mind and remained the beloved master, setting a remarkable example of tolerance for students' deviating ideas that Brücke, for one, followed in relation to his students. Brücke's teacher, Johannes Müller, is mentioned five times by Freud in his first paper (1877, pp. 1, 2, 7, 10, 13) for Brücke in addition to *Müller's Archiv*. Johannes Müller "in general strictly adhered to the orthodoxy" of the doctrine of the immutability of species but Du Bois-Reymond remembered that "on occasion" Müller "disclosed certain misgivings which troubled him." Du Bois-Reymond considered it sad that their great teacher "did not live to see the 'Katastrophe' which within a year of his death overtook the school of thought that had felt so secure" (1876, p. 10).

Bernfeld thought the best way to summarize the spirit and contents of Brücke's physiological lectures was "with the words used by Freud in 1929 to characterize psychoanalysis from its dynamic standpoint: 'The forces assist or inhibit one another, combine with one another, enter into compromises with one another, etc.'" We cannot agree with Bernfeld's claim that "very closely connected with this dynamic aspect of Brücke's physiology was its evolutionistic orientation" (1949, p. 172), although the elimination of purpose and supernatural design that made Darwin feel like he was committing murder and that aroused great outcries against Darwin's theory was exactly what the members of the Helmholtz school had started out to do in their attempt to fight vitalism and replace *Naturphilosophie* with physicalist physiology. This much we can perhaps grant as implicit in Brücke's viewpoint. However, the compatibility of the Helmholtzian philosophy with evolutionary theory hardly makes clear what position, if any, Brücke took on the many questions that we have seen were raised at the time by Darwin's theory. Perhaps, if we could obtain Brücke's letters to Du Bois-Reymond from 1841 to 1892 that E. Theo. Brücke acknowledged receiving through the kindness of Fraulein Estelle Du Bois-Reymond, we might find some references by Brücke to contemporaneous evolutionary issues in response to his friend's interest in, and closer involvement with, Darwin's theory. However, if the correspondence contains any reference by Brücke to Darwin or his theory, his grandson took no notice of it.

The picture that emerges at present from Brücke's works and biography is of a man not averse to Darwin's theory but not directly involved. According to his grandson, "the first year in Vienna Brücke had—true to the tradition of Müller's school—been busy with a series of special morphological questions, the form and structure of organisms. After that he left work on such problems mostly to his students"; Haeckel was one of those who worked on morphology in Brücke's institute. Brücke "himself turned to a completely general and fundamental problem of morphology, the question of the nature of animal and vegetable cells" (E. Theo. Brücke, p. 97).

Brücke's Institute of Physiology provided a congenial setting in which Freud could continue to pursue his evolutionary interests. The problem that Brücke suggested to Freud can be regarded as a very integral part of the researches into the "How" of evolution referred to by Bernfeld and Jones. Freud, however, did not attribute any evolutionary orientation to the suggestion made by Brücke. Freud simply stated in his *Autobiographical Study* that "Brücke gave me a problem to work out in the histology of the nervous system." In describing his shift from Brücke's institute to research in Meynert's Institute of Cerebral Anatomy Freud says that he, Freud, "nevertheless remained faithful to the line of work upon which I had originally started. The subject which Brücke had proposed for my investigations had been in the spinal cord of one of the lowest of the fishes (*Ammocoetes Petromyzon*); and I now passed on to the human central nervous system" (20:10). Freud's faithfulness was not merely to the study of the nervous system as he himself put it but also to the evolutionary orientation instilled in him by Claus.

In his work in Brücke's laboratory on the *Petromyzon Planeri* Freud discovered that the large nerve cells lying close to, and a little behind, the spinal cord at all levels, which had been studied by the Latvian-born professor of anatomy at Dorpat Ernst R. Reissner, by the German physician and pathological anatomist-discoverer of the insulin-producing cells in the pancreas Paul Langerhans, and others, also occurred in the larval form *Ammocoetes*, as later he was to discover that psychological characteristics of the adult human such as sexuality could also be found in some form in children. His second paper on the subject benefited from an improvement that he made in technique and described in a paper dated May 26, 1879, "Notiz über eine Methode zur anatomischen Präparation des Nervensystems" (Note on a method for anatomical preparation of the nervous system). That Freud was aware early in his scientific work of the importance of new and improved techniques for making discoveries is revealed here. Although this may be obvious today to the initiated, in *The Crayfish* (1880), to which Freud referred in a later paper, Huxley considered it desirable to point out to his readers that "new lights come with new methods of investigation" (p. vii). Later, in his treatment of hysteria, Freud was to recognize the value and limitations of Charcot's and Bernheim's hypnosis and of Breuer's cathartic method and to develop new techniques also for psychological investigation.

Freud was aware of the evolutionary import of his discovery that the Reissner cells were posterior spinal ganglion cell homologues, showing a variety of unipolar and bipolar ganglion cells that previously had been known only in higher vertebrates (unipolar) and lower animals (bipolar). He wrote: "These scattered cells mark the way which the spinal ganglion cells have made through their evolution" (1877–97 trans. in Bernfeld 1949, p. 170). Many years later he drew a connection between these researches and his findings on libidinal development. In one of the *Introductory Lectures on Psycho-Analysis* which he delivered at the Vienna Psychiatric Clinic during the winter terms of 1915–16 and 1916–17, he recalled that "when as a young student I was engaged under von Brücke's direction on my first piece of scientific work, I was concerned with the origin of the posterior nerve-roots in the spinal cord of a small fish of very archaic structure; I found that the nerve-fibres of these roots have their origin in large cells in the posterior horn of the grey matter, which is no longer the case in other vertebrates. But I also discovered soon afterwards that nerve-cells of this kind are present outside the grey matter the whole way to what is known as the spinal ganglion of the posterior root; and from this I inferred that the cells of these masses of ganglia had migrated from the spinal cord along the roots of the nerves. This is also shown by their evolutionary history. But in this small fish the whole path of their migration was demonstrated by the cells that had remained behind."

Freud the psychoanalyst was analogizing from his student discovery to the possibility that "in the case of every particular sexual trend some portions of it have stayed behind at earlier stages of its development, even though other portions may have reached their final goal" (1916–17, *SE* 16:340). The portion of a sexual trend that remained behind Freud called a "fixation." A return to such an earlier stage could also occur and this he called "regression." Therefore, the picture presented by sexual trends was reminiscent of his researches on *Petromyzon*. In both cases evidences of earlier stages of development were still present in the adult. As the study of the ontogenetic development of the *Petromyzon* had offered valuable insight also into the evolutionary development of spinal ganglia, it is not surprising that, when the developmental approach in psychoanalysis proved rewarding, Freud should also seek insights into the evolutionary history of man's personality.

From his work on *Petromyzon* and his next study, "Über den Bau der Nervenfasern und Nervenzellen beim Flusskrebs" ("On the structure of the nerve fibers and nerve cells of the fresh water [river] crayfish," filed with the Academy of Sciences Dec. 15, 1881, and published in the *Bulletin* January 1882), Freud clearly conceived the nerve cells and the fibrils to be one morphological and physiological unit, the later neurones. This anticipation of the neurone theory Freud did not venture to present to specialists in nerve histology. He threw it away instead in a cautious aside during a lecture before the Psychiatric Society shortly after leaving Brücke's institute to seek his fortune as a physician. "If we assume that the fibrils of the nerve fibre have the function of isolated conductive pathways, then we may assume that the pathways which are separated in the nerve fibre are confluent in the nerve cell; then the nerve cell becomes the beginning of all those nerve fibres which are anatomically connected to it. I would transgress the limitations which I have imposed on this paper were I to assemble the facts which are in favor of that assumption; I know that the existing material is not sufficient for a decision on this important physiological problem; yet if that assumption could be proved we would take a great step in the physiology of the elements of the nerve system. Then we could consider the possibility that the nerve as a unit conducts the excitation" (1884 [1882] trans. by Bernfeld 1949, p. 179).

In order to marry, Freud had to relinquish science for private practice. However, throughout his hospital training he was able to continue doing research in Meynert's Laboratory for Cerebral Anatomy. Here again he sought new techniques to further his research. From a hint by Paul Flechsig, Brücke's assistant and Meynert's rival in neurology, he developed a staining with gold chloride with which he was able to obtain a much clearer picture of the finer structure of the nervous system. Freud reported it in the English journal *Brain* as "a new histological method for the study of nerve-tracts in the brain and spinal cord" (1884).

Freud also devised a new method of study from another and more important discovery by Flechsig that the myelinization of the medullary sheaths of nerve fibers does not proceed simultaneously, but first with one group, then with another in precise steps which follow one another in an orderly fashion. Instead of following the standard procedure of studying consecutive slices of the adult brain in order to determine the course and connections of the nerve tracts, Freud studied a series of immature brains, first in kittens and puppies and then in embryos and infants. In the fetal phase one can observe simple pictures in which only a few tracts appear instead of the "inextricable picture of cross-sections, which permit hardly more than a superficial topographical survey" (1886, p. 247, trans. in Bernfeld 1951, p. 212). Freud's method was based on the assumption, which Freud clearly stated, that the earliest structures persist during the development, becoming more and more complicated but "nicht verschuttet" (never buried). He was later to find the persistence of earlier structures true also for psychological development, although more deeply buried.

As we have just seen, Freud in his early histological researches investigated the problem of evolution phylogenetically as well as through the ontogenetic study of the larval and adult forms of *Petromyzon*. In Meynert's Institute for Cerebral Anatomy Freud once again obtained fruitful results by taking the ontogenetic approach. It is not surprising that, when forced by the exigencies of life to turn his attention back to his original interest in the problems of the human personality, he should try the ontogenetic and phylogenetic approaches.

The Expression of the Emotions, Psychiatrie, and Studies on Hysteria

No less a person than the great Meynert, in whose
footsteps I had trodden with such deep veneration and
whose behaviour towards me, after a short period of
favour, had turned to undisguised hostility. . . . I had
carried on an embittered controversy with him in
writing, on the subject of male hysteria, the existence of
which he denied. When I visited him during his fatal
illness and asked after his condition, he spoke at some
length about his state and ended with these words: "You
know, I was always one of the clearest cases of male
hysteria." He was thus admitting, to my satisfaction and
astonishment, what he had for so long obstinately
contested.

Sigmund Freud, *The Interpretation of Dreams*

Psychiatry was the only branch of
medicine proper that held any attraction for Freud as a student. In 1879
he attended the psychiatry lectures given by Professor Theodor Meynert,
"by whose work and personality," Freud recalled many years later, "I had
been struck while I was still a student" (1925 [1924], *SE* 20:10). On leaving

Brücke's Institute of Physiology in 1882 Freud was able to continue his researches in Meynert's Institute of Cerebral Anatomy. In 1883 Freud served for six months as *Sekundararzt* (junior or house physician) in Meynert's Psychiatric Clinic. "One day Meynert, who had given" Freud "access to the laboratory even during the times when" Freud "was not actually working under" him, proposed that Freud "should definitely devote" himself "to the anatomy of the brain, and promised to hand over his lecturing work" to Freud. Meynert "felt he was too old to manage the newer methods." Freud declined "in alarm at the magnitude of the task. It is possible, too," Freud recalled, "that I had guessed already that this great man was by no means kindly disposed towards me."

In the spring of 1885 Freud "was appointed Lecturer [*Dozent*] in Neuropathology on the ground of" his "histological and clinical publications" (20:11–12). It was on Freud's return a year later from Paris with a report of Charcot's work on "male hysteria" that Freud's troubles with Meynert began. In Freud's words, "with my hysteria in men and my production of hysterical paralyses by suggestion, I found myself forced into the Opposition. As I was soon afterwards excluded from the laboratory of cerebral anatomy," of which Meynert was the chief, and "for terms on end had nowhere to deliver my lectures, I withdrew from academic life" (20:15).

Meynert's *Psychiatrie* was begun in 1877 shortly before Freud became Meynert's pupil. It was published in 1884 as Freud's association with Meynert and the Vienna Medical School was coming to an end. It takes note of Darwin's *Expression of the Emotions* (1872), a work to which Freud referred twice in his earliest psychological book, written with Josef Breuer, *Studies on Hysteria* (1893–95). Darwin's *Expression of the Emotions in Man and Animals* appeared in 1872. Freud's library at Maresfield Gardens contains a copy of the Stuttgart edition translated by Carus. Although inscribed "Sigmfreud," it is the one Darwin volume in which Freud did not put a date. There is a strong possibility that Freud obtained it between 1879, when he inscribed Darwin's *Insectivorous Plants* (London 1875) with a similarly condensed signature "SigmFreud," and the year in which he tardily completed his medical studies, 1881. After receiving his degree he inscribed "Dr. Sigmund Freud" in two English first editions, with "6/9/81" in *The Effects of Cross and Self-Fertilization in the Vegetable Kingdom* (London 1876) and with "6/6/83" in *The Variation of Animals and Plants under Domestication* (London 1868).

He probably used the European style of dating, which puts the month after the day. "DrSigmfreud 2/XI 81" was signed in volumes 1 and 2 of

Darwin's *Gesammelte Werke* containing Carus's 1875 translation of *Reise eines Naturforschers um die Welt* (*A Naturalist's Voyage: Journal of Researches etc.* [1860]) and his 1876 translation of *Über die Entstehung der Arten durch Natürliche Zuchtwahl; oder, Die Erhaltung der begünstigen Rassen im Kampfe um's Dasein* (*On the Origin of Species by Means of Natural Selection or The Preservation of Favoured Races in the Struggle for Existence* [1859]). In the early enthusiasm over his status as a medical student, he had written "Sigismundfreud Stud. med. 1875" in his first Darwin acquisition, the two-volume *Die Abstammung des Menschen* (*The Descent of Man*) published that year as volumes 5 and 6 of the *Gesammelte Werke*.

References to Darwin, as far as I have been able to determine, do not appear in Meynert's published works before his 1884 *Psychiatrie*. Nor did Meynert's interest in pursuing the lines opened up for psychiatry by Darwin's *Expressions of the Emotions* find a place in the body of his *Psychiatrie*. It required an appendix. In the author's preface dated Easter 1884 Meynert said of this appendix: "From the notes to be appended to the end of this work, the reader will gather wherein my views have been necessarily modified or supplemented by the investigations of other authors and my latest researches" (1968 [1884], p. vii). The appendix opens a window for us on Meynert's thinking while Freud was with him. Meynert continued the discussion of Darwin's work in a lecture "Mechanik der Physiognomik" at the 1887 Naturforscher-Versammlung (Society of Natural Scientists) at Wiesbaden. By this date Freud's break with Meynert had occurred and Freud had withdrawn from all academic life into private practice. Freud's references to Darwin's *Expression of the Emotions* in the *Studies on Hysteria* are related to Meynert's in the *Psychiatrie*, which Meynert had been preparing while Freud was still with him.

DARWIN'S *EXPRESSION OF THE EMOTIONS* IN MEYNERT'S *PSYCHIATRIE*

Meynert's writings reveal his role in directing Freud's attention to the relevancy for psychiatry of Darwin's work in *The Expression of the Emotions*. Meynert's appendix, "The Mechanism of Expression," opens with the statement that "through such movements as are involved in expression we obtain a clue to the inner life of others" (p. 271). In making use of the expression of emotions as clues in his *Studies on Hysteria* Freud referred to Darwin's work on the subject and utilized points from Darwin touched upon in Meynert's *Psychiatrie*.

The preface to Meynert's *Psychiatrie* reveals that Meynert "deemed it necessary to criticize in its proper connections, Darwin's theory of the inheritance of acquired faculties, as has been done before me by other German authors, among them Du Bois-Reymond and Weismann" (p. vii). The "proper connections" appear in the appendix, where Meynert dealt at length with Darwin's contribution. Although there were points of disagreement between Darwin and Meynert, there are also aspects of Darwin's work that both Meynert and Freud found useful. In Peter Amacher's excellent work on Freud's "Neurological Education and Its Influence on Psychoanalytic Theory," his interest in "Meynert and the Anatomy of Mind" highlighted the differences between Darwin and Meynert. We will be concerned as well with Meynert's positive transmission of Darwin's contribution.

But first their differences, typical of the difference between the study of the organism in England and in Germany. Darwin was not a physiologist and "related his ideas on the inheritance of behavioral patterns to the nervous system in a vague manner." This did not suit Meynert, who worked with the Germans' "relative precision" (Amacher 1965, pp. 36–37) of terms, which we have already seen Claus demand of himself and his colleagues and no doubt also of students like Freud. The concept of instinct as a behavioral determinant was too vague for Meynert. For Meynert, the baring of the teeth in rage described by Darwin was "not the result of reflex action but of cortical stimuli" (1968 [1884], pp. 255–56). According to Meynert, "not even his upright gait, which is surely a universal form of movement, is innate in man; it is acquired with difficulty only through imitation and cortical coordination" (p. 274). Darwin tried to explain many expressions of the emotions as "at first voluntarily performed for a definite object" (1872, pp. 352–53) and then inherited.

Meynert did not question the possibility of the inheritance of acquired characteristics per se. It was only its applicability to man that Meynert was denying (Amacher, personal communication, May 1969). In doing so, Meynert designated such inheritance "Darwin's theory" and taught Freud that the inheritance of acquired faculties and ideas is a "Darwinian doctrine." But for Meynert "the Darwinian doctrine that ideas are inherited and are not the result of perception and association, that movements, even mimical ones, are the result of innate motives, and have nothing to do with imitation and early reflexes," could "hardly be applied to man" (p. 274). According to Amacher, "both Exner and Freud discussed the same sort of behavior that Darwin and Meynert did. They agreed with Meynert that the determinants of behavior were not inherited" (p. 37). Exner's views probably did not differ from Meynert's, but Freud insisted on applying the inheritance of experience and acquired learning to man.

Darwin may not have been rigorous enough for Meynert in theorizing about expressions of emotions but his observations commanded Meynert's respect. Meynert found that in writing the appendix "The Mechanism of Expression," possibly as a rejoinder to Darwin's *Expression of the Emotions*, he was going to have "to refer again and again in the discussion on the pathological forms of physiognomical impulses to the many excellent observations of Darwin, whose views are based upon a larger number of facts than has been at the disposal of other physiognomists" (p. 274). Scientific physiognomy seems to have come into its own with Darwin's publication of *The Expression of the Emotions*. According to Meynert, "up to the time of Darwin" there was only one scientific physiognomist, the Scottish anatomist and Edinburgh professor of surgery Charles Bell. Sir Charles Bell's *Anatomy and Philosophy of Expression* (1806), referred to by Darwin in *The Expression of the Emotions*, contended that man's facial muscles had been specially created for the purpose of serving to express his emotions. Darwin claimed that a natural explanation consistent with the doctrine of evolution could be given in many cases already and would be possible in other cases by extension of his principles.

Darwin sought to understand the expression of the emotions in terms of their function as aids to survival currently or in the past. Freud extended Darwin's study of the expression of the emotions to include hysterical symptoms and verbal expressions. Both Darwin and Freud recognized that even the most minute detail must have meaning in terms of its function for survival, and that if meaning could not be found in terms of the present, then meaning had to be sought in the past. For Freud symptoms had to have meanings in just these Darwinian terms and could not be considered meaningless inherited characteristics or arbitrary productions of the patient. "All these sensations and innervations" in the hysterical patient "belong to the field of 'The Expression of the Emotions,' which, as Darwin has taught us, consists of actions which originally had a meaning and served a purpose" (1893–95, *SE* 2:181).

Recently Stephen Gould has confronted this view in evolutionary biology with the long-standing question of functionless characteristics like male nipples. But, fortunately, not before this evolutionary view had helped Freud to psychological discoveries. This would not be the first time that what might prove to have been a misconception led to an advance in science. Kepler sought the harmony of the spheres in the perfect circular orbits of the planets and to his dismay found ellipses. "I swept the Aegaean stables and found a heap of dung," Kepler is reputed to have said of his results. The now discarded phlogiston theory led Lavoisier to weigh substances before and after combustion, thus establishing modern chemistry with his discovery that something was lost, which he called oxygen, where phlogiston was supposed to be gained, and vice versa. Gould's example of male nipples, for which no use past or present can be found does not prove Darwin, nor Freud for that matter, wrong. Gould himself explains that "male mammals have nipples because females *need* them—and the embryonic pathway to their development builds precursors in all mammalian fetuses, enlarging the breasts later in females but leaving them small" without evident function "in the male" (1980, p. 16, italics added). Not being detrimental, male nipples do not require suppression or elimination.

Bell's creation theory had stifled further investigation of the causes of expression until Darwin. As Darwin pointed out, "No doubt as long as man and all other animals are viewed as independent creations, an effectual stop is put to our natural desire to investigate as far as possible the causes of Expression. By this doctrine, anything and everything can be equally well explained; and it has proved as pernicious with respect to Expression as to every other branch of natural history. With mankind, some expressions . . . can hardly be understood, except on the belief that man once existed on a much lower and animal-like condition. The community of certain expressions in distinct though allied species . . . is rendered somewhat more intelligible, if we believe in their descent from a common progenitor. He who admits on general grounds that the structure and habits of all animals have been gradually evolved will look at the subject of Expression in a new and interesting light" (1873 [1872], p. 12). Like Darwin, Meynert saw no value in the numerous earlier studies of physiognomy that attempted to recognize character from the study of the permanent forms of the features. For Meynert "the old prejudice about the possibilities of inferring the peculiar and special activity of the brain from the configuration of the face or other parts of the body (and that not by reason of knowledge which everyone can acquire, but, as Lavater, [the Swiss poet and mystic who founded 'the science of physiognomy,'] presumed to say, by dint of a special talent), does not deserve serious consideration" (p. 271).

Therefore, for Meynert only Charles Bell deserved to be regarded as a "scientific physiognomist . . . up to the time of Darwin" (p. 272).

Freud regarded Darwin's work as a landmark dividing the history of the physiology of laughter, as well he might from Meynert's teaching of the physiology of expression. In a footnote to his 1905 *Jokes and their Relation to the Unconscious* Freud wrote that "the theme of the physiological explanation of laughter—that is, the tracing back or interpretation of the muscular actions characteristic of laughter—has been treated at length both before and since Darwin, but has still not been finally cleared up" (*SE* 8:146 n. 2). Freud's footnote is appended to a quotation from Spencer's 1860 essay "The Physiology of Laughter." Freud's reference to Darwin introduced Freud's own attempt at an understanding of laughter as an expression of the emotions. "So far as I know, the grimace characteristic of smiling, which twists up the corners of the mouth, appears first in an infant at the breast as it falls asleep. Here it is a genuine expression of the emotions, for it corresponds to a decision to take no more nourishment, and represents as it were an 'enough' or rather a 'more than enough.' This original meaning of pleasurable satiety may have brought the smile, which is after all the basic phenomenon of laughter, into its later relation with pleasurable processes of discharge" (8:146–47 n. 2).

In *The Expression of the Emotions* Darwin had called attention to the value of a small point to which Meynert also referred, from Sir Charles Bell's *Anatomy and Philosophy of Expression* (1806), a work highly regarded for its study of the relationship between respiration and the movements of expression. The small point from Bell's book which Darwin picked up as throwing "a flood of light on several of the most important expressions of the human countenance" is that "the muscles around the eyes are involuntarily contracted during violent respiratory efforts, in order to protect these delicate organs from the pressure of the blood" (p. 2).

In his *Psychiatrie* twelve years after Darwin's *The Expression of the Emotions* Meynert stated that "the respiratory movements have great physiognomical value. Charles Bell, who up to the time of Darwin was the only scientific physiognomist, seems to have appreciated this fact, for he speaks of the facial—the nerve of mimical expression—as the respiratory nerve of the head." Meynert went on to discuss the small point from Bell to which Darwin called attention but did so quite differently, disagreeing with both Bell and Darwin. "Bell connected closure of the lids with respiratory movements. He thought that the former compressed the eyeball, and thus prevented the hyperaemia which might result from the pressure of expiration. But a condition of hyperaemia would be produced by laughing also, which is an aggressive reflex action; and yet there is no active closure of the lids accompanying that act. For this reason it will be better to suppose that closure of the lids is part and parcel of the repulsive reflex per se, and is calculated to screen the external world from the individual, instead of putting him, as it were, into possession of that world" (p. 273).

Meyert knew and taught "Bell's law of the conduction of nerve-force in a *centripetal* direction through the *posterior*, and in a *centrifugal* direction through the *anterior*, spinal roots" (p. 138). But without Darwin's reference would he have been aware of and discussed Bell's small point about the connection between the closure of the lids and respiratory movements, especially in the light of his disdain for all other physiognomy as unscientific until Darwin's *Expression of the Emotions?* A deeper study of Meynert's work would be required for a definitive answer. Here we will merely point out that Meynert himself linked the names of Charles Bell and Charles Darwin as the first two to recognize that "the respiratory movements have a great physiognomical value" (p. 272). Freud employed the idea of the relationship between respiration and the movements of expression in an 1895 paper "On the Grounds for Detaching a Particular Syndrome from Neurasthenia under the Description 'Anxiety Neurosis.'" In this early paper Freud related the symptoms of anxiety to the physiology of respiration in a sexually aroused state.

In the appendix Meynert referred to two aspects of Darwin's principles of the expression of emotions that we find also in Freud, allied (secondary) associations and the overflow of excess excitation or nerve-force. Although Darwin credited the idea of the overflow of excess excitation to Herbert Spencer as well as mentioning other proponents of this view, both Meynert and Freud refer to Darwin and not to Spencer in utilizing this idea. According to Meynert, "Darwin states that the overflow of psychical excitation, even such as may originate in our thoughts, and which gives rise to a change in our features, is equivalent to an excess of nerve-force, which is exhibited in certain typical forms of expression." Earlier on the same page Meynert had written that Darwin demonstrated that "a state of excessive pleasurable emotion may pass into a condition of maniacal excitement, as the result of a dilation of the arterial network of the brain or that a state of pleasurable confusion may end in a transitory swoon (the probable result of subcortical vasomotor stimulation)" (p. 275).

With regard to allied (secondary) associations Meynert found that "on this point Darwin gives a number of apt illustrations from his own experience and that of other authors. In regard to the emotions, it is evident that fear is associated with movements which would accompany the actual experience of the evil feared. A person fearing an accident will wring his hands as he would have done if the accident had actually occurred. Rage is accompanied by movements which would be useful in destroying the obnoxious object; by biting movements, by showing of the teeth, by a pounding with the fist, and by movements such as those of treading upon a disagreeable object and trampling it under foot. These movements are the expression of allied (secondary) associations, and are frequently not recognized as conscious movements" (pp. 275–76). In Meynert's *Psychiatrie,* "there is no evidence of the *unconscious* so well known to hypnotists of the same period." Meynert's "only reference to the unconscious is in the work of Darwin and the physical expression of emotions" (Serota in Ritvo 1970 [1969], p. 302).

In the next paragraph Meynert quoted almost verbatim from Darwin's *The Expression of the Emotions;* his "translator has, therefore, rendered this passage largely in the words of Darwin" (p. 276 n. 1). In continuation of his thought that "an equal interest attaches to other physiognomical movements which are the expression of allied associations, of parallel presentations attending any quiet train of thought" (p. 276), Meynert incorporated the following from Darwin's chapter 1, "The Principle of Serviceable Associated Habits": "A vulgar man, or one lost in fruitless thoughts, who scratches his head, acts as though he were experiencing a familiar uncomfortable sensation. Gratiolet remarks, that a man who rejects a proposition will shut his eyes or turn away his face; he acts as though he did not or would not see the thing; but if he accepts the proposition, he will, by nodding, bring his head nearer to the speaker, and will open his eyes widely, as if he clearly saw the thing." The French physician who studied the physiology of emotions, "Duchenne, remarks, that a person trying to remember something often raises his eyebrows, as if to see it" (Darwin, pp. 32–33; Meynert, p. 276).

FREUD'S APPLICATION OF DARWIN'S PRINCIPLES OF THE EXPRESSION OF THE EMOTIONS

In *The Expression of the Emotions*, through careful observations of his own and close study of such anatomical drawings as those of the German anatomist and pathologist Friedrich Gustav Henle, Darwin had arrived at three principles that he felt provided a fairly satisfactory explanation of many expressions of the emotions. Freud obviously was well acquainted with these principles. At the very start of his psychological work he explicitly used Darwin's first and third principles. Less clear is the contribution, if any, of Darwin's second principle of antithesis to Freud's findings about the role of antithesis in mental functioning. There is enough to suggest that Darwin's second principle may, at the very least, have contributed to Freud's early awareness of antithesis as a characteristic of mental functioning, the nature of which he later determined. It is very likely that Freud's dictum that psychological events are multiply determined applies to Freud's use of antithesis.

Darwin's First Principle: Associated Serviceable Habit

In the *Studies on Hysteria* (1893–95) Freud explicitly referred to Darwin in using Darwin's first principle, that of serviceable associated habit, in his discussion of the extensive use of symbolization by a very gifted hysteric. "When a hysteric" like his patient Frau Cäcelie M., "creates a somatic expression for an emotionally coloured idea by symbolization," it was Freud's opinion that it "depends less than one would imagine on personal or voluntary factors. In taking a verbal expression literally and in feeling the 'stab in the heart' or the 'slap in the face' after some slighting remark as a real event, the hysteric is not taking liberties with words, but is simply reviving once more the sensations to which the verbal expression owes its justification. For how has it come about that we speak of someone who has been slighted as being 'stabbed in the heart' unless it was identifiable by that sensation? What could be more probable than that the figure of speech 'swallowing something,' which we use in talking of an insult to which no rejoinder has been made, did in fact originate from the innervatory sensations which arise in the pharynx when we refrain from speaking and prevent ourselves from reacting to the insult?" Here, in case his readers had not recognized for themselves his indebtedness to Darwin's twenty-year old seminal work in psychology, Freud pointed out that "all these sensations and innervations belong to the field of 'The Expression of the Emotions,' which, as Darwin has taught us, consists of actions which originally had meaning and served a purpose."

These sensations and innervations "may now for the most part have become so much weakened that the expression of them in words seems to us only to be a figurative picture of them, whereas in all probability the description was once meant literally; and hysteria is right in restoring the original innervations. Indeed, it is perhaps wrong to say that hysteria creates these sensations by symbolization." It may even be that hysteria "does not take linguistic usage as its model at all, but that both hysteria and linguistic usage alike draw their material from a common source" (*SE* 2:180–81).

In a passage in "Lecture XXV Anxiety" of the *Introductory Lectures* (1916–17) Freud spoke of the hysterical attack as "the precipitate of a reminiscence" and suggested that normal affects are constructed on the same pattern. He combined the idea that ontogeny repeats phylogeny with Darwin's explanation of affects as relics of actions that originally had a meaning:

> An affect includes in the first place particular motor innervations or discharges and secondly certain feelings; the latter are of two kinds—perceptions of the motor actions that have occurred and the direct feelings of pleasure and unpleasure which, as we say, give the affect its keynote. But I do not think that with this enumeration we have arrived at the essence of affect. We seem to see deeper in the case of some affects and recognize that the core which holds the combination we have described together is the repetition of some particular significant experience. This experience could only be a very early impression of a very general nature, placed in the prehistory not of the individual but of the species . . . —an affective state would be constructed in the same way as a hysterical attack and, like it, would be the precipitate of a reminiscence. A hysterical attack may thus be likened to a freshly constructed individual affect, and a normal affect to the expression of a general hysteria which has become a heritage (*SE* 16:396).

In *A Phylogenetic Fantasy* (1915) Freud had, a little more than a year earlier, speculated on a scenario for this heritage (see "Freud's Interest in Lamarck," in chap. 2). But even in a public lecture where the scenario might have entertained his audience and made him more popular, he limited himself simply to "a general hysteria which has become a heritage."

In his important 1926 work *Inhibitions, Symptoms and Anxiety*, Freud repeated this view: "Anxiety is not newly created in repression; it is reproduced as an affective state in accordance with an already existing mnemic image. . . . Affective states have become incorporated in the mind as precipitates of primaeval traumatic experiences, and when a similar situation occurs they are revived like mnemic symbols. I do not think I have been wrong in likening them to the more recent and individually acquired hysterical attack and in regarding them as its normal prototypes"

(*SE* 20:93). Although in this work, too, Freud was primarily concerned with the affect of anxiety, he did not fail to state that he held this view for all affects: "In my opinion the other affects are also reproductions of very early, perhaps even pre-individual, experiences of vital importance; and I should be inclined to regard them as universal, typical and innate hysterical attacks, as compared to the recently and individually acquired attacks which occur in hysterical neuroses and whose origin and significance as mnemic symbols have been revealed by analysis." Freud would have liked "to be able to demonstrate the truth of this view in a number of such affects" but acknowledged that this "is still very far from being the case" (20:133).

In development of his first principle, that of associated serviceable habit, Darwin had in *The Expression of the Emotions* stated a corollary suggestive of the hierarchical view that Hughlings Jackson developed a decade later: "Some actions ordinarily associated through habit with certain states of the mind may be partially repressed through the will, and in such cases the muscles which are least under the separate control of the will are the most likely to act, causing movements which we recognize as expressive" (p. 28). Darwin, of course, was aware that the involuntary muscles were an earlier development than the voluntary, and Freud, too, would have known this in reading Darwin. According to the Jacksonian model used by Freud "the nervous system consists of a hierarchy of integrations in which the higher ones inhibit or control the lower, and damage to or suppression of the higher ones reinstates the function of the lower." This Jacksonian model, closely related to both the genetic and the topographic models in psychoanalysis, provided Freud with the "means for systematically coordinating those behavior phenomena which are not attended by voluntary control and/or consciousness with those which are" (Rapaport 1960, p. 23).

Darwin's Second Principle: Antithesis

Darwin established as his second principle for the understanding of the expessions of the emotions the principle of antithesis. Darwin's principle of antithesis is limited to observing that certain expressions of the emotions that cannot be understood in terms of any current or former usefulness can be understood as the antithesis, or opposite, of the useful forms of an antithetical emotion. In contrast to Freud's acknowledged applications in the *Studies on Hysteria* of Darwin's first and third principles, Darwin's second principle receives no direct mention in either Freud's work or

Meynert's *Psychiatrie*. In the *Studies on Hysteria* Freud did employ the mechanism of "putting into effect of antithetic ideas" in close juxtaposition to one of his references to Darwin's *The Expression of the Emotions*. After being reminded by the behavior of one of his patients, Frau Emmy von N., "of one of the principles," actually the third principle, "laid down by Darwin to explain the expression of the emotions—the principle of the overflow of excitation [Darwin 1872, chapter 3], which accounts, for instance, for dogs wagging their tails" (*SE* 2:91), Freud applied the concept of antithetical ideas to the understanding of some of her other behavior but without any specific reference to Darwin's principle of antithesis.

Darwin himself had closely intertwined his second principle of antithesis with his other two principles, to which Freud did refer directly. In the memorable paragraph in which Darwin illustrated his principle of antithesis by contrasting the antithetical postures of the hostile dog and of the happy dog with its wagging tail, Darwin started with the first principle of associated serviceable habit in describing the hostile dog; he also called attention to the third principle of the overflow of excess excitation to explain the movements of the happy dog. The paragraph is a beautiful example of Darwin's careful observations of bodily expression of the emotions to which scientists are returning today. The posture of the hostile dog is understandable as readying him for attack and thus is illustrative of the first principle of associated serviceable habit, which Darwin had discussed in a previous chapter. "When a dog approaches a strange dog or man in a savage or hostile frame of mind he walks upright and very stiffly; his head is slightly raised, or not much lowered; the tail is held erect and quite rigid; the hairs bristle, especially along the neck and back; the pricked ears are directed forwards and the eyes have a fixed stare; (see figs. 5 and 7). These actions, as will hereafter be explained, follow from the dog's intention to attack his enemy, and are thus to a large extent intelligible. As he prepares to spring with a savage growl on his enemy, the canine teeth are uncovered, and the ears are pressed close backwards on the head; but with these latter actions, we are not here concerned" (pp. 50–51).

What Darwin was concerned with here was the posture of the happy dog, which cannot be understood as serviceable to the dog. "Let us now suppose that the dog suddenly discovers that the man whom he is approaching, is not a stranger, but his master; and let it be observed how completely and instantaneously his whole bearing is reversed. Instead of walking upright, the body sinks downwards or even crouches, and is thrown into flexuous movements; his tail, instead of being held stiff and upright, is lowered and wagged from side to side; his hair instantly becomes smooth; his ears are depressed and drawn backwards, but not closely to the head; and his lips hang loosely. From the drawing back of the ears, the eyelids become elongated, and the eyes no longer appear round and staring." At this point Darwin called attention to the operation of his third principle, the overflow of excess excitation. "It should be added that the animal is at such times in an excited condition from joy; and nerve-force will be generated in excess, which naturally leads to action of some kind." However, the third principle does not account for the specific behavior of the happy dog. Nor is the first principle applicable. "Not one of the above movements, so clearly expressive of affection, are of the least direct service to the animal." For a complete understanding of the functionless movements of the happy dog, the second principle of antithesis is required in addition to the third principle of the overflow of excess excitation. "They are explicable, as far as I can see, solely from being in complete opposition or antithesis to the attitude and movements which, from intelligible causes, are assumed when a dog intends to fight, and which consequently are expressive of anger" (p. 51).

In the *Studies on Hysteria* Freud tried to understand some of his patient's behavior—"a more complicated method of conversion"—in terms of the "putting into effect of antithetical ideas." Darwin had gone from one type of behavior to its antithesis without the intervention of ideas or thoughts as we just saw in the above example of the dog. Freud later discovered that antitheses are compatible in the unconscious and that this compatibility is one of the features distinguishing the primary process of the id from the secondary process of the ego in mental functioning. This later discovery of Freud's reveals that the principle of antithesis is as automatically operative in the more primitive aspects of man's mental processes as it is in the automatic behavior observed and described by Darwin in animals.

Whether Freud's awareness of the usefulness of the concept of antithesis for understanding behavior comes from Darwin or another source would require a thorough study of the history of the concept of antithesis not only in science and psychology but also in philosophy, from which, as pointed out earlier, certain aspects of psychology were just beginning to be separated in Freud's student days. As Freud successfully used two of Darwin's three principles of the expression of the emotions, it is highly probable that he would have tried the effectiveness of the remaining one. But on this point we cannot be sure. Freud did not specifically relate his

183

mechanism of "the putting into effect of antithetic ideas" to Darwin's principle of antithesis. In the 1892–93 paper in which he originally introduced this mechanism, Freud does not mention Darwin.

In the *Studies on Hysteria* Freud employed it in the understanding of "some of the striking motor phenomena exhibited by Frau von N.," which Freud wrote "were simply an expression of the emotions and could easily be recognized in that light." Some of Frau Emmy von N.'s "striking motor phenomena" reminded Freud "forcibly of one of the principles laid down by Darwin to explain the expression of the emotions—the principle of the overflow of excitation [Darwin 1872, chapter 3], which accounts, for instance, for dogs wagging their tails." Darwin, as we saw, found the principle of the overflow of excitation insufficient to account fully for the tail-wagging of dogs. For such unserviceable behavior he also needed the principle of antithesis. Is it just coincidence that Freud's train of thought goes immediately from reference to Darwin's "principle of the overflow of excess excitation" and his famous dog example to employment of "the mechanism which" he had "described, in a short paper on the treatment of a case by hypnotic suggestion [1892b], as 'the putting into effect of antithetic ideas'" to explain "a more complicated method of conversion . . . revealed by Frau von N.'s *tic*-like movements, such as clacking with the tongue and stammering"?

According to Freud, "the process, as exemplified in" Frau von N.'s *tic*-like movements "would be as follows. Our hysterical patient, exhausted by worry and long hours of watching by the bedside of her sick child which had at last fallen asleep, said to herself: 'Now you must be perfectly still so as not to awaken the child.' This intention probably gave rise to an antithetic idea in the form of a fear that she might make a noise all the same that would wake the child from the sleep which she had so long hoped for. . . . In our patient's state of exhaustion the antithetic idea, which was normally rejected, proved itself the stronger. It is this idea which put itself into effect and which, to the patient's horror, actually produced the noise she dreaded" (*SE* 2:91–92).

As early as the *Studies on Hysteria* Freud thought that the mechanism of antithesis was operative in normal psychology though not to the same extent as in neurotics. "Similar antithetic ideas arise in us in a marked manner when we feel uncertain whether we can carry out some important intention." The only difference is that "neurotics, in whose self-feeling we seldom fail to find a strain of depression or anxious expectation, form greater numbers of these antithetic ideas than normal people, or perceive them more easily; and they regard them as of more importance" (2:92).

Darwin's Third Principle and the Overflow of Excess Excitation

In the introduction to *The Expression of the Emotions* Darwin acknowledged the usefulness of what he called Herbert Spencer's "general law that feeling passing a certain pitch, habitually vents itself in bodily action" and that "an overflow of nerve-force undirected by any motive, will manifestly take first the most habitual routes; and if these do not suffice, will next overflow into the less habitual ones" (p. 9). Darwin referred to excessive nerve-force as we saw above in his happy dog example of his second principle, that of antithesis. As we have already seen, the second and third principles were closely associated by Darwin in the very example of the wagging tail of the happy dog to which Freud referred in the case of Frau Emmy von N. Darwin's formulation of his third principle is "that certain actions, which we recognize as expressive of certain states of the mind, are the direct result of the constitutions of the nervous system, and have been from the first independent of the will, and, to a large extent, of habit. When the sensorium is strongly excited nerve-force is generated in excess, and is transmitted in certain directions, dependent on the connection of the nerve-cells, and, as far as the muscular system is concerned, on the nature of the movements which have been habitually practiced" (p. 66).

In the *Studies on Hysteria* Freud, like Meynert before him, attributed the principle of the overflow of excess excitation to Darwin and not to Spencer. Employing Darwin's concept of motor phenomena as expressions of emotions in his case of "Frau Emmy von N.," Freud credited Darwin with the principle of the overflow of excitation, which Darwin had used extensively in *The Expression of the Emotions*. "Some of the striking motor phenomena exhibited by Frau von N. were simply an expression of the emotions and could easily be recognized in that light. Thus, the way in which she stretched her hands in front of her with her fingers spread out and crooked expressed horror, and similarly her facial play. This, of course, was a more lively and uninhibited way of expressing her emotions than was usual with women of her education and race. Indeed, she herself was restrained, almost stiff in her expressive movements when she was not in a hysterical state. Others of her motor symptoms were, according to herself, directly related to her pains. She played restlessly with her fingers or rubbed her hands against one another so as to prevent herself from screaming. This reason reminds one forcibly of one of the principles laid down by Darwin to explain the expression of the emotions—the principle of the overflow of excitation [Darwin 1872, chapter 3], which accounts, for instance, for dogs wagging their tails." Freud followed Darwin's well-known example from man's best friend with one from our own human behavior. "We are all accustomed, when we are affected by painful stimuli, to replace screaming by other sorts of motor innervations. A person who has made up his mind at the dentist's to keep his head and mouth still and not to put his hand in the way, may at least start drumming with his feet" (*SE* 2:91).

In the theoretical discussion in the *Studies on Hysteria* Breuer, Freud's coauthor of this work, developed the overflow of excitation or nerve-force into what has come to be known in psychoanalysis as the constancy principle. However, Breuer attributed the constancy principle to Freud. Freud wrote with regard to these theoretical discussions that he and Breuer had discussed the material so long and so intimately that it was no longer possible to distinguish which ideas each had introduced. He always chose to give the credit to Breuer. However, the constancy principle Breuer attributed very specifically to Freud; and the posthumous publication of some earlier writings by Freud confirm that he did employ this concept earlier than Breuer's theoretical discussion in the *Studies on Hysteria*. Here is Strachey's translation of Breuer's words: "Thus the cerebral elements, after being completely restored, liberate a certain amount of energy even when they are at rest; and if this energy is not employed functionally it increases the normal intracerebral excitation. The result is a feeling of unpleasure. Such feelings are always generated when one of the organism's needs fails to find satisfaction. Since these feelings disappear when the surplus quantity of energy which has been liberated is employed functionally, we may conclude that the removal of such surplus excitation is a need of the organism. And here for the first time we meet the fact that there exists in the organism a *'tendency to keep intracerebral excitation constant'* (Freud).

"Such a surplus of intracerebral excitation is a burden and a nuisance, and an urge to use it up arises in consequence. If it cannot be used in sensory or ideational activity, the surplus flows away in purposeless motor action, in walking up and down, and so on, and this we shall meet with later as the commonest method of discharging excessive tensions" (2:197).[1]

According to Freud's theory as he formulated it in his magnum opus, *The Interpretation of Dreams* (1900), the activity of a hypothetical primitive psychic apparatus is "regulated by an effort to avoid an accumulation of excitation and to maintain itself so far as possible without excitation. For that reason it is built upon the plan of a reflex apparatus." According to this theory, "the accumulation of excitation . . . is felt as unpleasure and . . . sets the apparatus in action with a view to repeating the experience of satisfaction, which involved a diminution of excitation and was felt as pleasure" (*SE* 5:598). In the event that "the primitive apparatus is impinged upon by a perceptual stimulus which is a source of painful excitation, unco-ordinated motor manifestations will follow until one of them withdraws the apparatus from the perception and at the same time from the pain. . . . There will be an inclination in the primitive apparatus to drop the distressing memory-picture immediately, if anything happens to revive it, because if its excitation were to overflow into perception it would provoke unpleasure." Here, as Freud pointed out, we have "the prototype . . . of *psychical repression*" (5:600). And "the theory of repression," Freud declared in his "History of the Psycho-Analytic Movement" (1914), "is the corner-stone on which the whole structure of psycho-analysis rests" (*SE* 14:16).

13

Conclusion

Two statements by Freud provided the basis for the organization of this attempt to trace Darwin's influence as it might have reached Freud during his formative years, first as an adolescent still in *Gymnasium* and then as a biologist-in-training at the University of Vienna Medical School. Part I has had to rely entirely on circumstantial evidence. A plethora of material in the popularizations and the Darwin publications of this period supports and elaborates Freud's reference to the excitement and topicality of Darwin's theories. Much of it, even the unimportant or since forgotten, reappears in Freud's own writings. We have not been able to find any specific work by or about Darwin that we know Freud possessed, read, or had as an assignment as a *Gymnast*. But Freud's friend Silberstein could have recognized Darwin's *Voyage of the Beagle*, an ideal boys' adventure story of the period, as the inspiration for Freud's communication to him of an ambition for "a ship on the ocean with all the instruments the researcher needs" (Gay 1988, p. 26). And this same letter to Silberstein just before Freud started medical school reveals that Freud knew enough about the books of the English Darwinian scientists Tyndall, Huxley, Lyell, and Darwin to be confident that they "would always keep him a partisan of their nation" (p. 31).

Part II is on firmer ground. Exploration of Darwin's influence during Freud's medical school training proved richly rewarding. Two professors with whom Freud was closely connected taught aspects of Darwin's work that were crucial to Freud's later psychological work. Claus's prolific scien-

Conclusion

tific writings, *Text-Books*, and *Autobiographie* reveal that Freud's four years of intensive zoological pursuits, which included his very first research, were with a man who had shortly before visited Darwin at his home, whose contributions to Darwin's theory might already have been known to Freud from Fritz Müller's higher popular *Für Darwin*, and who was deeply involved in the issues and teaching of the new Darwinian biology. Not Brücke, as assumed until now from Freud's ontogenetic and phylogenetic researches in Brücke's laboratory, but Claus turned out to be the professor from whom Freud obtained his scientific evolutionary orientation. There is a striking consistency in the views maintained by Darwin, Claus, and Freud on aspects of Darwin's theory that were controversial at the time or subsequently became so. Some, like the genetic, are fundamental to Freud's work. Others, like use-inheritance, have been discredited scientifically but survive in Freud's writings as vestigial remains of what is now antiquated about Darwin's theory.

We also discovered that during Freud's lengthy association with Meynert, his professor of psychiatry and cerebral anatomy had come to appreciate from Darwin's *Expression of the Emotions* the value of expressions as clues to the inner workings of other people's minds. Meynert at this time also began to teach the two principles from Darwin's *Expression of the Emotions* that Freud explicitly used in the *Studies on Hysteria*. In addition, we had the good fortune with the aid of Freud's housekeeper to find eight Darwin volumes signed and/or dated by Freud between 1875 and 1883. Not among them was the one volume of the *Descent of Man* that Jones reported Freud had. There is good reason to believe that it remained in Jones's library at his death, Jones having been allowed to borrow it for the Freud biography.

The ideas now considered most basic to Darwin's theory have turned out to be basic to Freud's theory too. Aspects of Darwin's theories discarded with time may have seemed essential to Freud for his speculations in applied psychoanalysis but are no loss to his scientific structure. It is difficult to assess with any precision the exact amount of each specific influence to be assigned to Darwin. No claim can be made for Darwin as the *exclusive* source of any one of Freud's ideas. Darwin's achievement was the convincing synthesis of an enormous quantity of essential observations that threw new light on *old* ideas. It is the cumulative effect of these ideas as a consequence of Darwin's work that is impressive. It is probably also psychologically inaccurate to assume that any influence is exclusive, for, as Freud pointed out, psychological phenomena are overdetermined.

Conclusion

Natural selection comes closest to being original with Darwin's theory. Darwin had difficulty finding predecessors when he announced jointly with Wallace in 1858. At the time of his first public presentation of his theory to the Linnean Society, Darwin did not as yet know of the 1831 reference to natural selection by Patrick Matthew. In trying to make his theory palatable, Darwin opened by pointing to a Swiss botanist as one predecessor, at least for the struggle for existence. "De Candolle, in an eloquent passage, has declared that all nature is at war, one organism with another, or with external nature" (1958 [1858], p. 259). In the accompanying "Abstract of a letter from Charles Darwin to [his Harvard botanist friend] Professor Asa Gray of Boston, U.S.A., Dated Down, 5 September 1857" Darwin juxtaposed natural selection and the predecessors he found for the struggle for existence. "I think it can be shown that there is such an unerring power at work in *Natural Selection* (the title of my book), which selects exclusively for the good of each organic being. The elder de Candolle, W. Herbert, and Lyell have written excellently on the struggle for life; but even they have not written strongly enough" (p. 265). By the third edition of the *Origin* Darwin was able to include Patrick Matthew's 1831 recognition of "the full force of the principles of natural selection," which Matthew had "estimated . . . as a priori recognisable fact—an axiom requiring only to be pointed out to be admitted by unprejudiced minds of sufficient grasp" (pp. xiv–xv).

Wallace, with whom Darwin jointly announced the "Natural Means of Selection," is mentioned by Freud only once, half a century later and in connection with Darwin. Nor is he prominent in the writings of Haeckel and Claus, who were primarily occupied with what they regarded as Darwin's theories. From Freud's point of view it was "Darwin's theories" that inspired him to a life of science. In applying the idea of natural selection or survival value, as in the "Project," Freud thought of himself as "pursuing Darwinian lines of thought." Natural selection operates by eliminating the less fit. That which survives is useful or was at one time. The idea seems simple enough, but it was a difficult one for most scientists at the time, steeped in the creationist paradigm. Even Bronn, Darwin's first German translator, did not fully grasp it.

Darwin applied it to psychology in his first principle of expression, which Meynert taught and Freud applied in the *Studies on Hysteria*. Freud would already have learned from Claus that "it would be rash to claim," as Nägeli was doing, "that the so-called 'morphologic characteristics' which now seem useless and hence *appear* unimportant for the

190

struggle for survival were of absolutely no value even at the time of their occurrence" (1876 [1866–68], 3d ed., 1:67). Both Darwin and Freud recognized that even the most minute detail must have meaning in terms of its function for survival, and that if it could not be found in terms of the present, its meaning had to be sought in the past. Recently, Gould has pointed out another way to locate the function of useless features like male nipples: in the opposite sex because of the commonality of the earliest embryological form of the two sexes.

Freud extended the study of the expressions of the emotions to include hysterical symptoms and verbal expressions. He paid attention to such seemingly meaningless phenomena as parapraxes and dreams and found their value, their meaning often derived from the past. For Freud symptoms could no longer be considered meaningless inherited characteristics or arbitrary productions of the patient. "All these sensations and innervations" in the hysterical patient "belong to the field of 'The Expression of the Emotions,' which, as Darwin has taught us, consists of actions which originally had a meaning and served a purpose" (1893–95, *SE* 2:181). During Freud's formative years Darwin and his supporters acknowledged that it was yet to be determined how great a role in evolution should be attributed to natural selection. The progress of science has proved it to be not only Darwin's most original, but probably his most significant, contribution. Darwin's conceptualization of it in his first principle of expression is in itself a clear, direct, and significant contribution from Darwin to Freud.

None, least of all Darwin, claimed originality for the idea of evolution. It had been discredited as *Naturphilosophie* and covered with silence by German scientists in the era up to Darwin's announcement. For Freud and his generation of schoolboys Darwin was the inspirational source of the idea. "Evolution was the key to everything and could replace all the beliefs and creeds which one was discarding" (Goldschmidt 1956, p. 35). Haeckel proclaimed that the historical approach which Darwin had used with such world-shaking success to find a scientific solution to the problem of species was the key to every problem. Freud's application of this key or clue to the problems of the neuroses is basic to psychoanalysis and provides its genetic or Darwinian viewpoint.

Fritz Müller's application of the genetic approach in his testing of Darwin's theory led to a remarkable discovery, that of two distinct male *Tanais* with only a single female form. Classified traditionally as two species, they were identified by Müller as developing from the same nauplius form. Claus confirmed this exciting finding with his own observations on the

Conclusion

Copepoda of Messina and Nice. Applying the same approach to his observations of human behavior, Freud was able to recognize the genetic relationship of infantile behavior and two distinct classes of adult sexual behavior, normal and perverse.

Even Claus, who was more cautious than Haeckel, reported that "genetic questions attained prominence in all branches of biology" in the wake of Darwin's "successful final victory over the hypothesis of creation" (January 2, 1888, p. 4). Freud worked with success on genetic questions in his own researches in Brücke's Institute of Physiology and in Meynert's Institute of Cerebral Anatomy. Dr. Freud's youngest child and his scientific heir, Anna Freud, commented that "there never was any doubt about psychoanalysis as a *genetic* psychology. The genetic point of view had a recognized existence from the moment when psychoanalytic exploration turned from the neurotic problems of adult life to their forerunners in childhood and demonstrated the impact of early or later happenings and patterns" (1969, pp. 50–54), that is, from the moment Freud made this turn.

But it is not the whole of psychoanalysis, Anna Freud hastened to point out. "Psychoanalytic thinking, in classical terms, implied the specific demand that every clinical fact should be approached from four aspects: *genetically*, as to its origin; *dynamically*, as to the interplay of forces of which it is the result; *economically*, with regard to its energy charge; *topographically* (later *structurally*), concerning its localization within the mental apparatus" (p. 48), and, since Hartmann, also *adaptively*. As the pioneer of child psychoanalysis both clinically and scientifically Anna Freud may have felt responsible for the fact that the genetic viewpoint "for the moment" was "outstripping most other interests, and it may take some time until the other metapsychological aspects catch up again with the genetic one which has strayed ahead" (p. 52).

The genetic viewpoint has continued to be heuristic. Today we witness a burgeoning industry in infant research. The work of the late Margaret Mahler and her colleagues have added *separation-individuation* and the *rapprochement phase* to the vocabulary of trained preschool educators. The status of infant research is testified to by the entrance professionally of a great number of males into a field of observation more usually left to mothers and grandmothers. Darwin's observations of his own infants was a long-overlooked model. His father-in-law Josiah Wedgwood had confessed to "eavesdropping at the nursery door." Fliess had observed his children but Freud had to admit that the women would not permit him, Freud, into the nursery. A "hen-pecked" Freud? (Jones, who had the opportunity as a visitor to observe the Freud family from the perspective of a different culture, had found Freud "uxorious.")

Darwin, Claus, and Freud were all dedicated to development by gradation, or a continuum. Darwin wrote that it gave him "a cold shudder to hear any one speculating about a true crustacean giving birth to a true fish!" as the British geologist Murchison was doing. In Germany the idea that gave Darwin "a cold shudder" was seriously proposed and known as Kölliker's theory of heterogeneous generation. It was favored by such great scientists as von Baer, who conjectured that the sudden flowering of past types such as trilobites without apparent transitional stages could be accounted for, possibly in analogy with his embryological observations, by the greater plasticity and modifiability of newly arisen types that have become rigid with the passage of time.

Because of its identification with development by gradation, Darwin's theory was considered moribund at the turn of the century with the mistaken discovery of mutations by Hugo de Vries. Even Darwin's great champion, Huxley, criticized Darwin for his adamant insistence that "natura non facit saltum" (nature makes no jumps). Although it was at issue at this time, the concept was an ancient one. Freud would have been familiar with it from reading Goethe before encountering its application to development in Haeckel's popularizations, Darwin's own writings, Claus's teachings, or the controversies aroused over it by Darwin's theory. Haeckel credited Goethe with "guessing" at the unity of nature but gave Darwin the credit for establishing it scientifically as a continuum from the inorganic through the plant and animal kingdoms to the highest organic form. Darwin gave Lamarck credit for his "conclusion on the gradual change of species." Claus taught that modern geology also supported that idea; his authority was Lyell, who "has proved in a convincing way on geological ground . . . that the past history of the earth consists essentially of a gradual process of development" (1884 [1866–68], 1:66).

In defending himself against some of Haeckel's criticisms, Claus had to point out that classifications were still useful even though the reality was a continuum without breaks. Fifty years later Freud felt the same need to call to the attention of his listeners that his psychosexual stages were merely convenient divisions of what he regarded as a continuum from the beginning. He did not regard the continuum as obvious to his audience, although he was devoted to it in his own thinking just as Darwin had been. Neither Claus nor Freud seemed inclined at any time to join Huxley, von Baer, Kölliker, Murchison, de Vries, and others in accepting the possibility of development by sudden jumps. They were in complete accord with Darwin on the issue of development by gradation. The question has been reopened today by Gould.

Darwin's concept of evolution differed from Lamarck's on two essential points little thought of today, the roles of "will" or "volition" and of an inner orthogenetic force. Lacking the mechanism of natural selection, Lamarck introduced what Darwin called "the Lamarck nonsense of the slow willing of adaptation." In 1903 T. H. Morgan tried to correct what he considered a long-standing misconception of the importance of the role of will in Lamarck's theory and to relegate its function to the more acceptable "inheritance through exercise or use." Morgan's success may be responsible for the identification today of Lamarck's name with the belief in "use-inheritance."

Although today Freud's life-long insistence on use-inheritance has him labeled as Lamarckian, his own association with the name of Lamarck we found to be the older one of volition. In the second decade of this century Freud sought out Lamarck's *Philosophie Zoologique*, apparently for the first time, in hope of finding a biological basis in evolution for the concept he was developing of the ego as the organ of adaptation capable of will and volition. Nothing came of it. At the time he was also hoping for insights into mental illnesses from extension of his 1913–14 use in *Totem and Taboo* of the biological principle "ontogeny repeats phylogeny." Imagining scenarios for the ontogenetic origins of mental illnesses proved fruitless and were discarded by Freud. The recent discovery and posthumous publication of this failed effort may reinforce the twentieth-century misconception that Freud was "a Lamarckian and furthermore was substantially ignorant as to what Darwin was talking about" (Wright 1988, p. 30).

Darwin also criticized what he called "Lamarck's law of progressive development." It was revived with Darwin's theory by Nägeli, von Baer, and others who preferred an inner orthogenetic force toward perfection rather than the blind operation of natural selection on chance variations. Darwin's earliest German translator, Bronn, found an inner orthogenetic force easier to comprehend than natural selection. Freud, with but one exception, was never enough of an optimist to believe in inevitable progress. The best he could hope for was the reassertion of Eros in the eternal struggle with Thanatos.

Darwin's theory, unlike those based on an inner orthogenetic force toward progress, allowed a backward as well as a forward direction in development, retrogression (or regression) as well as progression; also fixation.

Conclusion

Freud himself drew an analogy in 1915 between what he termed "fixations" and his earlier evolutionary research. "When as a young student I was engaged under von Brücke's direction, on my first piece of scientific work,[1] I was concerned with the origin of the posterior nerve-roots in the spinal cord of a small fish of very archaic structure. . . . In this small fish the whole path of the migration [of the nerve cells] . . . also shown by their evolutionary history . . . was demonstrated by the cells that had remained behind." Freud's analogy was to the possibility that "in the case of every particular sexual trend some portions of it have stayed behind at earlier stages of development, even though other portions may have reached their goal" (1916–17 [1915–17], *SE* 16:340). A return to such an earlier stage also could occur and this Freud called "regression."

The model for Freud's highly sophisticated theories of regression has rightly been seen as Hughlings Jackson's hierarchy of neural levels. Jackson's evolutionary views derived from Spencer, not Darwin. Here we have proposed that Freud's early and deep involvement with Darwinian biology may account for Freud's unusually early receptivity in his book *On Aphasia* (1891) to Jackson's evolutionary ideas at a time when Jackson was otherwise almost unnoticed. More specifically we found that Darwin had developed in *The Expression of the Emotions* a corollary to his first principle that was suggestive of the hierarchical view which Jackson developed a decade later.

Darwin's theories created a Zeitgeist that gave greater emphasis than did Darwin himself to "conflict" and to the role of environment. Conflict dominated Freud's thinking throughout his life as it did the thinking of many German biologists of that era. After Freud's death Hartmann introduced the concept of the "conflict-free ego sphere" and demonstrated that conflict was not the complete story for psychoanalysis any more than it was for biology. Bernfeld had earlier traced Freud's predilection for two opposing forces to the views of what he misnamed the "Helmholtzian school," taught by Brücke. The reinforcing effect of two such important influences may account for Freud's single-minded devotion to conflict. It proved extremely useful to him throughout his life even if it kept him from enunciating Hartmann's concept for himself.

The experiential receded in Freud's theoretical formulations from a position of prime importance, to its proper place as part of the complemental series. Darwin, like Lamarck, Goethe, Haeckel, Claus, and, later, Freud, saw a role for both environment and heredity. Lamarck's "volition" and "law of progressive development" focused attention on internal causes for evolution so that his view of the role of environment was little noticed. Darwin's theory of natural selection led many to assume that environment was replacing the creationists' heredity as an exclusive explanation. Freud replaced the hereditary-taint etiology of hysteria that he had learned from Charcot with an environmental etiology, childhood seductions. When he realized that these seductions were, for the most part, fantasies and innate, he speculatively pushed the environmental or experiential back into the history of mankind.

Fortunately, Freud's use of the now discredited ideas of recapitulation and the inheritance of acquired characteristics were not crucial for his scientific theory any more than they were for Darwin's. They were used almost exclusively in connection with his speculations in applied psychoanalysis. In this connection he also utilized Darwin's primal horde hypothesis from *The Descent of Man*, the idea in the *Variation* introduced into biology by Darwin from the experiences of pigeon breeders that "too close interbreeding is detrimental to the species," and an observation Darwin had made concerning the behavior of savages. Freud agreed with Darwin that the incest taboo was not innate in man.

Darwin lent his great name to the revival of the theory of recapitulation, which in its nonevolutionary form of parallelism had been discredited by von Baer but was supported by Agassiz, an opponent of evolution. Haeckel, Claus, and Fritz Müller all contributed to and reinforced this idea. The critical Claus was completely uncritical of the idea of recapitulation. Freud would not have learned from either Claus or Darwin that anyone questioned it. It survived as a respectable idea in biology even longer than use-inheritance.

Inheritance through use and disuse was not questioned either while Freud was still a biologist. Darwin did not see it as a distinction between Lamarck's theory and his own. Nor did he credit it to Lamarck as Lyell had. In the *Variation* Darwin proposed a tentative hypothesis of heredity by pangenesis specifically intended to account for inheritance through use and disuse. Claus taught that the inheritance through use and disuse was the only physico-chemical principle for evolution as yet known. He assumed it was essential as the source of the variations on which natural selection operated. Like Darwin and Lamarck, Claus considered repetition essential for an experience to be inherited. And this is the form in which we find it in Freud. Freud even thought that the killing of the father in the primal horde would probably have recurred enough times in human history to account for its survival in man's unconscious as the Oedipus complex. The murderous intensity of the father hatred during the Oedipal stage convinced Freud of its hereditary origin in racial experience.

Natural selection and not use-inheritance was in question when Freud was involved in biology. Both Haeckel and Claus felt it was up to each individual to determine how much he thought should be attributed to natural selection. Darwin more and more with each new publication disclaimed his bias for natural selection and assigned a greater and greater role to use-inheritance. Meynert, in attacking the applicability to man of the inheritance of learning, taught that it was one of Darwin's doctrines. Freud did not know until late in life, when Jones called it to his attention, that it was no longer an acceptable scientific idea. He died before recapitulation had suffered a similar fate. Freud's speculations with these now antiquated biological ideas did no harm to his theory. They may have misled those who have read only his speculative writings on applied psychoanalysis, such as *Totem and Taboo, Civilization and its Discontents,* or *Moses and Monotheism,* into misjudgments about the scientific nature of Freud's many other contributions or his knowledge of Darwin.

Darwin used for his third principle of the expression of the emotions the idea of the overflow of excess excitation that he attributed to Spencer and others. Freud used it in the *Studies on Hysteria,* as Meynert had in his *Psychiatrie,* with attribution as Darwin's principle. Freud used it first to establish the constancy principle as the foundation of his theoretical formulations in the *Studies on Hysteria.* Later in 1920 he attributed the constancy principle to Fechner. A modern principle of evolutionary biology unavailable to Freud, T. C. Schneirla's biphasic theory of underlying approach and withdrawal,[2] was proposed in 1970 by Max Schur and the author as more suited to serve as the biological foundation for Freud's pleasure and unpleasure principles than the one available to him in his lifetime, Fechner's constancy principle.

The relationship of Freud's use of "antithetical ideas" in close juxtaposition with Darwin's other two principles of expression raises the question of the relationship, if any, of Darwin's second principle, that of antithesis, to Freud's discovery of the role of antithesis in mental functioning. It suggests further study into the history of the concept of antithesis, particularly in nineteenth-century Germany.

The effect of Darwin's work on Freud's appears to have been massive and primarily of a positive nature. Darwin's errors appear in Freud's writings but they are not seriously damaging. The overemphasis on conflict in the Darwinian Zeitgeist coupled with the "opposing forces" of the Helmholtz school carried Freud far. But it also blinded him to the nonconflict-ual, which was left for the next generation of psychoanalysts.

The excitement over Darwin's theories played a significant role in Freud's career choice. Freud studied zoology at a time when Darwin's accomplishment was having a revolutionary impact at the University of Vienna. Claus had just arrived to bring the zoology department into line with the new biology. Even a conservative, cautious German scientist like Claus taught and provided examples for such revolutionary ideas as "the need to make modification in the traditional conceptions . . . with new progress of experience." Claus also discussed all the different objections to, and mis-understandings of, Darwin's theories so that Freud might have experi-enced a déja vu and been fortified when his own theories encountered simi-lar misunderstandings and objections. Freud wrote about Darwin as an example of the fate of a scientist and his theory. He saw his own theory as adding the *psychological* blow to the *cosmological* and *biological* blows to man's narcissism dealt by Copernicus and Darwin, which Haeckel had called attention to in Freud's youth.

In 1938, shortly after his arrival in London as a refugee from the Nazi invasion of Austria, Freud was invited to sign the book of the Royal So-ciety, of which he had been a foreign member since 1936. Although the charter book of the Royal Society was rarely removed from its headquar-ters at Burlington House except to be taken to Buckingham Palace for the signature of its patron, the Monarch, "this special privilege was . . . extended to Professor Sigmund Freud . . . owing to his health" (1938, "Honor for Professor Freud," *London Times*, Sept. 5). Freud did not fail to note that, in signing, he was entering the company of Newton and Dar-win. He expressed his pleasure in a letter to his friend, the author Arnold Zweig, on June 28 in which he mentioned the many callers he had been receiving.

> The most pleasing was the visit of two secretaries of the Royal Society who brought me the hallowed book of the Society to sign, as a new pain (a bladder disturbance) prevented my going out. They left a facsimile of the book with me, and if you were at my house, I could show you the signa-tures from I. Newton to Charles Darwin. Good Company! (1968, p. 173)

Appendix A

Freud's References
to Darwin

Date	Freud's Writing	Nature of Reference to Darwin
1875	Letter from England to Eduard Silberstein, in Gay 1988, p. 31	"Tyndall, Huxley, Lyell, Darwin . . ." will keep him partial to England
1950 (1892–99)	"Extracts from the Fleiss Papers: *SE* 1:84	Malthusianism
1895	*Studies on Hysteria, SE* 2:91 and 191	Two references to *The Expression of the Emotions in Man and Animals*, including a lengthy quotation
1950 (1895)	"Project for a Scientific Psychology," *SE* 1:303	"A Darwinian line of thought"
1905	*Jokes and Their Relation to the Unconscious, SE* 8:146n	"The physiological explanation of laughter . . . before and since Darwin"
1907	"Letter to THE ANTIQUARIAN HINTERBERGER," *Letters of Sigmund Freud*, p. 268	*The Descent of Man*
1912 addition to 1901	*The Psychopathology of Everyday Life, SE* 6:148 and 148 n3	"The great Darwin," "Darwin's golden rule," and a quotation from *The Autobiography of Charles Darwin*

Appendix A

Date	Freud's Writing	Nature of Reference to Darwin
1913 (1912–13)	*Totem and Taboo, SE* 124 and 125	Quotations from *The Variation of Animals and Plants under Domestication* and from *The Descent of Man*
1914 addition to 1905	*Three Essays on the Theory of Sexuality, SE* 6:156	Natural selection
1915	"Thoughts for the Times on War and Death," *SE* 14:292	Darwin's primal horde concept in *The Descent of Man*
1916 (1915)	*Introductory Lectures on Psycho-Analysis, SE* 15:76	"The great Darwin made a golden rule"
1917 (1916–17)	*Introductory Lectures on Psycho-Analysis, SE* 16:285 and 399	"Darwin, Wallace and their predecessors" strike biological blow; Darwin on snake phobia from 2d ed. of *Expression of the Emotions* (1899)
1917	"A Difficulty in the Path of Psycho-Analysis," *SE* 17:140–41	Biological blow from "Charles Darwin and his collaborators and forerunners"
1920	*Beyond the Pleasure Principle, SE* 18:56	"Sober Darwinian lines of thought"
1921	*Group Psychology and the Analysis of the Ego, SE* 18:122	Darwin's primal horde concept from *The Descent of Man*
1925 (1924)	"Resistances to Psycho-Analysis," *SE* 19:221	Darwin's biological blow to man's narcissism
1925 (1924)	"An Autobiographical Study," *SE* 20:8 and 67	"The theories of Darwin . . . then of topical interest, strongly attracted me"; "Darwin's conjecture that men originally lived in hordes"
1927 addition to 1926	"Postscript to the Question of Lay Analysis," *SE* 20:252	"Training for analysts. . . . the study of evolution"
1933 (1932)	*New Introductory Lectures, SE* 22:173; 22:1, 66–67	"I was already alive when Darwin published his book on the origin of species." Darwin's theory of evolution

Appendix A

Date	Freud's Writing	Nature of Reference to Darwin
1939	*Moses and Monotheism, SE* 23:66, 81 and 130–31	"History of a new scientific theory, such as Darwin's theory of evolution"; "a statement of Darwin's [1872, 2, 362 F.] . . . that in primeval times primitive man lived in small hordes"

Appendix B

Darwin and Other Relevant
Works in Freud's Library
at Maresfield Gardens

DARWIN TITLES

Die Abstammung des Menschen und die geschlechtliche Zuchtwahl, vol. 1, Darwin's *Gesammelte Werke*, vol. 5, trans. J. Victor Carus. Stuttgart: F. Schweitzerbart'sche Verlagshandlung (E. Koch), 1875.
Signed: Sigismundfreud stud. med. 1875
Insectivorous Plants. London: John Murray, 1875; 2d thousand.
Signed: Sigmfreud 79 (day and month illegible)
Der Ausdruck der Gemüthsbewegungen bei den Menschen und den Thieren, trans. J. Victor Carus. Stuttgart: E. Schweizerbart'sche Verglagshandlung (E. Koch), 1872.
Signed: Sigmfreud
The Effects of Cross and Self-Fertilization in the Vegetable Kingdom. London: John Murray, 1876.
Signed: DrSigmfreud 6/9/81
Reise eines Naturforschers um die Welt, Ch. Darwin's *Gesammelte Werke*, vol. 1, trans. J. Victor Carus. Stuttgart: E. Schweizerbart'sche Verlagshandlung (E. Koch), 1875.
Signed: DrSigmfreud 2/XI 81
Über die Entstehung der Arten durch die natürliche Zuchtwahl; oder, Die Erhaltung der begünstigten Rassen im Kampfe um's Dasein 6th ed., *Darwin's Gesammelte Werke*, vol. 2, trans. J. Victor Carus. Stuttgart: E. Schweizerbart'sche Verlagshandlung (E. Koch), 1876.
Signed: DrSigmfreud 2/XI. 81
The Variation of Animals and Plants under Domestication, 2 vols. London: John Murray, 1868.
Signed in both volumes: DrSigmFreud 6/6 83

Appendix B

OTHER RELEVANT TITLES

Brücke, Ernst Theodor von. 1928. *Ernst Brücke*. Vienna: J. Springer.

Brücke, Ernst Wilhelm. 1866. *Die Physiologie der Farben für die Zwecke der Kunstgewerbe*. Leipzig: L. Voss.

———. 1876. *Grundzüge der Physiologie und Systematik der Sprachlaute für Linguisten und Taubstummenlehrer*, 2d ed. Vienna: C. Gerold.

Inscription on title page illegible.

———. 1891. *Schönheit und Fehler der menschlichen Gestalt*. Vienna: Wm. Braumüller.

Signed: "Dr. Sigm Freud," n.d.

———. 1861. Die Elementarorganismen, *Sitzungsberichte der mathematisch-naturwissenschaftlichen Classe der Kaiserlichen Akademie der Wissenschaften*, vol. 44. Vienna: K. Gerold.

Du Bois-Reymond, Emil Heinrich. 1876. *Darwin versus Galiani*. Berlin: A. Hirschwald.

Geddes, Patrick, and J. Arthur Thomson. No date. *Evolution, Home University Library of Modern Knowledge*. London: Williams and Norgate.

Gegenbauer, Carl. 1874. *Grundriss der vergleichenden Anatomie*. Leipzig: Verlag von Wilhelm Engelmann.

Signed: Sig. Freud stud. med 1874

Goethe, Johann Wolfgang von. 1877. *Faust: Eine Tragödie*. Bielefeld: Velhagen und Klasing.

———. 1912. (1748). *Italienische Reise*, ed. Georges von Gravenitz. Leipzig: Insel.

———. (1887–1919). *Werke*, ed. Gustav von Loper et al. on behalf of Sophie von Sachsen. Weimar: H. Bohlan. Labels inside some back covers read Max Lüttich, Hofsbuchbinder: Weimar.

Helmholtz, Herman Ludwig Ferdinand von. 1867. *Handbuch der physiologischen Optik, Encyclopädie der Physik*, vol. 9. Leipzig: L. Voss.

———. 1876. *Populäre wissenschaftliche Vorträge*, 3 vols. Braunschweig: F. Veweg.

Signed: Dr. Sigm Freud 3/26 82

———. 1884. *Vorträge und Reden*, 2 vols. in 1. Dedicated by Wilhelm Fleiss, 1892– (Christmas).

———. 1882–1895. *Wissenschaftliche Abhandlungen*, 3 vols. Leipzig: J. A. Barth. only vols. 1 and 2 in collection.

Signed: Dr. Sigm Freud 20/12 83 and 10/12 83

Huxley, Thomas, H. 1871. *Grundzüge der Physiologie in allgemeinverständlichen Vorlesungen*. Authorized trans. J. Rosenthal. Leipzig: Verlag von Leopold Voss.

Signed: from the private library of Martha Freud 16/Jan 83 (same handwriting as other inscriptions)

Kant, Immanuel. 1880. *Anthropologie in pragmatischer Hinsicht*, 3d ed. *Philosophische Bibliothek*, vol. 14. Leipzig: E. Koschny.

———. 1872–1873. *Kleinere Schriften zur Naturphilosophie*, 2 vols. in 1. *Philosophische Bibliothek*, vol. 49. Berlin: L. Heimann.

Signed: Dr. Sigm Freud 24/2 82

————. 1870. *Kritik der reinen Vernunft*, 2d ed. *Immanuel Kants sämtliche Werke*, vol. 1. Berlin: L. Heimann.
Signed: Dr. Sigm Freud 24/4 82

Kölliker, Albert von. 1855. *Handbuch der Gewebelehre des Menschen: Für Ärzte und Studierende*, 2d ed. Leipzig: W. Engelmann.
Signed: Dr. Sigm Freud 6/7 83 Also signed Westhof: Würzburg 1857 [previous owner]

————. 1889–1902. *Handbuch der Gewebelehre des Menschen: Für Ärzte und Studierende*, 6th rev. ed. 3 vols. Leipzig: W. Engelmann.
Signed: Dr. Freud

Lamarck, Jean. No date. *Zoologische Philosophie*. German by Dr. Heinrich Schmidt (Jena), with introduction and appendix "Das phylogenetische System der Thiere nach Haeckel." Leipzig: Alfred Kröner Verlag.

Lubbock, Sir John [Baron Avebury]. 1876. *Ursprung und Metamorphosen der Insecten. Bibliothek naturwissenschaftlicher Schriften für Gebildete aller Stände*, vol. 1, trans. W. Schlosser from 2d ed. Jena: Herman Gostenoble.

————. 1879. *Addresses: Political and Educational*. London: Macmillan.
Signed: Dr. Sigm. Freud 7/1/82

Maxwell, James Clark. 1876. *Matter and Motion, Manuals of Elementary Science*. London: Society for Promoting Christian Knowledge.
Signed: Sig Freud 31/7 77

Meynert, Theodor. 1876. *Skizzen über Umfang und wissenschaftliche Anordnung der klinischen Psychiatrie*. Vienna: Wm. Braumuller.

————. 1890. *Klinische Vorlesungen über Psychiatrie auf wissenschaftlichen Grundlagen für Studierende und Ärtzte, Juristen und Psychologen*. Vienna: Wm. Braumüller.

————. 1892. *Sammlung von populär-wissenschaftlichen Vorträgen über den Bau und die Leistungen des Gehirns*. Vienna: Wm. Braumüller.

Tyndall, John. 1876. The forms of water in clouds and rivers: Ice and glaciers, 6th ed. *The International Scientific Series*, vol. 1. London: H. S. King.
Signed: Sigm Freud 24/8 1878

Wagner, Rudolf (ed.) 1843–1855. *Handwörterbuch der Physiologie: Mit Rücksicht auf physiologische Pathologie*, 4 vols. in 5. Braunschweig: Veweg.
Signed: Sigm Freud 21/3 87

Appendix C

Who's Who: A Biographical Dictionary

Abraham, Karl (1877–1925), Freud's intimate friend and colleague, founder of the Berlin Psycho-Analytic Society (1910); editor of the *Zeitschrift;* president of the International Psycho-Analytic Association (1924). Thirty of his papers (1907–24) referred to in Freud's work.

Agassiz, Jean Louis Rodolphe (1807–1873), Swiss-American zoologist, associated with Cuvier and Humboldt at Paris (1831–32); professor of natural history, Neuchatel (1832–45); professor of geology and zoology at Harvard from 1847; remained a strong opponent of Darwin until his death.

Baer, Karl Ernst von (1792–1876), Baltic German naturalist and pioneer embryologist; librarian of the Academy of Sciences of St. Petersburg; author of *Über Entwicklungsgeschichte der Thiere* in 2 vols. (1828–73) and *Untersuchungen über die Entwicklung der Fische* (1835). Von Baer's cavity: the segmentation cavity of the blastoderm; von Baer's vesicle: the ovule.

Barrande, Joachim (1799–1883), French geologist and paleontologist, authority on Silurian formations, devoted himself to the investigation of the Paleozoic fossils of Bohemia, his adopted country; published twenty-two volumes of his *Système Silurien de la Bohème* during his lifetime; Darwin spoke highly of "his admirable labours on the development of Trilobites, and his most important work on his Lower or Primordial Zone" (*More Letters of Charles Darwin*, 1:81) and of "Barrande's new period Cambian" (ibid., p. 230); awarded the Wollaston Medal of the Geological Society of London (1855).

Bate, Charles Spence (1818–80), English invertebrate zoologist and practicing dentist; considered greatest authority of his time on Crustacea. Licentiate Royal College of Surgeons, fellow Linnean Society, Royal Society 1861, president Odontological Society 1885. Works: *Catalogue of the Specimens of the Amphipodus Crustacea* (1862); with John Obadiah Westwood, *History of the British Sessile-eyed Crustacea* (1863–68); *Report on the Crustacea Macrura dredged by*

H.M.S. Challenger during the Years 1873 and 1876 (1888); professional articles in dental journals.

Bateson, William (1861–1926), British naturalist, known especially for his work on Mendelism and the determination of sex; his works include *Materials for the Study of Variation* (1894), *Mendel's Principles of Heredity* (1902), and *Method and Scope of Genetics* (1908).

Beaumont. See Élie de Beaumont.

Becquerel, Antoine Henri (1852–1908). French physicist, professor at Paris École Polytechnique from 1895. Studied atmospheric polarization and the influence of the Earth's magnetism on the atmosphere. Shared with the Curies the 1903 Nobel Prize in Physics.

Bell, Sir Charles (1774–1842), Scottish anatomist; surgeon to Middlesex hospital (1812–36); professor of surgery, Edinburgh (1836) Discovery of distinct functions of sensory and motor nerves announced in *Anatomy of the Brain* (1811) and established by his *Nervous System* (1830). Royal Society medallist 1829; Bell's law: the anterior roots of the spinal nerves are motor and the posterior are sensory; Bell's palsy, facial paralysis; Bell's phenomenon: an outward and upward rolling of the eyeball on the attempt to close the eye, on the affected side in peripheral facial (Bell's) paralysis.

Bence-Jones, Henry (1813–1873), English physician and chemist, friend of Ernst Brücke; treated Darwin in 1865. Bence-Jones albumin, body, or protein: a peculiar albuminous substance, found in the urine, frequently but not exclusively, in cases of multiple myeloma; Bence-Jones albumosuria: the presence of Bence-Jones protein in the urine; Bence-Jones cylinders: cylindrical gelatinous bodies forming the contents of the seminal vesicles; Bence-Jones reaction: the precipitation of albumose by nitric acid redissolved by boiling and precipitated again on cooling.

Bernard, Claude (1813–1878), French physiologist, known as the founder of experimental medicine; investigated chemical phenomena of digestion, glycogenic function of the liver, and the sympathetic nervous system; author of *An Introduction to the Study of Experimental Medicine* (1865); three-time grand-prize winner of Academie des Sciences award in physiology; in a posthumous paper, which Pasteur believed he had "disproved," Bernard had rightly claimed that the process of fermentation did not necessarily require an organism. Bernard's canal: a supplementary pancreatic duct; Bernard's glandular layer, a layer of cells lining the acini of the pancreas; Bernard's puncture: puncture on a definite point of floor of the fourth ventricle causing diabetes.

Bernfeld, Siegfried (1892–1953), pioneer Viennese American psychoanalyst; Ph.D, University of Vienna, where he studied plant physiology, pedagogy, and psychology; early contributed to socialist and Zionist papers and knew leaders like Martin Buber; became thorough research worker, from 1914 contributing to scientific journals. In 1922 Freud sent him his first didactic case; later completed formal training analysis in Germany with Hanns Sachs. Works: *The New Youth and the Women* and *The Jewish People and Youth* (1914), *Kinderheim Baumgarten* (1921), *The Psychology of the Infant* and *Sisyphus or the Boundaries of Educa-*

Appendix C

tion (1925), *Psychoanalytic Education* published posthumously 1963, and many articles on adolescence and childhood.

Bleuler, Eugen (1857–1939), Swiss professor and psychiatrist at Burghölzli hospital near Zurich; promoted Kraeplin's views but later revised whole concept of dementia praecox, renaming it schizophrenia; opposition to Freud converted by Jung into support; with them coedited the six volumes (1909–14) of *Jahrbuch für psychoanalytische und psychopathologische Forschungen* and with them and a few others held a scientific meeting (Salzburg 1908); at next meeting (Nuremburg 1910) the International Psychoanalytic Association was formed; twelve articles (1904–19) among references in Freud.

Bonnet, Charles (1720–1793), Swiss naturalist and philosopher; described parthenogenesis among aphids; among his books are *Traité d'insectologie* (1745) and *Contemplation de nature* (1794–1765).

Brentano, Franz (1838–1917), Roman Catholic priest (1864–73); professor of philosophy in Würzburg (1872) and at the University of Vienna 1874–80; wrote on Aristotle, psychology, logic, and ethics.

Breuer, Josef (1842–1925), popular Viennese physician and physiologist trained in Brücke's institute; assistant to Oppolzer at the Clinic for Internal Medicine at the University of Vienna; *Privatdozent* (1875–85); elected to Vienna Academy of Science (1894); while working under Ewald Hering discovered the reflex regulation of respiration (the Hering–Breuer reflex), revolutionizing the idea of the relations of the vagus to respiration (1868); elucidated the function of the labyrinth of the ears (1875); in a period of forty years published five hundred pages in about twenty physiology papers; originator of the cathartic method of treating hysteria (1880); communicated to Freud his discovery that neurotic symptoms disappear when the unconscious becomes conscious; early collaborator with Freud on *Studies on Hysteria* (1893–95).

Broca, Pierre Paul (1824–1880), French anatomist, surgeon, and anthropologist; assistant professor at the Faculty of Medicine (1853–67), elected to chair of *pathologie externe* and professor of clinical surgery (1868); surgeon of the Central Bureau; held important posts in Paris hospitals including the Necker; active in the Anatomical Society of Paris and the Society of Surgery; from a lesion on the left inferior frontal gyrus (since known as Broca's convolution) of an aphasic patient, he located speech function there, a significant step toward proving that the cerebral hemisphere has localized areas of function; published extensively on cerebral localization, and on normal, comparative, and pathological brain anatomy; also on anthropology; elected life member of the French Senate, representing science, six months before he died. Broca's aphasia: atoxic aphasia; Broca's center: the speech center; Broca's fissure: the fissure surrounding the third left frontal convolution; Broca's formula: a full-grown man weighs as many kilograms as the number of centimeters his height exceeds 1 meter; Broca's plane: a plane passing through the visual axes of the two eyes; Broca's pouch: pudendal sac; Broca's space: central part of anterior lobe of the brain.

Brongniart, Adolphe Théodore (1801–1876), French botanist; professor at the Museum of Natural History; son of the geologist, mineralogist, and chemist, Alexandre, who with Cuvier studied and wrote on the geology of the Seine basin; pioneer in the study of vegetable physiology; author of an important work on vegetable fossils (1828–37) and of a valuable first account of pollen; helped establish the *Annales des sciences naturelle* and founded the Sociéte botanique de France.

Bronn, Heinrich Georg (1800–1862), German zoologist and paleontologist; professor at Freiburg and later at Heidelberg; author of work on rock formations and of *Geschichte der Natur;* earliest translator of Darwin's *Origin* into German.

Brücke, Ernst Wilhelm von (1819–1892), professor of physiology and director of the Physiological Institute at the University of Vienna; important member of the so-called Helmholtz school. Brücke's muscle: the longitudinal part of the ciliary muscle.

Buffon, Comte George Louis Leclerc de (1707–1788), French naturalist and author; from 1793 keeper of the Jardin du Roi (now the Jardin des Plantes) in Paris; devoted his life to his monumental *Histoire naturelle* (44 vols.; 1749–1804), a popular and brilliantly written compendium of data on natural history interspersed with Buffon's own speculations and theories, some of which foreshadowed Darwin.

Butler, Samuel (1835–1902), noted English author of *Erewhon* (1872), *The Way of All Flesh* (1903), and other works; opposed his friend Darwin's explanation of evolution, although not the theory, in *Evolution Old and New* (1879), *Unconscious Memory* (1880), and *Luck or Cunning as the Means of Organic Modification?* (1887).

Candolle, Augustin Pyrame de (1778–1841), Swiss botanist, whose *Théorie élémentaire de la botanique* (1813) materially advanced the natural system of classification.

Carpenter, William Benjamin (1813–1885), British zoologist, botanist, and physiologist; author of *Vegetable Physiology and Botany* (1884), *Zoology. A Systematizing Account*, 2 vols. (1845, 1857), *Mechanical Philosophy, Horology and Astronomy* (1857), *Introduction to the Study of Foraminifera* (1862), *Nature and Man: Essays Scientific and Philosophical* (1888).

Carus, Julius Victor (1823–1903), German zoologist; professor, Leipzig from 1853; author of a history of zoology; translator of Darwin's works after the death of Heinrich Bronn.

Carus Sterne, pseudonym of Dr. Ernst Ludwig Krause (1839–1903), German popular writer on science; contributed to spread of Darwin's theories; author of essay on Darwin's grandfather in the *Gratulationsheft* of the evolutionary journal *Kosmos* (1879) on Charles's seventieth birthday, which he enlarged and corrected for Darwin to publish in translation as *Life of Erasmus Darwin*, and author of *Charles Darwin und sein Verhältniss zu Deutschland* (1885) and *Geschichte der biologischen Wissenschaften im neunzehnten Jahrhundert* (1901).

Charcot, Jean Martin (1825–1893), professor of pathological anatomy at the University of Paris and director of the Clinic for Nervous Diseases at the Salpêtrière; famous neurologist best known for his work on hysteria. Charcot's disease or joint: tabetic arthropathy.

Claparède, Jean Louis René Antoine Édouard (1832–1871), Swiss naturalist; professor of comparative anatomy, Geneva; author of studies on infusoria, rhizopods, spiders, oligochaetes, and annelids.

Claus, Carl (1835–1899), professor of zoology and director of the Institute of Zoology and Comparative Anatomy at the University of Vienna from 1873; a founder of the Zoological Experiment Station at Trieste; author of the successful *Textbook of Zoology* and other zoological writings.

Correns, Carl Franz Joseph Erich (1864–1933), German botanist, docent at the University of Tübingen, where from 1894 he used methods of experimental breeding to study problems of heredity in maize, snapdragons, beans, peas, and lilies; published (1905) Mendel's letters to Nägeli; professor, Leipzig (1903), Münster (1909); director, Kaiser Wilhelm Institute of Biology, Berlin (1914).

Cuvier, Baron Georges Léopold Chrétien Frédéric Dagobert (1769–1832), French zoologist and geologist; founder of sciences of comparative anatomy and paleontology; divided animals into four groups (Vertebrata, Mollusca, Articulata, and Radiata) and compared forms only within each group; from his study of fossils and the Earth's development he rejected theories of continuous evolution and supported catastrophism; professor at the Collège de France (1800) and the Jardin des Plantes (1802); chancellor, University of Paris (1809).

Dallas, William Sweetland (1824–1890), excellent and busy translator; translated E. Krause's *Erasmus Darwin;* indexed *The Variation of Animals and Plants under Domestication;* prepared glossary of technical terms for sixth edition of the *Origin.*

d'Archiac, Vicomte. See Saint Simon.

Darwin, Erasmus (1731–1802), English physician and poet; grandfather of Charles Darwin and Francis Galton; cultivated 8-acre botanical garden at Litchfield; formed Lunar Society with Joseph Priestley, James Watt, and Josiah Wedgwood; founded Philosophical Society at Derby (1784). Author of *The Loves of the Plants* (1789) and *Economy of Vegetation* (1792), which were parts of his poetic work *Botanic Garden; The Temple Zoonomia,* which contained some evolutionary suggestions that anticipated Lamarck's views.

De Beaumont. See Élie de Beaumont.

De Bréau. See Quatrefages de Bréau.

De Saint Simon. See Saint Simon.

De Vries, Hugo (1848–1935), Dutch botanist; his study of discontinuous variations, especially in the evening primrose, led to his rediscovery of Mendel's laws of heredity and to the development of the theory of mutation expounded in *The Mutation Theory* (1901–03) and *Plant Breeding* (1907), in which he maintained that species remain unchanged between mutations; professor (1881–1918) at the University of Amsterdam; established an experimental garden at Kilversum.

Diderot, Denis (1713–1784), French encyclopedist and philosopher. Imprisoned for parts of his philosophic work *Lettres sur les Aveugles* (1740); released to work with d'Alembert on *Encyclopédie.* Labored 20 years (1751–72) aided by Voltaire, Montesquieu, Rousseau, Buffon, Turgot, Quesnay, and others to produce 28 volumes of *Encyclopédie ou Dictionnaire Raisonné des Sciences, des Arts et des Métiers,* supplemented by 6 volumes (1776–77) plus 2 volumes of tables

(1780), a work of practical value and an active force during the Enlightenment.

Dohrn, Anton Felix (1840–1909), German zoologist, studied with Haeckal at Jena, doctorate at Breslau; lecturer in zoology at Jena 1867–71; corresponded with Darwin 1867–82; science expeditions to Scotland and Messina; founded and directed Naples Zoological Station 1874–1909; Honorary Citizen of Naples, Fellow of the Royal Society 1899; research on origin and evolution of vertebrates (which he thought traceable to annelids), crustaceans, and other marine animals of Mediterranean and English coasts. Works: *Fauna und Flora des Golfen von Neapel, Der Ursprung der Wirbeltiere und das Prinzip des Funktionswechsels* (1875), and *Studien zur Urgeschichte des Wirbeltierkörpers* (1881–1907).

Driesch, Hans Adolf Eduard (1867–1941), German biologist and philosopher, advocate of vitalism; professor, Heidelberg (1911), Cologne (1920), Leipzig (1921); works include *Analytische Theorie der Organischen Entwicklung* (1894), *Geschichte des Vitalismus* (1905), *Leib und Seele* (1916), and *Parapsychologie* (1932).

Du Bois-Reymond, Emil Heinrich (1818–1896), German physiologist of French descent, pioneer in experimental physiology; known especially for investigations in animal electricity, physiology of muscles and nerves, and metabolic processes; a pupil of Johannes Müller with Brücke, Helmholtz, and Carl Ludwig; the relationship of these men is described in Siegfried Bernfeld, "Freud's Earliest Theories and the School of Helmholtz," *Psychoanalytic Quarterly* 13, no. 3 (July 1944). Du Bois-Reymond's law: it is the variation, not the absolute value of the density of stimulation at any given moment, that acts as a stimulus to a muscle or motor nerve.

Ehrenfels, Baron Christian von (1855–1932), German philosopher, introduced the term *Gestalt* into psychology; chief work, *System der Werttheorie* (2 vols., 1898–99), based ethics on a general theory of values; "Sexuales Ober- und Unterbewusstsein" in *Politisch-anthrop. Rev* (1903) referred to in Freud's *Jokes and their Relation to the Unconscious* (1905); *Sexualethik, Grenzfr. Nerv.- u. Seelenleb* (1907) referred to in Freud's "On the Sexual Theories of Children" (1908).

Élie de Beaumont, Jean Baptiste Armand Louis Léonce (1798–1884), French geologist, made a noted geological map of France begun in 1825; in *Notice sur les systèmes de montagnes* (3 vols., 1852) enunciated a theory relating age and orientation of mountain chains; professor at the School of Mines, Paris (from 1829), and at the Collège de France (from 1832); with Bureau of Mines (from 1824) and as inspector general (from 1847); senator (1852) and perpetual secretary (1853) of the Academy of Sciences.

Ewald, Julius Wilhelm (1811–1891), Berlin geologist, wrote on the Jurassic and the chalk formations of northern Germany and published a geologic map of the region between Magdeburg and the Hartz, 1864; coeditor of *The Complete Works of Leopold von Buch*, 1867–85.

Exner, Sigmund Ritter von (1846–1926), succeeded Brücke as professor of physiology in 1891; also became department head at the Ministry of Education; *Entwurf zu einer physiologischen Erklarung der psychischen Erscheinungen* (1894) referred to twice by Freud in "Project for a Scientific Psychology" (1950 [1895]) and three times by Breuer in his "Theoretical" chapter of *Studies on Hysteria;* Exner's plexus: a layer of nerve fibers near the surface of the cerebral cortex.

Appendix C

Fechner, Gustav Theodor (1801–1887), German physicist, philosopher, and experimental psychologist; a founder of psychophysics, professor of physics (Leipzig, 1833–40), working mainly on galvanism, electrochemistry, and theory of color; later devoted himself to psychophysics, natural philosophy, anthropology, and aesthetics; formulated Fechner's law (or the Weber–Fechner law, deduced from Weber's law) that the intensity of a sensation varies directly as the logarithm of the stimulus. Author of *Über die Physikalische und Philosophische Atomlehre* (1855); referred to by Freud: *Einige Ideen zur Schopfungs- und Entwicklungsgeschichte der Organismen* (1873) three times in "Project for a Scientific Psychology" (1950 [1895]); *Elemente der Psychophysik* (1889 [1860]) on the relations between physiology and psychology, twice in *The Interpretation of Dreams*, in *Jokes and their Relation to the Unconscious* (1905), and in *Introductory Lectures on Psycho-analysis* (1916–17 [1915–17]); and *Vorschule der Asthetik* (1897) in *Jokes and their Relation to the Unconscious*. Under pseudonym Dr. Mises: poems, and humorous and satirical essays; *Ratselbuchlein von Dr. Mises* (n.d. [1875]) referred to in *Jokes and their Relation to the Unconscious*.

Ferenczi, Sándor (1873–1933), Hungarian neurologist, psychiatrist, and psychoanalyst; prolific writer and inspiring lecturer in Hungarian and German on neurologic and psychiatric problems. M.D. Vienna (1894); chief neurologist, Elizabeth Poorhouse (1900); psychiatric expert to Royal Court of Justice, Berlin (1905). Close friendship with Freud started in 1908; accompanied Freud to Clark University (1909); provided a strong impetus to the practical application of Freud's findings; author of *Thalassia: A Theory of Genitality* (1924) and *Further Contributions to the Theory and Technique of Psychoanalysis* (1927). Thirty-three articles (1908–28) referred to by Freud.

Flechsig, Paul (1847–1929), professor of psychology at the University and director of the Psychiatric Clinic at Leipzig; disliked by Meynert as his rival in neurology; Flechsig's area: the anterior, lateral, and posterior areas on each half of the medulla oblongata, marked out by the vagus and hypoglossal nerves; Flechsig's cuticulum: a layer of flat cells on the external surface of the neuroglia; Flechsig's fasciculum: the anterior and lateral ground bundles; Flechsig's field: the myelogenetic field.

Fleischl von Marxow, Ernest von (1846–1891), Austrian pathologist. Fleischl's hemometer: an instrument for estimating the richness of hemoglobin by comparing blood color with a piece of red glass; Fleischl's test: urine test for bile pigments by heating in a strong solution of sodium nitrate and adding sulfuric acid to form colored layers.

Fliess, Wilhelm (1858–1928), Berlin otolaryngologist with a big consulting practice and wider medical and scientific interests; Freud's confidante at earliest stage of psychoanalysis (1887–1902); published on connection between the nose and the female genitals (1895 and 1897). *Neue Beitrage und Therapie der nasalen Reflexneurose* (1892) and "Die nasale Reflexneurose" (1893) cited by Freud in "On the Grounds for Detaching a Particular Syndrome from Neurasthenia under the Description 'Anxiety Neurosis'" (1895), and *Der Ablauf des Lebens* (1906) in Freud's "1909 Postscript" to *The Interpretation of Dreams* (1900), in a 1910 footnote added to *The Three Essays on the Theory of Sexuality* (1905 [1904]), in *In-*

troductory Lectures on Psychoanalysis (1917 [1916–17]), and in *Beyond the Pleasure Principle* (1920). Fliess therapy or treatment: anesthetization of the turbinated bones for the relief of pain in dysmenorrhea and in nervous stomach pains.

Flourens, Marie Jean Pierre (1794–1867), French physiologist; long a professor at the Collège de France; demonstrated the respiratory center in the medulla and the function of the cerebellum in muscular coordination and studied bone structure. Flouren's doctrine: the entire cerebrum takes part in every mental process.

Forbes, James David (1809–1868), Scottish physicist, professor of natural philosophy at Edinburgh 1833–59, dean Faculty of Arts 1837, principal St. Andrew 1859. Co-founder British Association 1831, three-time Keith medallist of Edinburgh Society, fellow of the Royal Society 1832 (Rumford and Royal medals), secretary 1840–51 of Royal Society of Edinburgh, member of the French Academy of Science 1842. Discovered polarization of heat 1834, experimentally established the identity of thermal and luminous radiation; first to study glacier movements; Agassiz and Tyndall contested his claim to first observations of the veined structure of glaciers. Author of *Travels through the Alps of Savoy and Other Parts of the Penine Chain with Observations on the Phenomena of Glaciers* (1843), and memoirs on the thermal springs of the Pyrenees, the extinct volcanoes of Vivarais (Ardêche), and Cuchillon and Eildon Hills.

Frazer, Sir James George (1854–1941), Scottish anthropologist, professor of social anthropology, (University of Liverpool, 1907); Order of Merit (1925). His great work *The Golden Bough*, a study of cults, myths, rites, and so forth, their origins and importance in the historical development of religions (1890), revised (1900), revised and expanded with further studies into 12 volumes (1915), and a one-volume abridgement (1921) with a supplement *Aftermath* (1936). Freud referred to various volumes of the 3d edition in *Totem and Taboo* (1913 [1912–13]), in *The Taboo of Virginity* (1918 [1917]), in *An Autobiographical Study* (1925 [1924]), and in *Moses and Monotheism* (1939 [1934–38]), and to *The Aborigines of New South Wales* in *Totem and Taboo*.

Freud, Anna (1895–1982), Freud's youngest daughter; educator and psychoanalyst; organizer and director of the Hampstead Child Therapy Clinic, London; author of *Psychoanalysis for Teachers and Parents* (1935), *The Ego and the Mechanisms of Defense* (1937), *Normality and Pathology in Childhood: Assessments of Development* (1965); and with Dorothy Burlingham, *War and Children* (1943) and *Infants without Families* (1943).

Galton, Sir Francis (1822–1911), English scientist born near Birmingham; graduated Cambridge 1844; in British Civil Service made study of meteorology; *Meteorographica* (1863), basis of modern weather maps; best known for work in anthropology and study of heredity; founded science of eugenics; devised system of fingerprint identification; author, *Hereditary Genuis* (1869), *Inquiries into Human Faculty and its Development* (1907 [1883]) referred to in Freud's *The Interpretation of Dreams* (1900), *Record of Family Faculties . . .* (1883), *Natural Inheritance* (1889), *Finger Prints, Essays on Eugenics*; Erasmus Darwin grandson, cousin to Charles Darwin. Galton's delta: triangular arrangement of the lines of a finger print near the base; Galton's law of regression: average par-

Appendix C

ents tend to produce average children, minus parents . . . produce minus children, plus parents . . . produce plus children, but extremes are inherited in a less marked degree; Galton's whistle: a metallic whistle used in testing hearing.

Gegenbauer, Karl (1826–1903), German anatomist; professor at Jena (1855–73) and Heidelberg (1873–1901); an influential teacher, he emphasized the value of comparative anatomy in the study of evolution and of homologies; he showed (1861) that the eggs of vertebrates are single cells; his most comprehensive work *Vergleichende Anatomie der Wirbeltiere* (2 vols., 1898–1901). Gegenbauer's cells: osteoblasts, cells that are developed into bone or that are directly active in the production of bony structures.

Geoffroy Saint-Hilaire, Étienne (1772–1844), French zoologist; professor in Paris at the Museum of Natural History (1793–1840) and at the Faculty of Sciences (from 1809); member (1798–1801) of Napoleon's scientific staff in Egypt; his theory in *Philosophie anatomique* (2 vols., 1818–22) and other works that all animals conformed to a single plan of structure attracted many supporters but was strongly opposed by Cuvier.

Goldschmidt, Richard Benedikt (1878–1958), German-born American zoologist and geneticist; Ph.D. Heidelberg (1902); taught at the University of Munich (1903–14) and at the Kaiser Wilhelm Institute, Berlin (1914–21), director there (1921–36); professor of zoology at the University of California (1936–48); author of *The Mechanism and Physiology of Sex Determination* (1923), *Ascaris: The Biologist's Story of Life* (1937), *Physiological Genetics* (1938), and *The Material Basis of Evolution* (1940).

Gratiolet, Louis Pierre (1815–1865), French anatomist, made comparative studies of human and primate brain lobes. Gratiolet's optic radiation: strand of fibers continuous with those of the corona radiata and optic tract.

Gray, Asa (1810–1888), American botanist; M.D. 1831; occupied the Chair of Natural History at Harvard, director of the Cambridge Botanical Garden (1842–72), and a founder of the National Academy of Arts and Sciences. Sir Joseph Hooker described Gray as "one of the first to accept and defend the doctrine of Natural Selection . . . so that Darwin, whilst fully recognizing the different standpoints from which they took their departures, and their divergence of opinion on important points, nevertheless regarded him as the naturalist who had most thoroughly gauged the *Origin of Species*, and as a tower of strength to himself and his cause" (*Proc. Roy. Soc.* 46 (1890); xv; *Letters of Asa Gray*, ed. Jane Loring Gray [2 vols., Boston, 1893]).

Groddeck, Georg (1866–1934), German physician and psychoanalyst; father of psychosomatic medicine, a term he despised as shallow and misleading; coined the term *Das es* (the It) later adopted by Freud and translated as "id." *Das Buch vom Es* (1923; *The Book of the Id* [1920]) referred to by Freud in *New Introductory Lectures on Psycho-Analysis* (1933 [1932]).

Haeckal, Ernst Heinrich (1834–1919), German biologist and philosopher; studied medicine and natural philosophy at Würzburg, Berlin, and Vienna; professor of zoology, Jena (1865–1908); on scientific expeditions to Canary Islands (1866–67), Red Sea (1873), Ceylon (1881–82), Java (1900–01), among others. First German advocate of organic evolution and early Darwin advocate; enunciated biogenetic

Appendix C

law that in the development of the individual animal the stages in the evolutionary history of the postulating species are repeated, postulating as illustration a hypothetical ancestral form (gastraea) represented by the gastrula stage of the individual; first to draw up a genealogical tree relating the various animal orders; exponent of monism; known also for his study of invertebrate marine organisms, especially Radiolaria. Works include *Monographie der Radiolaren* (1862), *Generelle Morphologie der Organismen* (1866), *Natürliche Schopfungsgeschichte Anthropogenie order Entwicklungsgeschichte* (1868), *des Menschen* (1874), *Studien zur Gastraeatheorie* (1877), *Monismus als Band zwischen Religion und Wissenschaft* (1892), and *Weltratzel* (1899). Haeckal's law: an organism, in developing from the ovum, goes through the same changes as did the species in developing from the lower to the higher forms of animal life.

Hall, G(ranville) Stanley, (1846–1924), American psychologist and educator, professor of psychology and pedagogics at Johns Hopkins (1883–88); founded and edited *American Journal of Psychology* [1887]; first president Clark University (1889–1919); first president, American Psychological Association 1891; invited Freud and Jung to Clark University (1909); author of *The Contents of Children's Minds* (1883), *Adolescence: Its Psychology and its Relation to Physiology, Anthropology, Sociology, Sex, Crime, Religion and Education* (2 vols., 1904) referred to by Freud in *Three Essays on the Theory of Sexuality* (1905), "A Synthetic Genetic Study of Fear" (1914) referred to in Freud's *Introductory Lectures on Psycho-Analysis* and in "From the History of an Infantile Neurosis" (1918 [1914]), (2 vols., 1904), *Educational Problems* (2 vols., 1917), *Senescence, The Last Half of Life* (1922), *Life and Confessions of a Psychologist* (1923).

Hartmann, Heinz (1894–1970), Viennese-born American psychoanalyst; one of psychoanalysis' greatest theoreticians and close associate of Freud; grandson of Freud's gynecology professor, Dr. Chrobak; with Anna Freud and Ernst Kris founded *The Psychoanalytic Study of the Child* (1945); author of *Ego, Psychology and the Problem of Adaptation* (1939) and other works; with S. Bettleheim "Ueber Fehlreaktionen des Gedachtnisses bei Korsakoffschen Psychose" (1924) referred to by Freud in *The Interpretation of Dreams* (1900) and in *New Introductory Lectures on Psycho-Analysis* (1932 [1931]).

Heer, Oswald (1809–1883), Swiss entomologist; professor of botany at the University of Zurich (1855–82); wrote chiefly on fossil plants (from 1841); published *Flora Tertiaria Helvetiae* (1855–59), *Flora Fossilis Arctica* (7 vols., 1869–83), *Die Urwelt der Schweiz* (1865), *Flora Fossilis Helvetiae* (1876–77) and numerous scientific papers; received the Wollaston medal of the Geological Society (1874) and a royal medal (1878).

Helmholtz, Hermann Ludwig Ferdinand von (1821–1894), physicist, physiologist, physician, mathematician, and philosopher; 1847 formulated the law of conservation of energy mathematically; invented the ophthalmoscope 1851; professor of physics at the University of Berlin from 1871 and director of the Physicotechnical Institute, Charlotennburg, from 1887. Helmholtz's ligament: the part of the anterior ligament of the malleus attached to the greater tympanic spine; Helmholtz's theory: each basilar fiber responds sympathetically to a definite tone and

Appendix C

stimulates the hair cells of Corti's organ resting upon the fiber to send a nerve impulse to the brain creating sound perception.

Henle, Friedrich Gustav Jakob (1809–1885), German anatomist and pathologist; greatest histologist of his day; professor at Göttingen (1852–85); worked on the microscopic structure of organs and tissues, especially of epithelium and hair; propounded a theory of microorganisms as the cause of infectious diseases and made a special study of sharks and rays; wrote *Handbuch der systematischen Anatomie* (3 vols., 1866–71) and other outstanding works. Henle's layer: the outer cells of the inner root sheath of the hair; Henle's loop: a U-shaped turn in a uriniferous tubule of the kidney; Henle's layer: lamina basalis, the transparent inner layer of the choroid in contact with the pigmented layer of the retina; sheath of Henle: connective tissue sheath of a nerve fiber outside the neurilemma.

Henslow, Reverend John Stevens (1796–1861), Cambridge Professor of Minerology (1822), of Botany (1827–61); "attended to every branch of natural science" (Darwin 1967 [1862 and 1873], p. 222). Darwin liked his lectures "much for their extreme clearness, and the admirable illustrations," particularly those to his pupils and senior university members on the "rarer plants and animals observed . . . during delightful field excursions, on foot, or in coaches to distant places, or in a barge down the river" (Darwin 1958 [1876–82], p. 60). Darwin, whom he helped obtain the post of naturalist on the *Beagle*, "always held him in high esteem" (p. 60 ed. n. 2) and attributed to him in large part his strong attachment to natural history. Founded the Cambridge Philosophical Society with Professor Adam Sedgwick (1785–1873) following their 1819 geological tour together of the Isle of Wight. Wrote a clear, somewhat philosophical treatise on *The Principles of Descriptive and Physiological Botany* (1830), *Roman Antiquities found in Norfolk* (1844), essays on *Diseases of Wheat Dictionary of Botanical Terms* (1846).

Herbert, Honorable and Reverend W., (1778–1847), Dean of Manchester, English horticulturist whom Darwin called "the great maker of Hybrids" (Charles Darwin, "Letter to C. Lyell" October 8 [845], in *Life and Letters of Charles Darwin*, ed. Francis Darwin [his son] [3 vols., London: John Murray, 1887], 1:343.

Hering, Ewald (1834–1918), German physiologist and psychologist; professor at Leipzig from 1895; investigated respiration and visual space perception; advanced a theory of color vision; opposed Fechner's psychophysical principles; regarded memory as a general function of organized matter; opposed Helmholtz's empirical theory with a nativistic one. Hering's test: testing for binocular vision with a blackened tube with a verticle thread across the far end and a small round body on one side of thread; Hering's theory: color sensation depends on decomposition and restitution of the visual substances, dissimulation producing red, yellow, and white, and restitution blue, green, and black; Hering–Breuer reflex: see Glossary. Pamphlet "Über das Gedachtnis als eine allgemeine Function der organisirten Materie" (1870) referred to in "Editor's Appendix A: Freud and Ewald" to Freud's "The Unconscious" (1915).

Hertwig, Oskar (1849–1922), German embryologist, studied with Haeckal and Gegenbaur, founder and director (1888–1922) of Anatomical Institute, Berlin; in 1875 established that fertilization is the fusion of male and female nuclei; investi-

Appendix C

gated malformations of vertebrate embryos; with brother Richard von Hertwig (1850–1937) developed the germ-layer theory.

Hooker, Sir Joseph Dalton (1817–1911), English botanist, friend and early supporter of Darwin, published *Antarctic Flora* (1843), *Genera Planetarum* (1862–63), *Flora of British India* (1892–1897), and other works, and succeeded his father, Sir William Jackson Hooker, as director of Kew Gardens, London.

Hutchinson, George Evelyn (1903–), American zoologist and ecologist, born and educated in Cambridge, England. Senior lecturer in zoology, Witwatersrand, South Africa (1926–28); rose from instructor to Sterling Professor of Biology, Yale University (1928–65), emeritus (1971–); North India expedition (1932). Cottrell Award, National Academy of Science (1974); Kyoto Award (1986). Member National Academy of Science, American Society of Zoologists, Ecological Society of America, American Society of Limnology and Oceanography (vice president 1939, president 1948). Wide-ranging contributions on limnology, biochemistry, aquatic Hemiptera, theoretical aspects of ecology, psychoanalytic aspects of evolution, medieval origins of biological iconography, random processes in human development. Works include *The Itinerant Ivory Tower; Scientific and Literary Essays* (1953). *The Enchanted Voyage and Other Studies* (1962), *El Bajo de Santa Fé* with Ursula M. Cowgill (1963), *The Ecological Theatre and the Evolutionary Play* (1965), *Ianula: an Account of the History and Development of* the Lago di Monterosi, Latium Italy with others (1970), *A Treatise on Limnology* (1975), *An Introduction to Population Ecology* (1978), and *The Kind Fruits of the Earth: Reflections of an Embryo Ecologist* (1979).

Huth, Henry (1815–1878), English banker and bibliophile of German descent; collected early English, Spanish, and German books; published works include *Ancient Ballads and Broadsides* (1867), *Inedited Political Miscellanies, 1584–1700* (1870), and *Fugitive Tracts, 1493–1700* (1875).

Huxley, Julian Sorell (1887–1975), English biologist and writer; son of Leonard Huxley; taught at Rice Institute, Houston (1912–16), Oxford (1919–25), and King's College, London (1925–35); president of National Union of Scientific Workers (1926–29); secretary of the Zoological Society of London (1935–42); director-general of UNESCO; wrote *Animal Biology* (with J. B. S. Haldane, 1927), *Scientific Research and Social Needs* (1934), *The Living Thoughts of Darwin* (1939), *Man in the Modern World* (1947), and *Heredity, East and West* (1949); edited T. H. Huxley's *Diary of the Voyage of H. M. S. Rattlesnake* (1935) and *The New Systematics* (1940).

Huxley, Thomas Henry (1825–1895), English biologist, Hunterian professor, Royal College of Surgeons (1863–69), Fullerian professor, Royal Institution (1863–67); president Royal Society (1883–85). Foremost advocate of Darwin's theory in England; author of *Zoological Evidence as to Man's Place in Nature* (1863), *Manual of the Comparative Anatomy of Vertebrated Animals* (1871), . . . *of Invertebrated Animals* (1877), *The Crayfish* (1880), *Science and Culture* (1881), *Evolution and Ethics* (1893). Huxley's layer: a layer of the root sheaths of a hair follicle within Henle's layer.

Jackson, John Hughlings (1834–1911), neurologist at the London Hospital and the National Hospital for the Paralyzed and Epileptic; studied aphasia, described unilateral convulsions (Jackson's epilepsy), and in the Croonean lectures for 1884 on the evolution and dissolution of the nervous system originated the doctrine of "levels" in the evolution of the nervous system. Jacksonian, or partial, epilepsy: localized spasm, mainly limited to one side and often to one group of muscles; Jackson's law: the nerve functions developed last are destroyed first.

James, William (1842–1910), American psychologist and philosopher; Harvard, M.D. (1869); taught anatomy, physiology, and hygiene, Harvard from 1872; professor of philosophy from 1881; known especially as one of the founders of pragmatism. Author of *The Principles of Psychology* (1890), *The Will to Believe and Other Essays* (1891), *The Varieties of Religious Experience* (1902), *Pragmatism* (1907), *The Meaning of Truth* (1909), *A Pluralistic Universe* (1909), and *Essays in Radical Empiricism* (1912).

Jelliffe, Smith Ely (1866–1945), New York neurologist and psychiatrist, pioneer in psychosomatic medicine; Brooklyn Polytechnic (1886); M.D. College of Physicians and Surgeons; maintained relationships with both Freud and Jung after the two split; managing editor of *The Journal of Nervous and Mental Disease* (1902–45), coauthor with William A. White of two-volume *Diseases of the Nervous System: A Text-Book of Neurology and Psychiatry* in six editions between 1914 and 1935, and with Louise Brink of *Psychoanalysis and the Drama* (1922).

Jones, Ernest (1879–1958), Welsh psychoanalyst, member of Freud's inner circle, a founder of the British Psycho-analytic Association (1913), author of earliest authorized full biography of Freud (1953–57), and crusader for psychoanalysis in Britain, Canada, and the United States. Met Freud 1908; first to present a psychoanalytic paper to a medical forum, the American Therapeutic Congress (1909); acclaimed Freud "the Darwin of the mind" (1910); didactic analysis with Ferenczi (1913); president of the International Psycho-Analytical Congress after World War I; helped fifty analysts gain refuge in Britain, some en route to America. Works: *Hamlet and Oedipus, Papers on Psycho-analysis* (1918), *Essays in Applied Psycho-analysis* (1923), *Social Aspects of Psycho-analysis* (1924), and *On the Nightmare* (1931).

Jung, Carl Gustav (1875–1961), Swiss psychiatrist at the Burghölzli in Zurich, until 1913 Freud's heir-apparent as editor of the *Jahrbuch für psychoanalytische und psychopathologische Forschungen* and first president of the International Psycho-analytical Society. Met Freud 1908 but broke with him to found analytical psychology based on psychic totality and energism; conceptualized two dimensions in the unconscious: personal (repressed life events) and collective; introduced concepts of introvert and extrovert, anima/animus. Member of the Royal Society. Works: *Psychologie der Dementia Praecox* (1907), *Wandlungen und Symbole der Libido* (1912), *Psychologische Typen* (1921), *Psychology and Religion* (1938), and *The Integration of a Personality* (1939).

Kalischer, Salomon (1845–1924), German Goethe scholar, coeditor of Goethe's complete works and champion of Goethe as a scientist.

Kant, Immanuel (1724–1804), German metaphysician and transcendental philosopher born in Königsburg; lectured in philosophy and various sciences at University of Königsburg from 1755 and was professor of logic and metaphysics in 1770. *Versuch ueber die Krankheiten des kopfes* (1764) and *Anthropologie in prag-*

matischer Hinsicht abgsflasst (1798) referred to by Freud in *The Interpretation of Dreams* (1900).

Kelvin, William Thomson, first Baron of Largs (1824–1907). Irish mathematician and physicist. He and his close personal friend Helmholtz were the foremost figures in transforming the science of nineteenth-century physics. As professor of natural philosophy at Glasgow from 1845 established the first British teaching laboratory. Best known for work on heat and electricity. Introduced the Kelvin, or absolute, scale of temperature. His work in thermodynamics of coordinating the theories of heat held by various leading scientists of his time established firmly the law of thermodynamics as proposed by Joule. Invented the reflecting galvanometer and the siphon recorder for telegraphic messages.

Kölliker, Albert von (1817–1905), Swiss anatomist, histologist, and zoologist; professor of physiology and of microscopic and comparative anatomy at Würzburg from 1847; his researches on animal tissue contributed to the development of embryology and histology; about 1870 visited Darwin, who "liked [him] extremely" (Darwin, *More Letters*, 2:359). Kölliker's fibrous layer: the mesiric, the substantia propria of the iris.

Kraeplin, Emil (1856–1926), German pioneer in modern psychiatry; divided mental diseases into dementia-praecox and manic-depressive groups; investigated fatigue and influence of alcohol on mental processes.

Krause, Ernst Ludwig. See Carus Sterne.

Kris, Ernst Ludwig (1900–1957), art historian and psychoanalyst; close friend of Freud; curator, Vienna Kunsthistorisches Museum until 1939; member Vienna Institute of Psychoanalysis (associate 1927); clinical professor of psychiatry, Yale University (1950–57); edited the *Imago* (from 1937) at Freud's request; a founder and managing editor, *The Psychoanalytic Study of the Child* (1945); founder of two psychoanalytic research programs; author of *Die Steinscheneidekunst* (1929), the *Catalogue of Goldsmithworks in the Vienna Museum* (1935), *Psychoanalytic Explorations in Art* (1952), among others; editor with Marie Bonaparte and Anna Freud, *On the Origins of Psychoanalysis* (1950).

Lamarck, Chevalier Jean Baptiste Pierre Antoine de Monet de (1744–1829), French naturalist noted for his study and classification of invertebrates and introduction of evolutionary theory; aided by Buffon, traveled as royal botanist (1781–82) collecting for the Academy of Sciences; keeper of the herbarium at the Jardin du Roi for a time and after 1793 professor of zoology at the Museum of Natural History; introduced the term *Invertebrata* and is considered founder of invertebrate paleontology. Cuvier's opposition to his theory of the gradual evolution of new species was influential in discrediting Lamarck during his lifetime.

Langerhans, Paul (1847–1888), German physician, authority on pathological anatomy, described the islands of Langerhans, insulin-producing cells in the pancreas, the malfunction of which causes diabetes, in his 1869 *Contribution to the Microscopic Anatomy of the Pancreas*.

Laugel, Antoine-August (1830–1914), French writer born at Strasbourg; attended l'École polytechnique (1849) and l'École nationale des mines (diploma of mine engineering 1854); secretary to Duke D'Aumale; administrator of the Paris-Lyons Railroad; under pseudonym A. Vernier wrote the scientific news for the *Temps*

Appendix C

from its founding until 1894; active on the *Revue de Géologie* and the *Revue des Sciences et de l'Industrie*. Scientific works: *Études scientifiques* (1859); *Science of Philosophie* (1862); *la Voix, L'Oreille et la Musique* (1867); *l'Optique et les Arts* (1869); *les Problèmes* (1873). Most popular works were historical essays and biographies.

Lavater, Johann Kaspar (1741–1801), Swiss poet, mystic, and writer on philosophy and theology; remembered for his work on physiognomy, the art of judging character from facial characteristics; works include lyric poems, dramas, and epics.

Le Bon, Gustave (1841–1931), French physician and sociologist; author of *L'Homme et les Sociétes* . . . (1881); *La Civilization des Arabes* (1884); *Les Lois Psychologiques de l' Evolution des Peuples* (1894), *La Psychologie des Foules* (1895, trans. 1920 as *The Crowd: A Study of the Popular Mind*), referred to by Freud in *Group Psychology and the Analysis of the Ego* (1921); *L' Evolution Actuelle due Monde* (1927).

Leuckart, Karl Georg Friedrich Rudolf (1823–1898), German zoologist, a founder of the science of parasitology, pioneer in animal ecology, made important discoveries in animal physiology and in comparative morphology and classification of invertebrates; also did valuable studies and writings on parasitic forms, including worms and insects.

Leydig, Franz (1821–1908), German zoologist; author of *Lehrbuch der Histologie des Menschen und der Thiere* (1857) and *Zelle und Gewebe* (1885). Leydig's cells: interstitial cells of the seminiferous tubules and of the mediastinum and connective tissue septa of the testes, believed to furnish the internal secretion of the testicle, or mucous cells that do not pour their secretion out over the surface of the epithelium; Leydig's cylinders: bundles of muscular fibers separated by partitions of protoplasm; Leydig's duct: the Wolffian duct.

Lichtheim, Ludwig (1845–1915), German physician; Lichtheim disease: subcortical sensory aphasia; Lichtheim's sign: subcortical aphasic patient unable to speak, can indicate with fingers the number of syllables in word he is thinking; Lichtheim's syndrome: subacute combined degeneration of the spinal cord.

Lockyer, Sir Joseph Norman (1836–1920). Clerk in war office London (1857); devoted leisure to astronomical studies; became professor of astronomical physics at newly founded Royal College of Science and director of the Solar Physics Observatory (1890–1913). Among the first to make spectroscopic examination of the sun and stars; devised method of observing solar prominences with the spectroscope in the daytime. Headed eight government expeditions to observe total eclipses of sun (1870–1905). Fellow of Royal Society (1869) and knighted (1897). Published *Contributions to Solar Physics* (1873), *The Sun's Place in Nature* (1897), and *Inorganic Evolution* (1900).

Loewenstein, Rudolph Maurice (1898–1976), Polish-born New York psychoanalyst and third member of the fruitful postwar collaboration with Hartmann and Kris which produced the series of classical papers that extended and integrated the newer developments of psychoanalytic theory. Served in French army; decorated with Croix de Guerre; charter member of the Paris Psychoanalytic Society and Institute; member of medical faculty University of Paris (1925–39), Yale (1948–52); president American Psychoanalytic Association (1957–58), New York

Psychoanalytic Institute (1959–61); vice president International Psycho-Analytical Association (1965–67). Translator for Marie Bonaparte of the French edition of Freud's five great case histories; author of *Christians and Jews: A Psychoanalytic Study* (1951); *Practise and Precept on Psychoanalytic Technique: Selected Papers* (1982); editor, *Drives, Affects, Behavior* (1953).

Lombroso, Cesare (1836–1909), Italian physician and criminologist; professor of psychiatry at Pavia 1862, later of criminal anthropology at Turin; 1876 pamphlet enlarged into famous 3-vol. *L' uomo deliguete* (5th ed. 1869–97; partial Eng. trans. *Criminal Man* [1911]) compared anthropological measurements, concluding that the average criminal was an atavistic type marked by distinct physical and psychological traits; focused attention on the nature of the criminal and circumstance and gave impetus to further scientific study of crime; Lombroso advocated humane treatment of criminals and less frequent use of the death penalty. Works in English translation: *The Female Offender* (partial, 1895), *The Man of Genius* (1891), *Crime: Its Causes and Remedies* (1911).

Lubbock, Sir John (1834–1913), first Baron Avebury. Darwin's neighbor. Writer of popular science books in archaeology and entomology; also published on botany and zoology. On a visit to Freud's library I found near Darwin's works, two volumes by Lubbock: *Addresses: Political and Educational* (London: Macmillan, 1879) and *Ursprung und Metamorphosen der Insecten*, trans. from 2d ed. (Jena: Hermann Gostenoble, 1876).

Lucretius (ca. 99 B.C.–ca. 55 B.C.), Roman poet; his *De rerum natura* sets in verse arguments founded on philosophical ideas of Democritus and Epicurus.

Ludwig, Karl Friedrich Wilhelm (1816–1895), German physiologist, world famous as professor (1865) and head of the Physiological Institute at the University of Leipzig; pioneered the study of physiology as related to the physical sciences and improved laboratory methods and apparatus. Ludwig's ganglion: a ganglion near the right auricle of the heart and connected with the cardiac plexus.

Lyell, Sir Charles, Bart., Fellow of the Royal Society (1797–1875), whose *Principles of Geology* (vol. 1, 1830; vol. 2, 1832), according to Huxley, "brings home to any reader of ordinary intelligence a great principle and a great fact—the principle that the past must be explained by the present, unless good cause be shown to the contrary; and the fact that, so far as our knowledge of the past history of life on our globe goes, no such cause can be shown—I cannot but believe that Lyell, for others, as for myself, was the chief agent in smoothing the road for Darwin" (Thomas Henry Huxley, *Life and Letters of Thomas H. Huxley* [2 vols., New York: D. Appleton, 1901], 1:181).

Meckel, Johann Friedrich (1781–1833), professor of anatomy and physiology at Halle; known especially for work on comparative anatomy. Meckel's cartilage or rod: that of the first branchial arch; Meckel's plane: a plane passing through the auricular and alveolar points.

Mendel, Gregor Johann (1822–1884), Austrian Roman Catholic priest whose systematic records of separately inherited characters of a great number of offspring of several generations of garden peas in precisely executed *Experiments in Plant Hybridization* (1866) established the laws known by his name: that separate characters (that is, height in peas) are inherited independently of one another; that each reproductive cell receives only one of a pair of alternative factors existing in the other body cells (the law of segregation); and that some factors are dominant over others (the law of dominance).

Meyer, Adolf (1866–1950), Swiss-born American psychiatrist; docent in psychiatry, Clark University (1895); professor of psychiatry, Cornell University Medical College (1904–09); and from 1910 at Johns Hopkins and director of Henry Phipps Psychiatric Clinic, Johns Hopkins Hospital.

Meynert, Theodor H. (1833–1892), brain anatomist, neurologist, and psychiatrist; professor of psychiatry and director of the Psychiatric Clinic at the University of Vienna. Meynert's bundle, *fasciculus retroflexus:* a small bundle of nerve fibers running from the habenula to the interpeduncular space.

Milne-Edwards, Henri (1800–1885), French naturalist; from 1843 professor at the Sorbonne and at the Museum of Natural History, Paris (director from 1864); wrote important works on the Crustacea, Mollusca, and corals and a noted textbook in zoology (1834); principal work a series of lessons on comparative anatomy and physiology (14 vols., 1857–81).

Morgan, Thomas Hunt (1866–1945), American zoologist noted for his demonstrations of the physical basis of heredity, using the fruit fly *Drosophila;* 1933 Nobel Prize in Physiology and Medicine for his theory that hereditary unit characters are dependent upon certain factors, or genes, in the chromosomes, the behavior of which he studied and mapped in detail; professor of experimental zoology at Columbia (1904–28) and from 1928 director of the laboratory of biological sciences at the California Institute of Technology.

Müller, Fritz Johann Friedrich Theodor (1822–1897), German zoologist, born in Erfurt, Thuringia; 1852 moved to south Brazil, taught mathematics at *Gymnasium*, Desterro; afterward held natural history post until 1891, when dismissed by Brazilian government for refusal to reside in Rio de Janeiro; author of *Für Darwin* (1864), published for Darwin in English as *Facts and Arguments for Darwin* (1869).

Müller, Johannes Peter (1801–1858), German physiologist, founder of scientific medicine in Germany and with Magendie of modern physiology; professor of physiology and anatomy at the University of Berlin from 1833; famed as a teacher and for researches in his own fields as well as in pathology, embryology, chemistry, and psychology; Müller's capsule (or Bowman's c.): the globular dilation forming the beginning of a uriniferous tubule within the kidney; Müller's duct: two ducts of the embryo that empty into the cloaca and are developed into uterus, vagina, oviducts, and other parts.

Murchison, Sir Roderick Impey (1792–1871), British geologist; served in the Napoleonic Wars; investigated the previously undifferentiated rock strata below the old red sandstone (1830s) and established the Silurian as a new geologic system (*The Silurian System*, 1838); later established the Devonian system with Darwin's teacher Adam Sedgwick; collaborated in the *Geology of Russia and the Urals* (1845); knighted (1846) and appointed (1855) director general of the Geological Survey of Great Britain.

Nägeli, Carl Wilhelm (1817–1891), born near Zurich. At Jena came under the influence of Schleiden, with whom he edited (1844–46) the single volume of the

Zeitschrift für Wiss enschaftlichen Botanik, in which he insisted on "development as a whole" as the only sound basis for classification; in *Über den Einfluss ausserer Verhältnisse auf die Varientenbildung* expressed his belief that the causes of variability are external to the organism; among his other writings are the *Theorie der Bastardbildung* (1866) and *Die Mechanisch-physiologische Theorie der Abstammungslehre* (1844). Professor of botany at Freiburg in Breisgar 1852–57, Munich 1857–91.

Nordmann, Alexander von (1803–1866), Ph.D. and professor of Zoology, Kaiser Alexanders University in Finland; described non-nauplius early stage in several parasitic Crustacea. Edited Lamarck's *Histoire naturelle des animaux sans vertèbres* (1835–45); author of two-volume *Mikrographische Beiträge zur Naturgeschichte der wirbellosen Thiere* (Berlin, 1832), *Palaeontologie Südrusslands* (Helsinki, 1858–60), and *Beiträge zur kentniss des knochen-baues der Rhytina stelleri* (Helsinki, 1863).

Oken, Lorenz (1779–1851), German naturalist and philosopher; sought to unify the natural sciences; his speculations foreshadowed theories of cellular structure of organism and of the protoplasmic basis of life; Oken's body (Wolffian body): the mesenephron or primitive kidney, the excretory organ of the embryo.

Paley, William (1743–1805), English theologian and utilitarian philosopher; archdeacon of Carlisle (1782); subdeacon of Lincoln (1795); author of *The Principles of Moral and Political Philosophy* (1785) and *Views of the Evidence of Christianity* (1794).

Pasteur, Louis (1822–1895), French chemist, first director of the Pasteur Institute; developed process of pasteurization from his studies of fermentation and also a technique of preparing a vaccine against anthrax that was successfully applied to hydrophobia. Pasteur's solution: a bacteriological culture medium for growing yeast and molds.

Peters, Christian August Friedrich (1806–1880), German astronomer; professor, University of Kiel 1874; wrote on nutation and on proper motion of Sirius.

Pictet de la Rive, François Jules (1809–1872), Swiss zoologist and paleontologist; wrote *Traité de Paléontologie* (1845–46).

Pouchet, Félix Archimède (1800–1872), French naturalist; author of works on the natural history of the nightshade, applied botany, and the anatomy and physiology of mollusks; his *Hétérogénie ou Traité de al Génération Spontanée* (1859), in which he advocated the doctrine of spontaneous generation, gave rise to controversy with Pasteur.

Preyer, Wilhelm Thierry (1841–1897), German physiologist and psychologist; advocate of Darwinism; wrote on child psychiatry, physiology, and hypnotism; his 1882 pioneer work on the developmental behavior of infants (*Die Seels des Kindes*) referred to as "well known" by Freud in the *Three Essays on Sexuality* (1905). Preyer's test: a test for carbon monoxide in the blood.

Pringsheim, Nathaniel (1823–1894), German botanist; one of first to demonstrate sexual reproduction in algae; investigated algoid fungi; published paper on alternation of generations in mosses and thallophytes.

Quatrefages de Bréau, Jean Louis Armand de (1810–1892), French naturalist and ethnologist, scion of an ancient family, his work was largely anthropological; his writings and lectures always combated evolutionary ideas; nevertheless he had a strong personal respect for Darwin and was active in obtaining his election at the Institut; author of *Histoire de l' Homme* (1867), *Charles Darwin et ses Précurseurs Français* (1870), and *Histoire Générale des Races Humaines* (1886–89); Quatrefage's angle: the pariental.

Rabi, I(sadore) I(saac) (1898–), Austrian-born American physicist; professor Columbia University (1937); known especially for study of radio frequency spectra of atoms and molecules; Nobel Prize in Physics (1944).

Rank, Otto (1884–1939), "active member of the Wednesday evening meetings in Freud's home where he was always seated at Freud's left hand" (Samuel Eisenstein, "Otto Rank: The Myth of the Birth of the Hero," in *Psychoanalytic Pioneers*, ed. Franz Alexander, Samuel Eisenstein, and Martin Grotjahn [New York: Basic Books, 1966], p. 39). Secretary of the Vienna Psychoanalytic Society (1906–1915). Started *Imago* with Sachs in 1912; editor of *Internationale Zeitschrift für Psychoanalyse* (1913–24); wrote *The Artist* (1904), *The Myth of the Birth of the Hero* (1909), *The Incest Motif in Poetry and Saga* (1912), and *The Double* (1914).

Reichert, Karl Bogislaus (1811–83), German zoologist, anatomist, and embryologist at Dorpat. Reichert's canal: Hensen's canal; Reichert's cartilages: cartilaginous bars in the outer side of the embryonical tympanum, from which develop the styloid processes, the styloid ligaments, and the lesser cornua of the hyoid bone; Reichert's membrane: Bowman's membrane; Reichert's recess: the cochlear recess; Reichert's scar: an area on the impregnated ovum consisting of a fibrinous membrane in place of the decidual tissue; Reichert's substance: the posterior portion of the anterior perforated space.

Reissner, Ernst R. (September 1824–September 1878), born at Riga; studied at University of Dorpat (1845–50); prosector to Karl Reichert; succeeded to chair in anatomy (1855) after Reichert left to replace Siebold at Breslau; named for him are the membranous canal of the cochlea (Reissner canal), the thin vestibular membrane between the cochlear canal and the scala vestibule (Reissner membrane), and the Reissner corpuscles, which he studied.

Romanes, George John (1848–1894), Canadian-born experimental biologist; early an intimate friend of Charles Darwin; University College, London, research on nervous and locomotor systems of medusae and echinoderms; applied Darwin's theory of evolution to development of mind in *Animal Intelligence* (1881), *Mental Evolution in Animals* (1883), and *Mental Evolution in Man* (1888); professor of physiology, Royal Institute of London (1888–91); upheld hereditability of acquired characteristics in *Examination of Weismannism* (1892); founded annual (1891) Romanes lecture at Oxford; developed in *Darwin and After Darwin* (3 vols., 1892–97) a theory of physiological selection hypothesizing possible evolution of distinct species from an isolated group of an original species.

Roux, Wilhelm (1850–1924), German anatomist; professor (1895–1921) at the University of Halle; pupil of Virchow and Haeckel; considered a founder of experimental embryology for his discoveries through experiments on frogs' eggs; called his field "developmental mechanics" and founded as its organ the *Archiv für Entwicklungsmechanik* (1894).

Appendix C

Rütimeyer, Ludwig (1825–1895), Swiss naturalist known for work in craniology and investigations in the mammalian paleontology of Switzerland.

Saint Simon, Étienne Jules Adolphe Desmier de, Vicomte d'Archiac (1802–1868), French geologist; author of *Histoire des Progrès de la Géologie.*

Savage, Thomas Staughton (1804–1880), American Protestant Episcopal clergyman and naturalist; established mission station in Liberia (1836–46); wrote on the gorilla, previously unknown to scientists, on the habits of the chimpanzee, and on termites of western Africa.

Schelling, Friedrich Wilhelm Joseph von (1775–1854), German *Naturphilosophe* and epistomologist; professor, University of Jena (1798), Würzburg (1803–08), Erlangen (1820–26), Berlin (1841–46); member, Royal Academy of Arts Munich (1808–20). Author of many philosophical works.

Serres, Antoine Étienne Renaud Augustin (1786–1868), French physician, anatomist, and embryologist; member of the Paris Academy of Science director of anatomical studies at the Paris School of Medicine; Serres's angle (metafacial angle): the angle between the base of the skull and the pterygoid process; Serres's glands: pearly masses of epithelial cells near the surface of the gum of the infant.

Spencer, Herbert (1820–1903), English philosopher; as subeditor, London *Economist* (1848–53), knew Huxley, Tyndall, George Eliot, and John Stuart Mill; advocated extreme individualism in *Social Statics* (1851); applied doctrine of evolution to sociology in *Principles of Psychology* (1855). Darwin's *Origins* (1859) provided documentary evidence for his speculations; *Systems of Synthetic Philosophy* (1862–96) covered physics, biology, psychology, and ethics in 8 volumes, a systematic account of all cosmic phenomena, including mental and social principles and influencing contemporary philosophy, psychology, and ethics throughout Europe, America, India, and Japan; author of a leading textbook, *Education* (1861), as well as *The Man versus the State* (1884) and *Autobiography* (1904).

Spielrein, Sabrina (1886–1942), pioneer Russian psychoanalyst, studied medicine in Zurich, analysand of Jung; regular contributions to discussions at Wednesday night meetings at Freud's home included 1911 pioneer speculations on destructive impulses in sexual drives, published as "Die Destruktion als Ursache des Werdens" (Destruction of the Cause of Becoming) in *Jahrbuch für psychoanalytische und psychopathologische Forschungen* (1912); shot with her two adult daughters by Nazi soldiers (1942).

Thomson, Sir Charles Wyville (1830–1882). Irish marine biologist, professor of natural history at Edinburgh (1870); lecturer in botany at Aberdeen (1850–51) and Marischal College (1851–52); chairs of natural history at Cork (1853) and Belfast (1854–68); scientific head of the *Challenger* expedition in the Atlantic, Pacific, and Antarctic oceans (1872–76), general account of which is in his *The Voyage of the Challenger* (1877). Using temperature variations as indicators, he produced evidence to suggest the presence of a vast mountain range in the depths of the Atlantic—the Mid-Atlantic Ridge—confirmed by 1925–27 German expedition.

Thomson, William. See Kelvin

Tschermak-Seysenegg, Erich von (1871–1962), Austrian botanist, specialist in plant breeding; became professor at the agricultural school in Vienna in 1909.

Appendix C

Tyndall, John (1820–1893), Irish physicist, geologist, microbologist, popularizer of science, friend of Huxley and Faraday, delivered final death blow to spontaneous generation by demonstrating that optically pure air, moteless and germless, was incapable of producing putrefaction in infusions (1870–76); at time of Freud's visit to England, Tyndall, a man of political conscience, was a powerful leader of British science as Faraday's successor to superintendent of the Royal Institution of Great Britain (1867–87). Studied at local mechanics institute at Carlow, and 1848–51 at Hesse Cassell, Marburg Ph.D. (1850), and Berlin; honorary degrees Cambridge (1865), Edinburgh (1866), Oxford (1873), University of Tübingen (1877) for researches on bacteria, Trinity College Dublin (1886), and Columbia (1887). Fellow of Royal Society (1852), council member (1856); president of the British Association for the Advancement of Science (1874). Studied glacial movement (1856–59), the effects of solar and heat radiation on atmospheric gases (1860–70), and Tyndall effect (the scattering of light particles in the atmosphere); introduced Tyndallization (intermittent sterilization), in which some time is permitted to elapse between the heatings to allow spores to develop into adult forms, which are more easily destroyed. Made bequest for fellowships at Harvard, Columbia, and Pennsylvania to encourage scientific research.

Virchow, Rudolf (1821–1902), German pathologist and political leader; worked also in archeology and anthropology; professor and director, Pathological Institute, Berlin, from 1856; founded cellular pathology; made sanitary reforms in Berlin; member of the Prussian National Assembly from 1862 and of the German Reichstag (1880–93); author of *Die Cellularpathologie* (1858) and *Handbuch der Speiellen Pathologie und Therapie* (6 vols., 1854–76). Virchow's angle: the angle between the nasobasilar and nasosubnasal lines; Virchow's disease: leontiassis osteum; Virchow's line: from the root of the nose to the lambda.

Vogt, Karl (1817–1895), German naturalist and physiologist; professor at the University of Giessen (1847–49), University of Geneva from 1852; a collaborator of Louis Agassiz and an ardent supporter of Darwin, he wrote textbooks and popular works on natural science. Vogt's angle: the angle between the nasobasilar and alneolonasal lines.

Wagner, Rudolf (1805–1864), German anatomist, anthropologist, and archaeologist; discovered the germinal spot in the human ovum (1835) named for him and, with Georg Meissner, the tactile end organs known as Meissner's corpuscles, Wagner's corpuscles (1852).

Wagner von Jauregg, Julius (1859–1940), Austrian neurologist-psychiatrist; Nobel Prize 1927 for discovery of maldaia therapy for general pareses, known as Wagner-Jauregg treatment.

Wallace, Alfred Russel (1823–1913), English naturalist who from his study of comparative biology in Brazil and the East Indies independently arrived at a theory of evolution similar to Charles Darwin's, which friends arranged for them to announce jointly to avoid any problem of priority.

Walsh, Benjamin Dann (1808–1869), London-born American entomologist; Cambridge classmate of Darwin and his early advocate; in England published separate works and wrote *Blackwood's Magazine;* farmed in Illinois (1838–50); in lumber business and some real estate until retirement (1858), when he began

225

Appendix C

studies in entomology; collection of some 10,000 species destroyed in Chicago fire of 1871; contributed on insect pests to agricultural newspaper; over 800 items, some as coauthor, in *American Entomologist;* about a dozen scientific articles in *Proceedings of Boston Society of Natural History* and *Transactions of American Entomological Society* (1862–66); associate editor and then editor, *Practical Entomologist.* Demonstrated growth of insect population resulting from American farming practices; early advocate of importation of foreign predators to control imported pests. Appointed second state entomologist at urging of farmers and horticulturists, issued single report in *Transactions of Illinois State Horticultural Society.* Letters from Darwin in American Philosophical Society Library.

Weismann, August (1834–1914), German biologist, originator of the germ-plasm theory, which stresses the unbroken continuity of the germ plasm and noninheritability of acquired characteristics; taught zoology at University of Freiburg (1866–1912); works translated into English include *The Germ Plasm* (1892) and *Essays upon Heredity and Kindred Biological Problems* (2 vols., 1891–92).

Wernicke, Carl (1848–1905), German neurologist; authority on aphasia and hemianopia. Wernicke's fissure: fissure that sometimes demarcates the parietal and temporal lobes from the occipital lobe; Wernicke's sign: the hemiopic pupillary reaction.

Westermarck, Edward Alexander (1862–1939), Finnish philosopher and anthropologist; works include *The History of Human Marriage* (1891) and *The Origin and Development of the Moral Ideas* (2 vols., 1906–08) referred to by Freud in *Totem and Taboo;* also *Early Beliefs and Their Social Influences* (1932) and *Christianity and Morals* (1939).

Wilberforce, Samuel (1805–1873), called "Soapy Sam" because of his versatile facility; Anglican prelate; Bishop of Oxford 1845, of Winchester 1869; author of criticism of Darwin in *Quarterly Review*, July 1860.

Wundt, Wilhelm Max (1832–1920), German physiologist and psychologist; founded the first laboratory for experimental psychology at Leipzig (1879), where he was professor (1875–1917); believed that psychology must be based directly on experience; correlated the mathematical, psychophysical, physiological, and experimental principles in psychology; author of books on physiology, psychology, and ethics. Wundt's tetanus: tetanic contraction in a frog's muscle produced by injury or electric current.

Zweig, Arnold (1887–1968), born at Gross-Glogau, Silesia; author of *Novellen um Claudia* (1913) translated into English as *Claudia, The Case of Sergeant Grischa* (1927), *Education before Verdun* (1935), and other works. Studied history, philosophy, and literature at various German universities. Volunteered in World War I and left army a confirmed pacifist. Emigrated via France to Palestine in 1933; returned to native East Germany in 1948 on invitation of East German government. President of East German Academy of Arts; awarded Lenin Peace Prize from Soviet Union for his series of antiwar novels. Died in East Berlin almost blind.

Notes

INTRODUCTION

1. In 1915 Freud formulated the economic, topographic, and dynamic points of view; since 1923 the structural point of view has gradually supplanted the topographic. The adaptive was later made specific by Hartmann.
2. Freud attempted in 1920 to replace the instinctual drive of aggression with the controversial death instinct.
3. An uncompleted work, *An Outline of Psycho-Analysis* (1940 [1938]), was published posthumously.
4. World War II had exposed many Americans to seemingly miraculous cures of the war neuroses by psychoanalysts, leading to the euphoric expectations with which the American mental health movement welcomed psychoanalysis after the war as a messiah that would cure all mankind's ills, including war. Psychoanalysts, knowing with Freud that "the best we can hope for is to turn neurotic suffering into ordinary suffering," were concerned about inevitable disillusionment and backlash from this overevaluation.
5. At the time of his first public presentation of his theory to the Linnean Society Darwin did not as yet know of the 1831 reference to natural selection by Patrick Matthew. In trying to make his theory palatable, Darwin opened by pointing to a Swiss botanist as one predecessor, at least for the struggle for existence. "De Candolle, in an eloquent passage, has declared that all nature is at war, one organism with another, or with external nature." In the accompanying "Abstract of a letter from Charles Darwin to [his Harvard botanist friend] Professor Asa Gray of Boston, U.S.A., Dated Down, 5 September 1857" Darwin juxtaposed natural selection and the predecessors he found for the struggle for existence. "I think it can be shown that there is such an unerring power at work in *Natural Selection* (the title of my book), which selects exclusively for the good of each

organic being. The elder de Candolle, W. Herbert, and Lyell have written excellently on the struggle for life; but even they have not written strongly enough." By the third edition of the *Origin* Darwin was able to include Patrick Matthew's 1831 recognition of "the full force of the principles of natural selection," which Matthew "estimated . . . as a priori recognisable fact—an axiom requiring only to be pointed out to be admitted by unprejudiced minds of sufficient grasp." One, therefore, cannot discuss Darwin's influence in terms of a *new* idea or ideas but must assess the reactions and issues his work evoked in the time and place under consideration.

CHAPTER 1. HAECKAL'S POPULARIZATIONS OF DARWIN

1. German interjective used when something falls with a clatter.
2. The controversy was recently replayed in the U.S. Supreme Court. The unanimous decision that creationism is religion and not science failed to note that the theory of creationism had once been accepted and used by such respected scientists as Louis Agassiz and therefore might rightly be taught, not as religion or as current science but as part of the history of science.
3. The relationship of Brücke, Helmholtz, Carl Ludwig, and Emil Du Bois Reymond, all pupils of Johannes Müller, is described in S. Bernfeld, "Freud's Earliest Theories and the School of Helmholtz," *Psychoanalytic Quarterly* 23 (July 1944).
4. Preformationists subdivided into the opposing camps of ovists, who believed that from the beginning the egg contained tiny but complete organisms, and spermaticists, who were equally sure that complete organisms were contained in the sperm. The aberrations of the early microscopes enabled keen and imaginative observers to discern in egg or sperm the outlines of homunculus.
5. For the Darwinian as well as the other viewpoints essential to psychoanalysis see D. Rapaport, "The Structure of Psychoanalysis: A Systematizing Attempt," *Psychological Issues* 2, no. 2, mono. 6. New York: International Universities Press, 1960.
6. J. Breuer 1880–82, "Case History 1. Fraulein Anna O.," in Breuer and Freud, *Studies on Hysteria SE* 2:21–47.
7. "The frothy science" or "soft science," what today might be denounced as "hot-air science."
8. In the flush of victory over the French, the Prussian state established its first university, where science, conqueror of nature, usurped the traditional primacy of humanism in the universities. The appointment of Du Bois-Reymond as chancellor is symbolic and his attack on a Goethe specialist represents an opening salvo in the war declared by Prussian science, not only on nature, but on traditional higher education.

CHAPTER 2. DARWIN, LAMARCK, AND LAMARCKISM

1. See also Lucille B. Ritvo, "Darwin as the Source of Freud's Neo-Lamarckism," *Journal of the American Psychoanalytic Association* 13 (July 1965), 499–517.

2. Max Schur, Freud's personal physician, took issue with the Strachey translation (1972, personal communication). I have chosen to use the Schur translation as more consistent with the gradualism and developmental viewpoint characteristic of Freud's thinking. "Neutral English words and static passive constructions have rather consistently replaced affect-laden German terms and dynamic, active constructions" (Brandt 1966, p. 50). During the past decade several authors have been chipping away at the Anglican overtones of some of the Strachey translation (see glossary entry "instinctual drive"). Bettelheim (1983), Kernberg (1982), and Ornston (1978, 1982, 1985a, 1985b, 1988) in the United States and Mahoney (1984, 1989) in England have been attempting to capture a flavor each considers closer to Freud's own.
3. The self-regulating mechanism of breathing controlled by the vagus nerve unraveled by Breuer while working as a medical student under [the distinguished physiologist] Ewald Hering (Sulloway, p. 51).
4. See *Reader* August 13 and 20, 1864, for Kölliker's arguments in detail.
5. See J. Huxley (1958), "The Emergence of Darwinism" in *Journal of the Linnean Society of London, Zoology* 45:1–14, *Botany* 56:1–14.
6. A period of time that may be short relative to the vast expanse of 4.6 billion years conceived by modern scientists as the age of the Earth could have seemed lengthy enough to constitute gradualism for Darwin, who grew up when biblical time of four millennia prevailed in science.

CHAPTER 3. ADAPTATION AND CONFLICT

1. Also called "overdetermination."

CHAPTER 4. IDEAS FROM DARWIN'S PUBLICATIONS DURING FREUD'S *GYMNASIUM* DAYS

1. Microbiologists "now know that mutations to phage and streptomycin resistance are *not expressed until several generations* after the change in DNA sequence has occurred [Luria, S. E. and Delbruck, M. *Genetics* 28:491–511, (1943)]" (Cairns, Overbaugh, and Miller 1988, 335:18, italics added).
2. See Stanley W. Jackson, "The History of Freud's Concepts of Regression," *Journal of the American Psychoanalytic Association* 17 (July 1969): 743–84.
3. An extinct African animal with stripes whose name was mistakenly applied to the zebra.

CHAPTER 5. "ONTOGENY RECAPITULATES PHYLOGENY"

1. For a discussion of earlier recapitulationists see A. W. Meyer, "Some Historical Aspects of the Recapitulation Idea," *Quarterly Review of Biology,* 10 (December 1935): 379–96.
2. "Object" as used in psychoanalysis. See glossary.
3. Ferenczi's "actual quotation reads somewhat differently: 'It is to be assumed that we shall some day succeed in bringing the individual stages in the development of the ego, and the neurotic regression-types of these, into a parallel'" (Freud [1987 (1915)], p. 16, n. 36).

CHAPTER 6. FREUD'S USE OF DARWIN'S
PRIMAL HORDE HYPOTHESIS

1. *An Outline of Psycho-Analysis* (1940 [1938]) was unfinished when Freud died in 1939 and was published posthumously.

CHAPTER 8. "IN MANY OF US THE PATH TO THE SCIENCES
LED ONLY THROUGH OUR TEACHERS"

1. See Alvar Ellegard, *Darwin and the General Reader* (Göteborg: Göteborgs Universitets Arskrift, 1958).

CHAPTER 9. CARL CLAUS AND THE NEW DARWINIAN BIOLOGY

1. Where no significant change from the editions of 1872 or 1876 occurred, I have used Sedgwick's admirable English translations of Claus's near-impossible *Akademische-Deutsch*.
2. For a complete list of Claus's publications see Claus's *Autobiographie*, pp. 26–35.
3. George Cuvier, "Sur un nouveau rapprochement à établir entre les classes qui composent le règne animau," *Annales des Musées d'Histoire* 19 (1812).

CHAPTER 10. FRITZ MÜLLER, CLAUS'S
EXEMPLARY DARWINIAN BIOLOGIST

1. Thomas Huxley, "On the Anatomy and Affinities of the Family of Medusae," in *Philosophical Transactions* (London, 1849).
2. See p. 228 (chap. 1, note 5).

CHAPTER 12. *THE EXPRESSION OF THE EMOTIONS*, MEYNERT'S
PSYCHIATRIE, AND *STUDIES ON HYSTERIA*

1. For a discussion of the significance of the constancy principle and of its many occurrences throughout Freud's writings, see Strachey's "Editor's Appendix" to Freud's first paper on *The Neuro-Psychoses of Defence* (1894, *SE* 3:65).

CHAPTER 13. CONCLUSION

1. Once again Freud excluded his earlier research with Claus at the Trieste Marine Laboratory.
2. T. C. Schneirla 1957, "The concept of development in comparative physiology." For full discussion see Max Schur and Lucille B. Ritvo 1970, "The concept of development and evolution in psychoanalysis," and "A principle of evolutionary biology for psychoanalysis."

Glossary

Darwin was asked for a glossary and provided one in the sixth edition of the *Origin*. I have reproduced the relevant definitions here followed by —D. Definitions copied or adapted from Gould's *Ontogeny and Phylogeny* are followed by —G.

ADAPTIVE (psychoanal). Ego function involving intrapsychic changes and modifications of the environment necessary to attain a harmonious relationship among instinctual drives, internalized restraints, and the external world.

ALCA IMPENNIS. Great auk, a flightless bird, now extinct.

ALLOPLASTIC. Denotes a form of adaptation altering the environment rather than the self.

ALTERATION OF GENERATIONS. This term is applied to a peculiar mode of reproduction which prevails among many of the lower animals, in which the egg produces a living form quite different from its parent, but from which the parent-form is reproduced by a process of budding, or by the division of the substance of the first product of the egg.—D.

AMPHIMIXIS. Union of the germ plasm of two individuals in sexual reproduction; interbreeding.

AMPHIOXUS. Synonym of Branchiostoma, the genus to which belong the common European lancelet and other species with paired gonads and symmetrical metapleura.

ANALOGY. The resemblance of structures which depends upon similarity of function, as in the wings of insects and birds. Such structures are said to be analogous, and to be analogues of each other.—D. A similarity between two organisms due to independent evolution of the similar feature of each—for example, the wings of a bat and a butterfly.

ANTHERS. The summits of the stamens of flowers, in which the pollen or fertilising dust is produced.—D.

Glossary

ANXIETY-HYSTERIA. A psychic disorder characterized by manifest anxiety, some-times also by conversions.

APHASIA. Loss or impairment of the power to use or understand speech resulting from brain lesion or, sometimes, from functional or emotional disturbance.

A POSTERIORI. Characterizing the kind of reasoning deriving propositions from ob-servation of facts or arriving at principles by generalizing from facts; hence, des-ignating what can be known only through experience.

A PRIORI. Deducing consequences from self-evident definitions or principles; that which can be known by reason alone and not through experience.

ARACHNIDA. Class of arthropods comprising mostly air-breathing invertebrates, in-cluding the spiders and scorpions, mites, and ticks, having a segmented body di-vided into two regions, the anterior one bearing four pairs of legs but no antennae.

ARTHROPODA. Phylum of animals with articulated body and limbs; its most impor-tant classes are insects, arachnids, and crustaceans.

ARTICULATA. A great division of the Animal Kingdom characterised generally by having the surface of the body divided into rings, called segments, a greater or less number of which are furnished with jointed legs (such as Insects, Crusta-ceans and Centipedes).—D.

ASCIDIA. The tunicata marine chordates with cuticular outer covering of the body.

ASTOMATOUS. Lacking a mouth, especially a cystostoma (mouth-like opening in many unicellular organisms) as in certain ciliates.

ATAVISM. Revival or resurrection of former shapes.

AUTOPLASTIC. Denotes a form of adaptation directed toward altering the total per-sonality rather than the environment.

BARBATE. Bearded; beset with long stiff hairs.

BLASTODERM. The blastodisk of a fully formed vertebrate blastula.

BLASTODISK. The embryo-forming, protoplasmic disk on the surface of a yolk-filled egg, such as in reptiles, birds, and some fish.

BLASTULA. A hollow sphere of cells characteristic of the early metazoan embryo.

BRANCHIAE. Gills or organs for respiration in water.—D.

BRANCHIAL FILAMENT. Thread-like part of a gill.

BUCCALA. Fleshy growth around the chin.

CATASTROPHISM (geol). The doctrine, opposed by Uniformitarianism, that changes in the earth's crust have generally been effected suddenly by physical forces or catastrophes.

CATHARTIC METHOD. The discharge of anxiety and tension through the recall, ex-pression, and, possibly, further exploration of significant unconscious material; introduced by Breuer (1895), who discovered that the symptoms of hysteria dis-appeared when forgotten memories were recalled with appropriate affect during a state of hypnosis.

CATHECT (psychoanal). Invest or charge with psychic or instinctual energy.

CEPHALOPODS. The highest class of the Mollusca, or soft-bodied animals, charac-terised by having the mouth surrounded by a greater or less number of fleshy arms or tentacles, which, in most living species, are furnished with sucking-cups. (Examples, Cuttle-fish, Nautilus).—D.

232

Glossary

CHELIFORM. Having a movable joint or finger closing against the next segment to it, or a projecting part of that segment, so as to form a forcep-like organ, as a crab's claw; pincerlike.

CIRRIPEDES. An order of Crustaceans including the Barnacles and Acorn-shells. Their young resemble those of many other Crustaceans in form; but when mature they are always attached to other objects, either directly or by means of a stalk, and their bodies are enclosed by a calcareous shell composed of several pieces, two of which can open to give issue to a bunch of curled, jointed tentacles, which represent the limbs.—D.

CLAVATE. Club shaped; gradually thickening near one end.

COELENTERATA. Phylum of invertebrate, usually radially symmetrical, animals, including corals, sea anemones, jellyfishes, and hydroids, with an internal digestive cavity that may be produced into tubular extensions, but no separate vascular system or perivisceral cavity.

COMPLEMENTAL SERIES (psychoanal). A series in which neither nature nor nurture (heredity nor environment) operates in isolation from the other but "in which the diminishing intensity of one factor is balanced by the increasing intensity of the other" (Freud 1905b, *SE* 7:239–40).

CONVERSION HYSTERIA. The manifesting of a bodily symptom, such as paralysis or anesthesia, as a result of psychic conflict.

COPEPODA. A large subclass of crustaceans, mostly minute in size, found in both fresh and salt water.

CORYPHAEOUS. The leader of the chorus, especially in the Greek drama.

CRUSTACEANS. A class of articulated animals, having the skin of the body generally more or less hardened by the deposition of calcareous matter, breathing by means of gills. (*Examples*, Crab, Lobster, Shrimp, &c.).—D.

CYCLOPES. Marine and fresh-water Copepoda characterized by grasping antennae in the males and paired dorsal egg sacs in the females.

DECAPODAL CRUSTACEA. Largest and most highly organized order including shrimps, lobsters, crabs; five pairs of legs on thorax, one pair of mandibles, two of maxillae, three of maxillipeds, carapace covering head and thorax forms a gill chamber on each side.

DEMENTIA PRAECOX. Now called schizophrenia; a group of psychotic reactions characterized by fundamental disturbances in reality relationships, by a conceptual world determined excessively by feeling (autism), and by marked affective, intellectual, and overt behavioral disturbances.

DICOTYLEDONS OR DICOTYLEDONOUS PLANTS. A class of plants characterised by having two seed-leaves, by the formation of new wood between the bark and the old wood (exogenous growth) and by the reticulation of the veins of the leaves. The parts of the flowers are generally in multiples of five.—D.

DILUVIAL (geol). Effected or produced by a flood or deluge of water.

DIMORPHIC. Having two distinct forms. Dimorphism is the condition of the appearance of the same species under two dissimilar forms.—D.

DIOECIOUS. Having the organs of the sexes upon distinct individuals.—D.

DIPHASIC SEXUALITY (psychoanal). The division of sexual life in man into two distinct periods separated by latency from about the end of the fifth year to puberty.

DROSOPHILA. Genus containing the common fruit fly, members of which inhabit chiefly fermenting fruits and liquids like wine, beer, and cider.

DYNAMIC (psychoanal). Psychological forces involved in behavior, particularly the conflict between instinctual drives and restraining influences past and present.

ECHINODERMATA. Ancient and distinct phylum of marine animals consisting of starfish, sea urchins, and other forms with radial symmetry, calcareous exoskeleton, coelom, blood vascular and nervous systems, and a water-vascular system connecting with small tubular appendages as tentacles or tube feet.

ECONOMIC (psychoanal). Deployment of, and increases or decreases in, psychological energies.

EDENTATA. A peculiar order of Quadrapeds, characterized by the absence of at least the middle incisor (front) teeth in both jaws. (*Examples*, the Sloths and Armadillos).—D.

ENTELECHY. With H. Driesch and other vitalists, a supposititious supramechanical agency, immanent in the organism, directing the vital process toward the realization of the normal whole or perfect organism.

ENTOMOLOGY. Study of insects.

ENTOMOSTRACA. A division of the class Crustacea, having all the segments of the body usually distinct, gills attached to the feet or organs of the mouth, and the feet fringed with fine hairs. They are generally of small size.—D.

FIXATION (psychoanal). Arrested development of a component instinct causing it to remain cathected at that infantile stage or associated with a certain infantile narcissistic mortification, making further advance more difficult, and increasing the likelihood of regression to the point of fixation in the face of later obstacles.

FOLIACEOUS. Leaflike in form or mode of growth; having the texture or nature of a foliage leaf.

FORAMINIFERA. A class of animals of very low organisation, and generally of small size, having a jelly-like body, from the surface of which delicate filaments can be given off and retracted for the prehension of external objects, and having a calcareous or sandy shell, usually divided into chambers, and perforated with small apertures.—D.

FURCULA. The forked bone formed by the union of the collar-bones in many birds, such as the common Fowl.—D.

GANGLION. A swelling or knot from which nerves are given off as from a centre.—D.

GASTRAEA. Haeckal's hypothetical adult ancestor of all higher animals, inferred from the . . . gastrula as a common stage in early ontogeny of higher animals.—G.

GASTRULA. The early embryonic stage of higher animals produced by invagination of the blastula to form inner and outer germinal layers.—G.

GENERA (pl.), GENUS (sing.). Classification between family and species of a group of structurally or phylogenetically related species or of an isolated, unusually differentiated species.

Glossary

GENETIC (psychoanal). History of the drive processes and ego functioning expressed in behavior, and history of the subject's relation to the situation in which the behavior occurs.

GERMANAPHONE. German speaking.

GERMINAL SPOT OR VESICLE. A minute vesicle in the eggs of animals, from which the development of the embryo proceeds.—D.

GERM-PLASM THEORY. Hereditary characteristics can be transmitted only by the germ cells.

HEBEPHRENIA. A subgroup of schizophrenia, or dementia praecox, usually at puberty, characterized by silly behavior and rapid loss of mentality.

HERING–BREUER REFLEX. The nervous mechanism that tends to limit the respiratory excursions. Stimuli from the sensory endings in the lungs and perhaps in other parts passing up the vagi tend to limit both inspiration and expiration in ordinary breathing.

HETEROGAMY. Conjugation of gametes of unlike size and structure in higher organisms; alternation of two kinds of sexual generation, parthenogenetic and dioecious.

HIERARCHICAL. Characterizing organization in ranks and orders each subordinate to one another, for example, integrations of the nervous system in which "the higher [or later] ones inhibit or control the lower [or earlier], and damage to or suppression of the higher ones reinstates the function of the lower" (Rapaport 1960, p. 23).

HISTOLOGY. Study of the minute structure of animal and vegetable tissues.

HOMOLOGY. That relation between parts which results from their development from corresponding embryonic parts, either in different animals, as in the case of the arm of man, the fore-leg of a quadruped, and the wing of a bird; or in the same individual, as in the case of the fore and hind legs in quadrupeds, and the segments or rings and their appendages of which the body of a worm, a centipede, &c., is composed. The latter is called *serial homology*. The parts which stand in such a relation to each other are said to be *homologous*, and one such part or organ is called the *homologue* of the other. In different plants the parts of the flower are homologous, and in general these parts are regarded as homologous with leaves.—D.

HYPEREMIA. A superabundance or congestion of blood in any part.

INFUSORIA. A class of microscopic Animalcules, so called from their having originally been observed in infusions of vegetable matters. They consist of a gelatinous material enclosed in a delicate membrane, the whole or part of which is furnished with short vibrating hairs (called cilia), by means of which the animalcules swim through the water or convey the minute particles of their food to the orifice of the mouth.—D.

INSTINCTUAL DRIVE (psychoanal). "A certain quota of energy . . . [arising] from sources of stimulation within the body . . . which presses in a particular direction. It is from this pressing that it derives its name of 'Trieb'" (Freud 1933 [1932]), *SE* 22:96). Strachey used the English word "instinct" instead of "drive," thus losing the distinction Freud chose to make between *Instinkt* and *Trieb*.

INTERMAXILLARY BONE. Between the maxillary bones of the jaw or the maxillae in insects.

JURASSIC. Designating the period and its system of rocks of the Mesozoic era succeeding the Triassic and before the Comanchean; the seas ruled by ichthyosaurus, plesiosaurus, and other reptiles invaded great areas of Europe, Asia, and western North America; dinosaurs, pterosaurs, and other forms abounded.

LABRUM. The upper or anterior lip of insects, crustaceans, other arthropods, consisting of a single median piece or flap immediately in front of the mandibles. The external margin of a gastropod shell.

LARVA (pl. LARVAE). The first condition of an insect at its issuing from the egg, when it is usually in the form of a grub, caterpillar, or maggot.—D.

LEPIDOPTERA. An order of Insects, characterised by the possession of a spiral proboscis, and of four large more or less scaly wings. It includes the well-known Butterflies and Moths.—D.

LIBIDO (psychoanal). The psychic energy responsible for human sexual activity.

MAXILLAE, in Insects. The second or lower pair of jaws, which are composed of several joints and furnished with peculiar jointed appendages called palpi, or feelers.—D.

MAXILLIPEDA. One of the mouth appendages of Crustacea, behind the maxillae.

MEDULLA (bot). The pith or central portion of parenchyma, when enclosed by a definite vascular cylinder as in the stems of dicotyledons and gymnosperms. (anat) The marrow of bones; the deep or inner substance or tissue of an organ or part, as of the kidney or of a hair.

MEDULLARY SHEATH (bot). The primary xylem zone surrounding the medulla in certain stems. (anat) The layer of myelin surrounding a medullary nerve fiber.

MEDUSA. A jellyfish or free-swimming acaleph or coelenterate.

METAPSYCHOLOGY (psychoanal). Literally "beyond psychology"; introduced by Freud for the assumptions of psychoanalysis that went beyond the academic psychology of the day, which equated "mental" with "conscious." As the highest level of abstraction in the continuum from clinical observation to psychoanalytic theory, it is a conceptual tool for establishing a framework around which to organize clinical data and lower level psychoanalytic propositions.

MONISM (biol). Oneness of origin; the theory of the development of all living things from a single cell.

MORPHOLOGY. The law of form and structure independent of function.—D.

MOTHER LIQUOR. A residual liquid resulting from crystallization and remaining after the substances that readily or regularly crystallize have been removed.

MYELINATION. The process of acquiring a medullary sheath.

MYRIAPODA. A group of arthropods formerly regarded as a class, related to the hexapod insects, but having the body made up of numerous similar segments, nearly all of which bear true jointed legs. They have one pair of antennae, three pairs of mouth organs, and numerous tracheae, similar to those of true insects; divide into two classes, Diplopoda, the millepedes, and Chelopoda, the centipedes.

NARCISSISM (psychoanal). A concentration of psychological interest upon the self.

NATATORY. Adapted for the purpose of swimming.

Glossary

NATURPHILOSOPHIE. A romantic movement in late eighteenth- and early nineteenth-century German biology—a search for unification of all natural phenomena and processes through such transcendental and developmental beliefs as that the history of the universe is the history of spirit, beginning in primal chaos, striving upward to reach its highest expression in man.—G.

NAUPLIUS FORM. The earliest stage of the development of many Crustacea, especially belonging to the lower groups. In this stage the animal has a short body, with indistinct indications of a division into segments, and three pairs of fringed limbs. This form of the common fresh-water Cyclops was described as a distinct genus under the name of Nauplius.—D.

NOSOLOGY. Descriptive classification of disease.

OBJECT (psychoanal). What an instinctual drive depends on for satisfaction of its aim, whether the subject's own body, or more often, external to it.

OBSESSIONAL NEUROSIS. Characterized by ego-alien repetitive ideas and actions as defense against an ambivalent oscillation, leading to an inability to make decisions and to compulsive doubts as symptom or neurotic character traits.

OPERCULUM. A calcareous plate employed by many Mollusca to close the aperture of their shell. The opercular valves of Cirripedes are those that close the aperture of the shell.

ORTHOGENESIS. The theory that evolution, once started in certain directions, cannot deviate from its course, even though it leads a lineage to extinction.—G.

ORTHOGENETIC FORCE. Internal predetermining factors predestining progressive evolution independent of natural selection or other external factors.

OVERDETERMINED (psychoanal). Multiply determined; having more than one cause, some more important than others.

PALEOZOIC. Of an era of geological history from the Proterozoic to the Mesozoic, or the group of rocks formed then; in its later epochs land plants, amphibians, and reptiles first appeared.

PALEONTOLOGY. Based on the study of fossils, a science that informs about the phylogeny and relationships of modern animals and plants and about the chronology of the history of the earth.

PARADIGM. "Universally recognized scientific achievements that for a time provide model problems and solutions to a community of practitioners" (Kuhn 1963).

PARANOIA. A (rare) psychosis characterized by an extensive but relatively isolated system of delusions of grandeur and persecution defended with much appearance of logic and reason.

PARTHENOGENESIS. Reproduction by the female parent alone, leading to the development of an organism from an unfertilized egg.—G.

PEDUNCLE. Stem or stalk.

PETIOLATE. Having a slender leaf stalk or a peduncle such as the slender abdominal segment(s) in certain insects, as wasps and ants.

PHANEROGAM. A seed plant or flowering plant; a spermatophyte.

PLANULA. The very young, free-swimming larva of coelenterates, usually of flattened oval or oblong form.

POSTERIOR (bot). On the side next the axis of blossoming or flowering.

PRECONSCIOUS (psychoanal). The portion of the mental apparatus containing the unconscious mental elements capable of becoming conscious with relative ease.

PREFORMATIONISM. The notion that all major structures of the adult are already preformed in the sex cell (egg or sperm, depending on your preference) and that ontogeny is the unfolding ("evolution") of this prebuilt complexity.—G.

PROTISTA. Unicellular organisms, including both protozoans and unicellular plants.

PROTOPHYTE. Any unicellular plant, like slime molds, bacteria, yeasts, blue-green and simpler green algae.

PROTOZOA. The lowest great division of the Animal Kingdom. These animals are composed of a gelatinous material, and show scarcely any trace of distinct organs. The Infusoria, Foraminifera, and Sponges, with some other forms, belong to this division.—D.

PUPA (pl. PUPAE). The second stage in the development of an Insect, from which it emerges in the perfect (winged) reproductive form. In most insects the pupal stage is passed in perfect repose. The chrysalis is the pupal state of Butterflies.—D.

QUAGGA. A South African wild ass, now extinct, allied to the zebra; or erroneously, a zebra.

RADIOLARIA. An extensive order of minute marine rhizopods having a siliceous skeleton of spicules and radiating threadlike pseudopodia.

RAPPROCHEMENT. The third subphase of the separation-individuation process described by Mahler; begins around the fifteenth month and continues through at least the end of the second year.

RECAPITULATION. The supposed repetition in the development of the individual of the principal stages or phases in the history of its race. (Biol) The repetition of ancestral adult stages in embryonic or juvenile stages of descendants.-G.

REDUCTIONISTS (biol). Those who sought to explain the evolution and behavior of the biosphere in terms of the law of physics.

REGRESSION (psychonal). Return of a repressed wish or its energy to an earlier developmental stage for discharge.

REISSNER CELLS. Cells in the thin membrane separating the vestibular and cochlear canals of the inner ear or in the band of fibers arising from the roof of the midbrain in many vertebrates, passing along the aqueduct and fourth ventricle to enter the central canal of the spinal cord, ending in the region of the spinal nerves, being especially large in fishes.

RETROGRESSION (biol). Backward development. When an animal, as it approaches maturity, becomes less perfectly organised than might be expected from its early stages and known relationships, it is said to undergo a retrograde development or metamorphosis.—D.

REVERSION (biol). Revival or resurrection of former shape.

RHIZOPODS. A class of lowly organized animals (Protozoa), having a gelatinous body, the surface of which can be protruded in the form of root-like processes or filaments, which serve for locomotion and the prehension of food. The most important order is that of the Foraminfera.

SALTUS (biol). Break of continuity.

Glossary

SARCODE. The gelatinous material of which the bodies of the lowest animals (Protozoa) are composed.—D.

SCAPULA. The shoulder blade; in most mammals the principal, or sometimes the only, bone of the pectoral arch.

SCHIZOPHRENIA. A group of psychotic reactions characterized by fundamental disturbances in reality relationships, by marked affective, intellectual, and overt behavioral disturbances; once called dementia praecox.

SEPARATION-INDIVIDUATION. The process described by Mahler (1968) "by which the normal baby, step by step, established a viable identity and sense of him- or herself as a separate entity" (1988, p. 139).

SESSILE. Not supported on a stem or footstalk.—D. (bot) Attached directly by the base; not raised upon a stalk or peduncle. (zool) Permanently attached; not free to move about.

SETA (bot and zool). Any slender, bristlelike organ or part.

SILURIAN SYSTEM. A very ancient system of fossiliferous rocks belonging to the earlier part of the Paleozoic series.

SPONTANEOUS GENERATION. The generation of living from nonliving matter; from a belief now abandoned that organisms found in putrid organic matter arose from it spontaneously.

STOMA. Any of various small mouthlike openings, especially in the lower animals or in the epidermis of plants.

STRUCTURAL THEORY (psychoanal). Divides the mind, or *psychic apparatus*, into the three functional groups, *ego*, *id*, and *superego*, corresponding to how the mind is observed to function in situations of conflict over an instinctual drive.

SUBLIMATION (psychoanal). An ego defense that redirects the energy of an impulse from its primitive aim to one that is culturally or ethically higher.

TARSUS (pl. TARSI). The jointed feet of articulate animals, such as Insects.—D.

TERTIARY (geol). The latest geological epoch, immediately preceding the establishment of the present order of things.—D.

THORAX. Part of body in mammals, between neck and abdomen, in which the heart, lungs, esophagus, and other parts are situated; in insects, the middle of the three chief divisions of the body.

TOPOGRAPHIC (psychoanal). Freud's early theory of the *conscious, preconscious,* and *unconscious* conceptualized as regions of the mind or *mental apparatus* according to their relationship to *consciousness* rather than anatomically or spatially.

TRICHINA. A small slender nematode worm that, in the larval state, is parasitic in the voluntary muscle of man and other animals.

TRILOBITES. A peculiar group of extinct crustaceans, somewhat resembling the wood lice in external form, and, like some of them, capable of rolling themselves up into a ball. Their remains are found only in the Paleozoic rocks, and most abundantly in those of Silurian age.

TRIMORPHIC. Presenting three distinct forms.

UNCONSCIOUS (psychoanal). The id, and parts of the ego and superego, which can only become conscious after the censorship between the systems Cs. and Ucs. has been eliminated.

Glossary

UNIFORMITARIANISM (geol). The principle introduced in 1785 by James Hutton and developed by Lyell in his *Principles of Geology* (1830) that the geological agents seen operating today could, given sufficient time, have produced everything that happened in the past history of the earth.

URPFLANZE. Archetypal plant or ideal primitive form upon which all plants seem to be organized.

URTIER. Archetypal organism or ideal primitive form upon which all animals seem to be organized.

VITALISM. The doctrine that the processes of life are not explicable by the laws of physics and chemistry alone and that life is in some part self-determining instead of mechanistically determined.

WERNICKE–LICHTHEIM SCHEMES. Postulates by two neurologists about the supposed connections of brain centers to account for the bewildering combinations of speech losses in aphasia.

WISSENSCHAFTEN. Science.

ZOEA-STAGE. The earliest stage in the development of many of the higher Crustacea, so called from the name of Zoea applied to these young animals when they were supposed to constitute a peculiar genus.—D.

References

Note: For all authors except Freud the original publication date in parentheses follows the date of the edition cited. Standard practice in dating Freud's works follows the style established by James Strachey and his collaborators in *The Standard Edition of the Complete Psychological Works of Sigmund Freud* (24 vols., 1953–74); the original date of publication is followed by the date(s) of composition in parentheses. For a complete list of Freud's biological writings, see "A Freud Bibliography," *SE* 24:47.

Agassiz, Louis. 1857–62. *Essay on Classification* (1857), *Contributions to the Natural History of the United States of America*. 4 vols., Boston: Little Brown, vol. 1, pt. 1.

Amacher, Peter. 1965. Freud's neurological education and its influence on psychoanalytic theory. *Psychological Issues* 4, no. 4, monograph 16. New York: International Universities Press.

Andersson, Ola. 1962. *Studies in the Prehistory of Psychoanalysis: The Etiology of Psychoneurosis and some Related Themes in Sigmund Freud's Scientific Writings and Letters, 1886–1896*. Stockholm: Svenska Bokförlaget/Norstedts.

Baer, Karl Ernst von. 1828. *Beiträge zur Entwicklungsgeschichte der Thiere: Beobachtung und Reflexion*. 2 vols., Königsberg: Gebrüder Bornsträger.

———. 1876. Über Darwins Lehre. *Reden gehalten in wissenschaftlichen Versammlurgen und kleinere Aufsätze vermischten Inhalts*. St. Petersburg: H. Schmitzdorf, 1:235–480, 2:241.

Beer, Gavin E. de. 1930. *Embryology and Evolution*. Oxford: Oxford University Press.

———. 1965. *Charles Darwin: A Scientific Biography*. Garden City: Doubleday.

Benjamin, J. 1961. The innate and the experiential in child development. *Lectures*

References

on Experimental Psychiatry, ed. H. W. Brosin. Pittsburgh: University of Pittsburgh Press.

Bernfeld, Siegfried. 1944. Freud's earliest theories and the school of Helmholtz. *Psychoanalytic Quarterly* 13, no. 3 (July).

———. 1949. Freud's scientific beginning. *American Imago* 6, no. 3 (September).

———. 1951. Sigmund Freud, 1882–1885. *International Journal of Psychoanalysis* 32, pt. 3 (July): 204–17.

Bettelheim, B. 1983. *Freud and Man's Soul*. New York: Knopf.

Boring, Edward G. 1950 (1929). *A History of Experimental Psychology*, 2d ed. New York: Appleton-Century-Crofts.

Brandt, L. W. 1961. Some notes on English Freudian terminology. *Journal of the American Psychoanalytical Association*, 9:331–339.

———. 1966. Process or structure? *Psychoanalytical Review*, 55:374–378.

Breuer, Josef. 1893–95. Case history 1. Fräulein Anna O. in Josef Breuer and Sigmund Freud. *Studies on Hysteria, Standard Edition of the Complete Psychological Works of Sigmund Freud*, trans. under general editorship of James Strachey in collab. with Anna Freud assist. Alix Strachey and Alan Tyson, 2:21–47.

———. 1893–95. Theoretical. *Studies on Hysteria* 2:183–251.

Brosin, Henry. 1960. Evolution and understanding diseases of the mind. *The Evolution of Man*, vol. 2, Sol Tax, ed., *Evolution after Darwin*, 3 vols. Chicago: University of Chicago Press, pp. 373–422.

Brücke, Ernst. 1893 (1845). Anatomische Untersuchungen über die sogenannten leuchtenden Augen bei den Wirbelthieren. Reprint J. Müller, *Archiv für Anatomie, Physiologie u.s.w.*, in *Das Augenleuchten und die Erfindung des Augenspiegels*, ed. Arthur König. Hamburg: Leopold Voss, pp. 1–11.

———. 1893 (1847). Über das Leuchten der menschlichen Augen. Reprint J. Müller, *Archiv für Anatomie, Physiologie u.s.w.*, in *Das Augenleuchten und die Erfindung des Augenspiegels*, ed. Arthur König. Hamburg: Leopold Voss, pp. 35–40.

———. 1856. *Grundzüge der Physiologie und Systematik der Sprachlaute für Linguisten und Taubstummenlehrer*. Vienna: Druck and Carl Gerold's Son.

———. 1866. *Die Physiologie der Farben*. Leipzig: L. Voss.

———. 1868. Über das Aufsuchen von Ammoniak in thierischen Flüssigkeiten und über das Verhalten desselben in einingen seiner Verbindungen. *Sitzungsberichte der mathematisch-naturwissenschaftlichen Classe der Kaiserlichen Akademie der Wissenschaften*. Vol. 57 (January).

———. 1875 (1873–74). *Vorlesungen über Physiologie unter dessen Aufsicht nach stenographischen Aufzeichnungen herausgegeben*, 2d improved ed., 2 vols., Vienna: Wilhelm Braumüller.

Brücke, E. Theo. 1928. *Ernst Brücke*. Vienna: Julius Springer.

Burnham, John C. 1974. Medical origins of instinctual drive theory. *Psychoanalytic Quarterly* 43, no. 2 (April): 193–217.

———. 1983. *Jelliffe: American Psychoanalyst and Physician; and His Correspondence with Sigmund Freud and C. G. Jung*, ed. William McGuire, with forward Archangelo R. T. D'Amore. Chicago and London: University of Chicago Press.

References

Cairns, John, Julie Overbaugh, and Stephan Miller. 1988. The origin of mutants. *Nature* 335, no. 6186 (Sept. 8): 142–45.

Carpenter, William B. 1871–1876. *Zoology.* London: Bell & Sons.

Claus, Carl. 1863. *Über die Grenze des thierischen und pflanzlichen Lebens.* Leipzig: W. Englemann.

————. 1866. *Die Copepodenfauna von Nizza: Ein Beitrag zur Characteristik der Arten und deren Abänderungen "im Sinne Darwins."* Marburg: Elwert's Verlag.

————. 1872 (1866–68). *Grundzüge der Zoologie zum Gebrauche an Universitäten und höheren Lehranstalten sowie zum Selbststudium,* 2d ed., 2 vols., Marburg and Leipzig: N. G. Elwerts Universitäts-Buchhandlung; 3d ed., 1876.

————. 1875. *Cuviers Typenlehre und E. Häckel's sogenannte Gastraea-Theorie.* Vienna: Manz.

————. 1876. *Untersuchungen zur Erforschung der genealogischen Grundlage des Crustaceen-Systems: Ein Beitrag zur Descendenzlehre.* Vienna: Carl Gerold's Son.

————. 1882. Charles Darwin, *Wiener Medizinische Blätter: Zeitschrift für die gesammte Heilkunde,* no. 17 (April 27).

————. 1884 (1883). *Elementary Text-Book of Zoology,* trans. and ed. Adam Sedgwick from *Lehrbuch der Zoologie.* 2 vols., New York: Macmillan.

————. 1888a. Lamarck als Begründer der Descendenzlehre: Vortrag gehalten im wissenschaftlichen Club im Wien am 2. Januar 1888. Vienna: Alfred Hölder.

————. 1888b. Über die Wertschätzung der natürlichen Zuchtwahl als Erklärungsprincip: Vortrag gehalten im wissenschaftlichen Club im Wien am 5. und 9. April 1888. Vienna: Alfred Hölder.

————. 1899. *Autobiographie,* until 1873, completed by Prof. v. Alth. in Vienna. Marburg: N. G. Elwert's Verlag.

Colp, Ralph, Jr. 1977. *To Be an Invalid: The Illness of Charles Darwin.* Chicago: University of Chicago Press.

Cuvier, Georges. 1812. Sur un nouveau rapprochement à établir entre les classes qui composent le règne animal. *Annales des Musées d'Histoire* 19.

Darwin, Charles. 1958 (1857). Abstract of a letter from Charles Darwin to Professor Asa Gray of Boston, U.S.A., dated Down, 5 September 1857. Reprint in Charles Darwin and Alfred Russel Wallace, *Evolution by Natural Selection,* foreword Sir Gavin de Beer. Cambridge: University Press.

————. 1870 (1858). Auszug aus einem noch nicht veröffentlichten Werke über den Artbegriff; Derselbe ein Abschnitt eines Briefes an Professor Asa Gray; Alfred Russel Wallace, Über das Gesetz, welches das Entstehen neuer Arten reguliert hat. *Proceedings of the Linnean Society,* 1859. Trans. A. B. Meyer. Erlangen.

————. 1958 (1858). On the variation of organic beings in a state of nature: On the natural means of selection; on the comparison of domestic races and true species. Reprint in Charles Darwin and Alfred Russel Wallace, *Evolution by Natural Selection,* foreword Sir Gavin de Beer. Cambridge: University Press.

————. 1950 (1859). *On the Origin of Species* (reprint of 1st ed., 1859). London: Watts & Co., 2d ed.; London: John Murray, 1860. 3d ed. with additions and corrections, 1861. 4th ed. additions and corrections, 1866; German trans. by Victor Carus, Stuttgart: Schweizerbart's Verlag, 1867. 5th ed. additions and corrections, 1869. 6th ed. 1872 reprint New York: D. Appleton, 1873, 1902.

———. 1862. *Über die Einrichtungen zur Befruchtung britischer und ausländischer Orchideen durch Insekten und über die günstigen Erfolge der Wechselbefruchtung*, ed. and trans. H. G. Bronn from *On the Various Contrivances by which Orchids are Fertilized by Insects*. Stuttgart: Schweizerbart's Verlag.

———. 1967 (1862 and 1873). Darwin's recollections of J. S. Henslow, *Darwin and Henslow: The Growth of an Idea: Letters 1831–1860*, ed. Nora Barlow. Berkeley and Los Angeles: University of California Press.

———. 1868 (1859). *The Variation of Animals and Plants under Domestication.* 2 vols., London: John Murray.

———. 1888 (1871). *The Descent of Man.* 2 vols., London: John Murray. 2d ed., 1874.

———. 1873 (1872). *The Expression of the Emotions in Man and Animals.* 2d ed., New York: D. Appleton.

———. 1876. *The Effects of Cross and Self-Fertilization in the Vegetable Kingdom.* London: John Murray.

———. 1887 (1876–82). Autobiography, *Life and Letters of Charles Darwin*, ed. Francis Darwin (son). London: John Murray.

———. 1958 (1876–82). *The Autobiography of Charles Darwin, 1809–1882*, with original omissions restored, ed. with appendix and notes by Nora Barlow (granddaughter). London: Collins.

———. 1887–88. *The Life and Letters of Charles Darwin*, ed. Francis Darwin (son). 3 vols., London: John Murray.

———. 1903. *More Letters of Charles Darwin*, ed. Francis Darwin (son) and A. C. Seward. 2 vols., London: John Murray.

Dorer, M. 1932. *Historische Grundlagen der Psychoanalyse*. Leipzig: Felix Meiner.

Du Bois-Reymond, Emil. 1868. Voltaire und seine Beziehung zur Naturwissenschaft.

———. 1876. *Darwin versus Galiani*. Address in public meeting of Royal German Academy of Science in celebration of Leibnitz anniversary on 6 July 1876. Berlin: August Hirschwald.

———. 1883 (Oct. 15, 1882). *Goethe und kein Ende*. Leipzig: Veit.

Eaton, Howard O. 1930. *The Austrian Philosophy of Values*. Norman: University of Oklahoma Press.

Eiseley, Loren. 1958. *Darwin's Century*. Garden City: Doubleday.

Eisenstein, Samuel. 1966. Otto Rank (1884–1930): The myth of the birth of the hero. *Psychoanalytic Pioneers*, ed. Franz Alexander, Samuel Eisenstein, and Martin Grotjohn. New York: Basic Books.

Ellegard, Alvar. 1958. *Darwin and the General Reader*. Göteborg: Göteborgs Universitets Arskrift.

Fagg, C. D. 1923. The significance of Freudian psychology for the evolutionary theory (presidential address). *Proceedings and Transactions of the Croydon Natural History and Scientific Society* 9:137–164, esp. 150.

Ferenczi, Sándor. 1954 (1913). Stages in the development of the sense of reality. *First Contributions to Psycho-Analysis*, trans. E. Jones. London: Hogarth Press.

References

———. 1968 (1924). *Thalassa: A Theory of Genitality*, trans. H. A. Bunker. New York: Norton.

Fisher, Sir Ronald Aylmer. 1930. *The Genetical Theory of Natural Selection*. Oxford: Clarendon Press.

Freud, Anna. 1969. *Difficulties in the Path of Psychoanalysis: A Confrontation of Past and Present Viewpoints*. New York: International Universities Press.

Freud, Sigmund. 1877a. Über den Ursprung der hinteren Nervenwurzeln im Rückenmarke von Ammocoetes (Petromyzon Planeri) (Vorgelegt in Sitzung am 4. Jan. 1877 bei Prof. Brücke). *Sitzungsberichte der mathematisch-naturwissenschaftlichen Classe der Kaiserlichen Akademie der Wissenschaften*, pt. 3, vol. 75, (1), pp. 15–27.

———. 1877b. Beobachtungen über Gestaltung und feineren Bau der als Hoden beschriebenen Lappenorgane des Aals (Vorgelegt in Sitzung am 15. März 1877 bei Prof. Claus). *Sitzungsberichte der mathematisch-naturwissenschaftlichen Classe der Kaiserlichen Akademie der Wissenschaften*, pt. 1, vol. 75 (4), pp. 419–43.

———. 1878. Über Spinalganglion und Rückenmark des Petromyzon (Vorgelegt in Sitzung am 18. Juli 1878 bei Prof. Brücke). *Sitzungsberichte der mathematisch-naturwissenschaftlichen Classe der Kaiserlichen Akademie der Wissenschaften*, pt. 3, vol. 78 (2), pp. 81–87.

———. 1879. Notiz über eine Methode zur anatomischen Präparation des Nervensystems. *Centralblatt für die medicinischen Wissenschaften*, May 26, vol. 17, pp. 468–69.

———. 1882 (1881). Über den Bau der Nervenfasern und Nervenzellen beim Flusskrebs (Vorgelegt in Sitzung am 15. Dec.). *Sitzungsberichte der mathematisch-naturwissenschaftlichen Classe der Kaiserlichen Akademie der Wissenschaften*, pt. 3, vol. 85, pp. 9–46.

———. 1884 (1882). Die Struktur der Elemente des Nervensystems. *Jahrbuch für Psychiatrie*, 5 (no. 3): 221.

———. 1884a. A new histological method for the study of nerve-tracts in the brain and spinal cord. *Brain* 7:86–88.

———. 1884b. Über Coca. *Centralblatt für die gesammte Therapie* 2:289–314.

———. 1886. Über den Ursprung des Nervus acusticus. *Monatsschrift Ohrenheilkunde* new series 20 (8, 9), 243–51, 277–82.

———. 1954 (1887–1902). *The Origins of Psycho-Analysis, Letters to Wilhelm Fliess, Drafts and Notes: 1887–1902*, ed. Marie Bonaparte, Anna Freud, Ernst Kris, authorized trans. Eric Mosbacher and James Strachey. New York: Basic Books.

———. 1985 (1887–1904). *The Complete Letters of Sigmund Freud to Wilhelm Fliess*, trans. and ed. Jeffrey Moussaieff Masson. Cambridge and London: Belknap Press of Harvard University Press.

———. 1891. *Zur Auffasung der Aphasien, Eine kritische Studie*. Leipzig and Vienna: Franz Deuticke.

———. 1987 (1915). *A Phylogenetic Fantasy*, ed. and essay Ilse Grubrich-Simitis, trans. and foreword Alex Hoffer and Peter T. Hoffer.

———. 1952. *Gesammelte Werke*, vol. 15; London: Imago.

References

————. 1953–74. *The Standard Edition of the Complete Psychological Works of Sigmund Freud*, trans. under general editorship of James Strachey in collab. Anna Freud assis. Alix Strachey and Alan Tyson. vols. 1–24; London: Hogarth Press.

Vol. 1. 1892–94. Preface and footnotes to Charcot's *Tuesday Lectures*.

    1950 (1895). Project for a scientific psychology.

Vol. 2. 1893–95. Case histories. *Studies on Hysteria*.

Vol. 3. 1894. The neuro-psychoses of defence.

    1895 (1894). On the grounds for detaching a particular syndrome from neurasthenia under the description 'anxiety neurosis.'

Vols. 4 and 5. 1900. *The Interpretation of Dreams*.

Vol. 6. 1901. *The Psychopathology of Everyday Life*.

Vol. 7. 1905 (1901). *Fragment of an analysis of a case of hysteria*.

    1905. *Three Essays on the Theory of Sexuality*.

Vol. 8. 1905. *Jokes and their Relation to the Unconscious*.

Vol. 10. 1909. Notes upon a case of obsessional neurosis.

Vol. 13. 1913 (1912–13). *Totem and Taboo*.

    1913. The claims of psycho-analysis to scientific interest.

    1914. Some reflections on schoolboy psychology.

Vol. 14. 1914a. On the history of the psychoanalytic movement.

    1914b. On narcissism: an introduction.

    1915a. Instincts and their vicissitudes.

    1917 (1915)a. A metapsychological supplement to the theory of dreams.

    1917 (1915)b. Mourning and melancholia.

    1915b. Thoughts for the times on war and death.

Vol. 15. 1916–17 (1915–17). *Introductory Lectures on Psycho-Analysis*.

Vol. 16. 1917 (1916–17). *Introductory Lectures on Psycho-Analysis* (continued).

Vol. 17. 1918 (1914). From the history of an infantile neurosis.

    1917. A difficulty in the path of psycho-analysis.

    1919. A child is being beaten: A contribution to the study of the origin of sexual perversion.

Vol. 18. 1920. *Beyond the Pleasure Principle*.

    1921. *Group Psychology and the Analysis of the Ego*.

Vol. 19. 1923. *The Ego and the Id*.

    1925 (1924). The resistances to psycho-analysis.

Vol. 20. 1925 (1924). *An Autobiographical Study*.

    1935. Postscript to *An Autobiographical Study*.

    1926 (1925). *Inhibitions, Symptoms and Anxiety*.

    1927. Postscript to *The Question of Lay Analysis* (1926).

Vol. 21. 1930 (1929). *Civilization and Its Discontents*.

    1931 (1930). The expert opinion in the Halsmann case.

Vol. 22. 1933 (1932a). *New Introductory Lectures on Psycho-Analysis (Lectures XXIX–XXXV)*.

    1933 (1932b). Why war? (Einstein and Freud).

    1933. Sándor Ferenczi.

Vol. 23. 1939 (1934–38). *Moses and Monotheism: Three Essays*.

References

1940 (1938). *An Outline of Psycho-Analysis.*

1937. Analysis terminable and interminable.

———. 1960. *The Letters of Sigmund Freud,* select. and ed. Ernst L. Freud, trans. Tania Stern and James Stern. New York: Basic Books.

——— and Abraham, Karl. 1965. *A Psycho-Analytic Dialogue: The Letters of Sigmund Freud and Karl Abraham,* ed. Hilda C. Abraham and Ernst L. Freud, trans. Bernard Marsh and Hilda C. Abraham. New York: Basic Books.

Freud, Sigmund, and Jung, C. G. 1974. *The Freud/Jung Letters: The Correspondence between Sigmund Freud and C. G. Jung,* ed. William McGuire, trans. Ralph Manheim and R. F. C. Hull. Princeton: Princeton University Press.

Freud, Sigmund, and Zweig, Arnold. 1968. *Briefwechsel,* ed. Ernst L. Freud. Frankfurt am Main: S. Fischer.

Garstang, W. 1922. The theory of recapitulation: A critical restatement of the biogenetic law. *Journal of the Linnean Society, Zoology* 35:81–101.

Gay, Peter. 1988. *Freud: A Life for Our Time.* New York: Norton.

Gegenbauer, Karl. 1874. *Grundriss der vergleichenden Anatomie.* Leipzig: Wilhelm Engelmann.

Gillispie, Charles Coulston. 1959. Lamarck and Darwin in the history of science. *Forerunners of Darwin: 1745–1859,* ed. Bentley Glass et al. Baltimore: Johns Hopkins Press.

Goldschmidt, R. B. 1956. *Portraits from Memory: Recollections of a Zoologist.* Seattle: University of Washington Press.

Gould, Stephen Jay. 1977. *Ontogeny and Phylogeny.* Cambridge: Belknap Press of Harvard University Press.

———. 1980. *The Panda's Thumb.* New York: Norton.

———. 1982. Darwinism and the expansion of evolutionary theory. *Science.*

———. 1987. Freudian slip, *Natural History,* February.

Gray, Asa. 1876 (1875). Do varieties wear out, or tend to wear out? *Darwiniana: Essays and Reviews Pertaining to Darwinism.* New York: D. Appleton. Published originally in the *New York Tribune and American Journal of Arts and Sciences,* February 1875.

———. 1893. *Letters of Asa Gray,* ed. Jane Loring Gray. 2 vols., Boston.

Haeckel, Ernst. 1866. *Generelle Morphologie der Organismen: Allgemeine Grundzüge der organischen Formen-Wissenschaft, mechanisch begründet durch die von Charles Darwin Descendenz-Theorie.* Berlin: G. Reimer.

———. 1868. Über die Entstehung und den Stammbaum des Menschengeschlechts: Zwei Vorträge. *Sammlung gemeinverständlicher wissenschaftlicher Vorträge,* series 3, nos. 52, 53. Berlin: C. G. Luderitss'sche.

———. 1876 (1868). *The History of Creation: Or the Development of the Earth and Its Inhabitants by the Action of Natural Causes,* trans. E. Ray Lankester. 2 vols., New York: D. Appleton.

———. 1874. Die Gastraea-Theorie, die phylogenetische Classification des Thierreichs und der Keimblätter. *Jenaische Zeitschrift für Naturwissenschaft* 9.

———. 1905 (1874). *Evolution of Man: A Popular Scientific Study,* trans. from 5th (enlarged) ed. Joseph McCabe. 2 vols., London: Watts.

———. 1879. *Freedom in Science and Teaching.* New York: D. Appleton.

References

———. 1903. (1894). *The Confession of Faith of a Man of Science*, trans. J. Gilchrist. London: Adam & Charles Black.

———. 1900. *The Riddle of the Universe*, trans. Joseph McCabe. New York and London: Harper & Brothers.

———. 1906. *Last Words on Evolution*, trans. from 2d ed. with intro. Joseph McCabe. London: A. Owen.

Hartmann, Heinz. 1958 (1939). *Ego Psychology and the Problem of Adaptation*, trans. David Rapaport. New York: International Universities Press.

———, E. Kris, and R. M. Loewenstein. 1964. Papers on psychoanalytic psychology. *Psychological Issues* 4, no. 2, mono. 14. New York: International Universities Press.

Heer, O. 1865. *Die tertiäre Flora der Schweiz, sowie die Urwelt der Schweiz.* Zurich.

Holmes, S. J. 1947. K. E. von Baer's perplexities over evolution. *Isis* 37, pt. 172, nos. 107, 108 (May): 7–14.

Holt, Robert R. 1963. Two influences on Freud's scientific thought. *The Study of Lives*, ed. Robert W. White. New York: Atherton Press.

Hooker, Joseph. 1918. *Life and Letters of Sir Joseph Dalton Hooker*, ed. Leonard Huxley. 2 vols., London: John Murray.

Huxley, Julian. 1958. The emergence of Darwinism. *Journal of the Linnean Society of London, Zoology* 45:1–14, *Botany* 56:1–14.

Huxley, Thomas Henry. 1849. On the anatomy and affinities of the family of Medusae. *Philosophical Transactions.*

———. 1871 (1860). The origin of species. Reprint from *The Westminster Review* (April), in *Lay Sermons, Addresses, and Reviews.* New York: D. Appleton.

———. 1880. *The Crayfish: An Introduction to the Study of Zoology.* London: C. K. Paul.

———. 1887. On the reception of the "origin of species." In Charles Darwin, *The Life and Letters of Charles Darwin*, ed. Francis Darwin. 3 vols., London: John Murray.

———. 1893. *Collected Essays.* 2 vols., London: Macmillan.

———. 1901. *Life and Letters of Thomas Huxley*, ed. Leonard Huxley (son). 2 vols., New York: D. Appleton.

Jackson, Stanley W. 1969. The history of Freud's concepts of regression. *Journal of the American Psychoanalytic Association* 17, no. 3 (July).

Jelliffe, Smith Ely. 1937. Sigmund Freud as a neurologist. *Journal of Nervous and Mental Disease* 85, no. 6 (June).

Jones, Ernest. 1953–1957. *The Life and Work of Sigmund Freud.* 3 vols., New York: Basic Books.

Kalischer, S. 1878. Goethes Verhältniss zur Naturwissenschaft und seine Bedeutung in derselben. *Goethes Werke.* Berlin: Biederman.

———. 1883. *Goethe als Naturforscher und Herr du Bois-Reymond als sein Kritiker: Eine Antikritik.* Berlin: Gustav Hempel.

Kandel, Eric. 1979. Psychotherapy and the single synapse: The impact of psychiatric thought on neurobiologic research. *New England Journal of Medicine*, November 8.

References

Kernberg, O. 1982. Self, ego, affects, and drives. *Journal of the American Psychoanalytical Association* 30:893–917.

Kölliker, Albert. 1864. *Über die Darwin'sche Schöpfungstheorie: Ein Vortrag.* Leipzig.

Kraus, Oskar. 1876. *Was für ein Philosoph manchmal Epoche macht.* Vienna: Hartleben.

Krause, Ernst. 1885. *Charles Darwin und sein Verhältniss zu Deutschland.* Leipzig: Ernst Gunthers.

Kris, Ernst. 1951. Psychoanalytic propositions. *Psychological Theory: Contemporary Readings,* arr. and ed. Melvin H. Marx. New York: Macmillan.

——. 1956. Freud in the history of science. *The Listener,* 55. London: BBC, May.

Kroeber, Alfred L. 1960. Evolution, history and culture. *The Evolution of Man,* vol. 2, S. Tax, ed., *Evolution after Darwin,* 3 vols., Chicago: University of Chicago Press.

Kuhn, Thomas. 1963. *The Structure of Scientific Revolutions.* Chicago: University of Chicago Press.

Lamarck, J. B. 1802. *Recherche sur l'organisation des corps vivants.* Paris.

——. 1963 (1809). *Zoological Philosophy,* trans. with intro. Hugh Elliot (1914). New York: Hafner.

Lovejoy, Arthur O. 1936. *The Great Chain of Being.* Cambridge: Harvard University Press.

——. 1959. Recent criticism of the Darwinian theory of recapitulation: Its grounds and its initiator. *Forerunners of Darwin: 1745–1859,* ed. Bentley Glass, Owsei Temkin, and William L. Strauss, Jr. Baltimore: Johns Hopkins Press.

Lyell, Sir Charles. 1832. *Principles of Geology.*

——. 1870 (1863). *The Geological Evidences of the Antiquity of Man with Remarks on Theories of the Origin of Species by Variation.* 2d American ed., Philadelphia: J. B. Lippincott.

——. 1881. *Life, Letters, and Journals of Sir Charles Lyell,* edit. Mrs. Lyell (sister-in-law). London: John Murray.

MacBride, E. W. 1917. Recapitulation as a proof of the inheritance of acquired characteristics. *Scientia* 22:425–34.

McCabe, Joseph. 1906. Introduction to his translation of the 2nd edition of Ernst Haeckel. *Last Words on Evolution.* London: A. Owen.

Magoun, H. W. 1960. Evolutionary concepts of brain function following Darwin and Spencer. *The Evolution of Man,* vol. 2, S. Tax, ed., *Evolution after Darwin.* 3 vols., Chicago: University of Chicago Press, pp. 187–209.

Magnus, Rudolf. 1949 (1906). *Goethe as a Scientist,* trans. Heinz Norden from *Goethe als Naturforscher.* New York: Henry Schuman.

Mahler, Margaret S. 1968. *On Human Symbiosis and the Vicissitudes of Individuation,* in collaboration with Manuel Furer. New York: International Universities Press.

——. 1988. *The Memoirs of Margaret S. Mahler,* compiled and ed. Paul E. Stepansky. New York: Free Press.

Mahony, Patrick J. 1984. Further reflections on Freud and his writing. *Journal of the American Psychoanalytical Association* 32:847–864.

References

Mahony, Patrick J. 1989a. *Freud as a Writer*, rev. and enlarged ed. New Haven: Yale University Press.

———. 1989b. *On Defining Freud's Discourse*. New Haven: Yale University Press.

Mayr, Ernst. 1959. Agassiz, Darwin, and evolution. *Harvard Library Bulletin* 13, no. 2 (Spring): 165–94.

Meyer, A. W. 1935. Some historical aspects of the recapitulation idea. *Quarterly Review of Biology* 10, no. 4 (December): 379–96.

Meynert, Theodor H. 1870. Beiträge zur Theorie der maniakalischen Bewegungs-erscheinungen nach dem Gange und Sitze ihres Zustandekommens. *Archiv für Psychiatrie und Nervenkrankheiten* 2, pt. 3. Berlin: August Hirschwald, pp. 622–42.

———. 1877. Die Windungen der convexen Oberfläche des Vorder-Hirnes bei Menschen, Affen und Raubthieren. *Archiv für Psychiatrie und Nervenkrankheiten* 7, pt. 2. Berlin: August Hirschwald, pp. 257–86.

———. 1873. Skizze des menschlichen Grosshirnstammes nach seiner Äusseren Form und seinem inneren Bau. *Archiv für Psychiatrie und Nervenkrankheiten* 4. Berlin: August Hirschwald, pp. 386–431.

———. 1968 (1884). *Psychiatry: A Clinical Treatise on Diseases of the Fore-Brain Based upon a Study of its Structure, Function, and Nutrition* (facsimile of 1885 ed. trans. from 1884 *Psychiatrie* B. Sachs, under authority of author) with a new introd. Stanley Jackson. New York: Hafner.

———. 1892 (1887). Mechanik der Physiognomik: Vortrag gehalten in der 2. Allgemeinen Sitzung der 60 Naturforscher Versammlung in Wiesbaden 1887. *Sammlung von populär-wissenschaftlichen Vorträgen über den Bau und die Leistungen des Gehirns* (1868–1891). Vienna: Wilhelm Braumüller, pp. 111–38.

Morgan, Thomas Hunt. 1903. *Evolution and Adaptation*. New York: Macmillan.

———. 1909. For Darwin. *Popular Science Monthly*.

Müller, Fritz. 1869 (1864). *Facts and Arguments for Darwin*, trans. *Für Darwin* W. S. Dallas. London: John Murray.

Nordenskiöld, Erik. 1929. *History of Biology*, trans. from Swedish Leonard Bucknail Eyre. New York: Knopf.

Nunberg, Herman, and Ernst Federn, eds. 1962 (1906–08). *Minutes of the Vienna Psychoanalytic Society*, trans. from German with intro. Herman Nunberg. New York: International Universities Press.

Oppenheimer, Jane. 1969. An embryological enigma in the *Origin of Species*, in *Forerunners of Darwin: 1745–1859*, ed. Bentley Glass, Owsei Temkin, and William L. Strauss, Jr. Baltimore: Johns Hopkins Press, pp. 292–323.

Ornston, Darius Gray, Jr. 1978. On projection. A study of Freud's usage. *Psychoanalytical Study of the Child* 33:117–166.

———. 1982. Strachey's influence. *International Journal of Psychoanalysis* 63:409–426.

———. 1985a. Freud's conception is different from Strachey's. *Journal of the American Psychoanalytic Association* 33, no. 2.

———. 1985b. The invention of 'cathexis' and Strachey's strategy. *International Review of Psycho-Analysis* 12:391.

References

——. 1988. How standard is the "Standard Edition"? In *Freud in Exile*, ed. E. Timms and N. Segal. New Haven: Yale University Press.

Proceedings of the Linnean Society of London (October 1899).

Rádl, Emanuel. 1930 (1909). *The History of Biological Theories*, rev. by author and trans. and adapted E. J. Hatfield. London: Oxford University Press.

Rapaport, David. 1960. The structure of psychoanalytic theory: A systematizing attempt. *Psychological Issues* 2, no. 2, mono. 6. New York: International Universities Press.

Ritvo, Lucille B. 1963. Darwin of the mind. Master's thesis, Yale Medical Historical Library.

——. 1965. Darwin as the source of Freud's neo-Lamarckism. *Journal of American Psychoanalytic Association*, vol. 13, trans. and reprinted as Freud's neo-lamarckistische Darwin-Interpretation. *Psyche* 27, no. 5 (1973).

——, reporter. 1970. The ideological wellsprings of psychoanalysis. *Journal of American Psychoanalytic Association*, 18, no. 1 (January).

——. 1970. Carl Claus as Freud's professor of the new Darwinian biology. *International Journal of Psycho-Analysis* 53, pt. 2; trans. and reprinted as Carl Claus, Freud und die Darwinsche Biologie. *Psyche* 27, no. 5 (1973).

Romanes, George John. 1893 (1881). *An Examination of Weismannism*. 2d ed., Chicago: Open Court Publishing.

Roux, Wilhelm. 1881. *Der Kampf der Theile im Organismus*. Leipzig.

Russell, E. S. 1916. *Form and Function*. London: J. Murray.

Schneirla, T. C. 1957. The concept of development in comparative psychology. *The Concept of Development: An Issue in the Study of Human Behavior*, ed. C. B. Harms. Minneapolis: University of Minnesota Press, pp. 78–108.

Schur, Max. 1966. The id and the regulatory principles of mental functioning. *Journal of American Psychoanalytical Monograph Series 4*. New York: International Universities Press.

——, and Lucille B. Ritvo. 1970a. The concept of development and evolution in psychoanalysis. *Development and Evolution of Behavior*, ed. Lester R. Aronson, Ethel Tobach, Daniel S. Lehrman and Jany S. Rosenblatt. San Francisco: W. H. Freeman, pp. 609–19.

——. 1970b. A principle of evolutionary biology for psychoanalysis: Schneirla's evolutionary and developmental theory of biphasic processes underlying approach and withdrawal and Freud's pleasure and unpleasure principles. *Journal of American Psychoanalytic Association* 18, no. 2 (April): 422–39.

Sedgwick, Adam. 1884. Preface to the English translation of Carl Claus, *Elementary Text-book of Zoology*, trans. and ed. Adam Sedgwick, with assistance of F. G. Heathcote. 2 vols., New York: Macmillan.

Serota, Herman. 1970. The ego and the unconscious before Bernheim and Breuer in Lucille B. Ritvo, reporter, "Panel report: The ideological wellsprings of psychoanalysis," Miami, May 1969. *Journal of American Psychoanalytic Association* 18, no. 1 (January).

Shumway, Waldo. 1932. The recapitulation theory. *Quarterly Review of Biology* 7, no. 1 (March): 93–99.

References

Stauffer, Robert C. 1957. Haeckel, Darwin and ecology. *Quarterly Review of Biology* 32, no. 2 (June).

Sterba, Richard F. 1982. *Reminiscences of a Viennese Psychoanalyst*. Detroit: Wayne State University Press.

Sulloway, Frank J. 1979. *Freud: Biologist of the Mind*. New York: Basic Books.

Tax, Sol, ed. 1960. *Evolution after Darwin*. 3 vols., Chicago: University of Chicago Press.

Temkin, Owsei. 1959. The idea of descent in post-romantic German biology: 1848–1858. *Forerunners of Darwin: 1745–1859*, ed. Bentley Glass, Owsei Temkin, and William L. Strauss, Jr. Baltimore: Johns Hopkins Press.

Veith, Ilza. 1960. Panel four: The evolution of the mind. *Issues in Evolution*, vol. 3, Sol Tax, ed., *Evolution after Darwin*. 3 vols., Chicago: University of Chicago Press, pp. 175–206.

Virchow, Rudolf. 1878. *Freedom of Science in the Modern State*. London: John Murray.

Wagner, Moritz. 1870. Über den Einfluss der geographischen Isolirung und Colonienbildung auf die morphologischen Veränderungen der Organismen. *Sitzungsberichte der Kaiserlichen Akademie zu München*.

Wagner, Rudolf. Louis Agassiz's Prinzipien der Classification, etc. mit Rucksicht auf Darwins ansichten. Reprint *Gottingschen Gelehrten Anzeigen*.

Weismann, August. 1868. *Über die Berechtingung der Darwin'schen Theorie*. Academy Lecture at the University of Freiburg (July). Leipzig: Wilhelm Engelmann.

———. 1872. *Über den Einfluss der Isolirung auf die Artbildung*. Leipzig: Wilhelm Engelmann.

———. 1894. *The Effect of External Influences upon Development*. London: Henry Frowde.

———. 1904 (1902). *The Evolution Theory*, trans. with author's cooperation by J. Arthur Thomson and Margaret R. Thomson. 2 vols., London: Edward Arnold.

Westermarck, E. 1906–08. *The Origin and Development of the Moral Ideas*. 2 vols., London (in Freud Library as trans. Leopold Katscher 1907–09. *Ursprung und Entwicklung der Moralbegriffe*. 2 vols., Leipzig: W. Klinkhardt.)

Winslow, John. 1971. *Darwin's Victorian Malady: Evidence for its Medically Induced Origin*. Philadelphia: American Philosophical Society.

Wittels, Fritz. 1912. *Alles um Liebe: Eine Urweltdichtung*. Berlin.

Wright, Robert. 1988. Why men are still beasts. *New Republic* (July 11), pp. 27–32.

Young-Bruehl, Elisabeth. 1988. *Anna Freud: A Biography*. New York: Summit Books.

Index

Anxiety, 42, 94, 177; affects, 180–81; hysteria, 93–95; infantile, 95. *See also* Hysteria

Associated serviceable habit, Darwin's principle of, 179–82. *See also* Allied (secondary) associations

Astronomy, 138, 141–42, 163

"Autobiographical Study, An" (Freud), 9, 21, 100, 101, 117, 157, 166, 200

Autobiography (Darwin), 64, 66, 79, 82, 199

Baer, Karl Ernst von, 14, 20, 27, 38–39, 44, 45, 79, 80–82, 89, 90, 127, 193, 194, 196

Beagle, 114, 188

Beetles, collectors of, 35–36

Bell, Charles, 174–77

Bence-Jones, Henry, 163–64

Bernard, Claude, 20, 63, 164

Bernfeld, Siegfried, 3, 26, 56, 62, 158, 161–62, 165–66, 195, 228

Beyond the Pleasure Principle (Freud), 18, 25, 59, 129, 200

Biogenesis: law, 87, 159; viewpoint, 161

"Biology is destiny," 44

Breeders, 36, 104–05. *See also* Domestic animals

Brentano, Franz, 115

Breuer, Joseph, 3, 6, 19, 40, 69, 75, 128, 186, 229. See also *Studies on Hysteria* (Breuer and Freud)

Bronn, Heinrich Georg, 10, 13, 34, 35, 38, 66, 141, 153, 190, 194

Brücke, Ernst Wilhelm, 3, 6, 11, 15, 24, 25, 26, 28, 62, 81, 115–17, 130, 161–69, 189, 192, 195, 228

Buffon, George Louis Leclerc de, 20, 29, 33

Carus, Julius Victor, 10, 38, 64, 72, 133, 144

Castration, 77–78, 96–97

Charcot, Jean Martin, 3, 19, 26, 40, 74–75, 155, 196

Children, 87, 88, 95, 101, 184

Childhood, 40, 88, 93–94, 106, 167, 192; and animals, 76–77, 101; phylogenetic, 76; psychosexual development, 87; of the race; 41; seduction, 40, 41

Civilization and Its Discontents (Freud), 152, 197

Classification, 122, 129, 131; natural system of, 124; traditional systems of, 119. *See also* Types

Claus, Carl, 6, 11, 16, 17, 19, 24–27, 66, 82–87, 109, 113–16, 188–89, 191–93, 196, 198, 230; biographical information, 118–24; and Brücke, 162–63; criticism of, 193; with Darwin at Down, 11; Freud and, 6, 11, 124, 130–31; Goethe and, 148–49; Haeckel and, 122, 125–31; 193; laboratory, 124; Lamarck and, 145–48; Müller and, 150–51, 154–59; natural selection and, 131–35; objections to Darwin's theory and, 135–45, 158–60; ontogenetic recapitulation and, 158–60, *See also specific titles*

Climate: direct action of, 66–68; and varieties, 144, 147

Complemental series, 40, 42, 44–45, 63, 195

Conflict, 2, 29, 95; and adaptation, 61–63, 195, 197

Conflict-free ego sphere, 2, 63

Consanguinity, 107–08; in Darwin's and Freud's marriages, 105

Harmony, 94, 123, 149; of the organism, 62

Hartmann, Heinz, 2, 47, 51, 53, 62, 63, 78, 192, 195

Heer, Oswald, 45, 136–37

Helmholtz, Hermann Ludwig Ferdinand von, 62, 81, 137, 164–65, 228

Helmholtz school, 3, 62, 161–62, 165–66, 195, 197–98, 228; viewpoint, 133

Henle, Friederich Gustav Jakob, 34, 178

Herbert, W., 190, 228

Heredity, 40–42, 45, 78, 97, 143, 148, 195–96; adaptation and, 132; "hereditary taint," 155, 196

Heritage, archaic, 77; of ego, 78–79; of hysteria, 180

Hermaphrodites, 104, 105, 157

Heterogeneous generation, 44, 193

Hierarchical viewpoint, 4, 158, 181, 195

Historical (or genetic) approach, 2, 5, 28, 79, 108–09, 115, 189, 191; Darwin, 29; Freud, 21; Haeckel, 18

"Historical Sketch of the Recent Progress of Opinion on the Origin of Species, An" (Darwin), 35–37, 46

History, 5, 10, 18, 32, 82, 109, 139; cultural, 15; developmental, 41, 92, 124; of the earth, 193; of the evolution of Crustacea, 151; of life, 137; of mankind, 39, 100, 196; patients', 41; primeval, 40; of race, 88, 121; of species, 41, 158; syphilitic, 40

History of Creation, The (Haeckel), 20–21, 23, 64, 82

Homunculus, 29, 30, 228

Hooker, Joseph Dalton, 33, 35, 43, 119, 139

Horde, 94. *See also* Primal horde

Human, 107; behavior, 192; family, 102; race, 94

Huxley, Julian, 46, 229

Huxley, Thomas Henry, 10, 13–14, 15, 16, 20, 43, 45, 50–51, 54, 121, 137, 167, 188, 193, 199

Hypnosis, 101–02, 167

Hysteria, 19, 61, 94–95, 128, 155–57, 179–81; 184–87; conversion, 92–95; etiology of, 40. *See also* Anxiety; Neuroses; *Studies on Hysteria* (Breuer and Freud)

Ice Age, 94–95; post-, 96

Id, 61, 129, 183; and ego, 26, 39, 68, 78, 130

Identification, 69, 93, 97, 148

Imagination, 130–50; Darwin's, 91; Freud's, 91, 131

Immutability, 144–45

Inbreeding, 103–08

Incest, 77, 79; abhorrence of, 105–08; inbreeding and, 105–08; taboos, 108, 148, 196

Inheritance, 58, 60, 101, 146; of acquired characteristics, 5, 31–32, 37, 43, 53, 58, 60, 69–71; Darwin and, 173, 196–97; Freud and, 41, 72–73, 196–97; of learning, 72, 79, 197; ontogenetic recapitulation and, 88–98; of schema, 77. *See also* Use-inheritance

Inhibitions, Symptoms and Anxiety (Freud), 180

Innate, the, 40, 41. *See also* Incest; Orthogenetic drive

Insectivorous Plants (Darwin), 65

Insects, 87, 118–19, 143

Instinct, 59, 128, 136, 173; animal,